Do Unto Others
and Then Run

A collection of columns by
Barry Saunders

The News and Observer Publishing Company
Raleigh, North Carolina

Printed in the United States of America.

ISBN: 0-935400-40-0

Cover and author photos by Gary Allen.
Jacket and book design by Bill Herrin.
Copy editing by Millicent Fauntleroy.

The News and Observer Publishing Co.
215 South McDowell Street
Raleigh, North Carolina 27601
www.newsobserver.com

Dedication

This book is lovingly dedicated to my aunt and uncle, Jennie and Johnny Reddick, who raised me; to my cousin, Henry Everette who inspired me; to my dad, Leonard Saunders; to my son, Wesley; and to Glenn Sumpter, editor of the Richmond County Daily Journal, who first hired me.

It is also dedicated — not so lovingly — to all of the girls at Richmond Senior High School, class of '75, who wouldn't go out with me — which was all of the girls at Richmond Senior High School, class of '75.

A few comments about Barry Saunders' columns

black' hu'mor: a form of humor that regards suffering as absurd rather than pitiable, or that considers human existence as ironic or pointless, but somehow comic.

Leave it to Barry Saunders to rewrite the dictionary.

Ever since this American griot of humor has been writing his column, he has been dispensing quintessential black humor. That's logical. Barry is black.

His brand of humor may sometimes regard suffering as pitiable, but never absurd, human existence as comically ironic, but never pointless.

So, really, what can a group of white guys sitting around an ivory-cloistered tower know about black humor, compared to a black dude whose lifetime of listening to brothers and sisters rapping in the ghetto gave him insights for a textbook?

With his column, Barry Saunders has accepted the torch of laughter from Langston Hughes' "Simple," Al Duckett's "Big Mouth," and Dan Burley's "brother in the suburbs."

But Barry Saunders is more than an American griot of humor or a 20th-century Mark Twain wit. He is notice-server.

Three times a week, Barry blends a lacerating jocularity with self-deprecating irreverence to serve notice to his readers that he holds these truths to be self-evident...

...That he acknowledges no sacred cows, that no prisoners will be taken (especially if they are hypocrites), that freedom of speech means exactly what the First Amendment says...

...That he will "comfort the afflicted and afflict the comfortable," that he will defend "a brother" whenever he can, but will skewer "bro" just as quickly when Barry is convinced the brother has screwed up...

...That he will be a lightning rod for information, that race relations is only one part of his beat, but one whose historical symbiosis cries out for a no-holds-barred analysis...

...And that he believes passionately that "an injustice anywhere is injustice everywhere" and if a reader can't get justice, Barry's column is available as a court of last resort. That includes for EVERYBODY, because Barry is a crossover columnist.

Did I forget to mention that Barry has guts or what the Spanish call, "cojones?" I mean, the brobdingnagian kind because any black columnist who mercilessly skewers America's premier crossover icon, Michael Jordan, for rejecting support for a famished university black cultural center is either courageous or crazy.

Bet on the former. Barry Saunders is a middle-class, middle-of-the-road paradigm of middle American sanity.

He just enjoys having a ball, even when scampering through the most trenchantly serious subject. He expects you to join the party.

Ironically, most of the choleric mail following his butt-kicking column on Michael Jordan came from white readers who woodshedded him with vitriolic whacks. More irony — proof of Barry's crossover appeal.

What that racial disparity in readers response may have signified, however, is that Barry can tap into a deep lodestone of ethnicity that sometimes agree with him while others think he is no longer shuffling a full deck.

Barry Saunders is also a worrier. He worries about a young brother who spent much of his high school years going to basketball games and went to a second-rate university just to play basketball, hoping the pros would anoint him.

But, one day, lamented a Barry column, you'll drive up to a fast food stand and Arizona's basketball star, Henry Bibby, will come up to your car and ask, "Hey, bro, do you want a milkshake with those fries?"

Barry worries about a black women's sorority that got so strung out in its rejection of African American standards of beauty that it banned a young woman from its cotillion ball because she wore dreadlocks.

His column was quoted in a Raleigh N&O front page story, transmitted by the Associated Press and picked up by the Los Angeles Times which ran a story on the young black woman's aesthetic plight.

I speak from 40 years of writing a column for three African American newspapers and a syndicated column when I say the overwhelming majority of black columnists are serious because the majority of white columnists are serious. Very few black columnists are humorous, even though they came out of a history and culture whose laughter enabled them to survive.

Occasionally, I tried a humorous column, but I usually pontificated on a George Willian or Krauthammerian soapbox of turgidity.

Thank goodness, there is an Art Buchwald or Dave Barry to bring the sunshine of humor into our lives.

Move over, guys. Barry Saunders has just joined your club.

— Chuck Stone

Chuck Stone is the Walter Spearman Professor at the School of Journalism and Mass Communication, UNC-Chapel Hill and Founding president of the National Association of Black Journalists.

Is it too much to ask that black men not degrade their race?

If I weren't afraid he'd knock my teeth out, I'd walk right up and slap Larry Johnson.

Shoot, it might be worth losing a couple of molars to hit Johnson, the massive-shouldered, gold-tooth-wearing forward for the Charlotte Hornets, for the stupidity of those shoe commercials in which he dresses up like an old lady and plays hoops.

I like the Hornets, but I figure the sooner they are out, the better — because that means the networks will stop showing those insulting commercials. Just think about it: What message is conveyed in a commercial showing a black man in drag? It's hard enough for us to be taken seriously under the best of circumstances. But now we have to deal with some skirt-wearing, hyper-glandular rich black jock portraying a slam-dunking, trash-talking, testosterone-laden grandmother. That demeans black women and men.

I consider grandmothers to be God's greatest invention. Mamas are cool, too, but there ain't nothing like the warmth and security of a grandmother's lap.

Some people may think I've hit my head on the backboard one too many times for making an issue of this, what with all the other important stuff going on. But ask yourself: Would a white athlete have subjected himself to the degradation that Larry Johnson has submitted to? Not likely. For most people, white and black, there are things money can't buy — like integrity. Johnson makes about $3 million a year, so he won't be in Kmart waiting for a blue-light special regardless of whether or not he dons a skirt and acts like a fool in the name of a pair of over-priced athletic shoes.

And my! How the Charlotte media love that crap. When Johnson was selected for the all-star team, the Charlotte Observer's headline read: "Grandmama makes the all-stars." Or something stupid like that.

I'm not going to slap Larry Johnson — I might be crazy, but I'm no fool — but his grandmama should.

To be fair, though, Johnson isn't the only black dude who obviously worships at the shrine of Flip Wilson, the creator of the despicable drag queen "Geraldine." Others who've sold their souls include comedian Martin Lawrence, who plays a walking racial insult named ShaNaynay. And that dude on "In Living Color" who plays a grotesque character named "Wanda." Fortunately they, like Wilson, will soon fade into well-deserved obscurity.

If I could ask these guys one question, it would be: "Have y'all no shame?"

Racism has nothing to do with any of this. Nobody, black or white, put a gun to their heads and forced them to denigrate themselves and their race this way. What distresses me as much as this idiocy, though, is the response of other blacks. I asked 10 of my friends ... Well, OK, you're right. I don't have 10 friends. So I asked some people I know whether they were offended by Johnson and all the black male entertainers who dress up like women. Nobody else was. The most common justification was: "He's gettin' paid."

Hell, Stepin Fetchit was getting paid, too, when he portrayed black men as lazy, shiftless, no-account, head-scratching, eye-bugging clowns who mumbled: "Feets don't fail me now."

Johnson and these other dudes are quick to capitalize off their names, but are equally quick to deny responsibility for being role models to kids. Charles Barkley, the bubble-headed round mound of rebound who plays for the Phoenix Suns, hasn't put on a dress, but his latest shoe ad has turned him into a hideous, slobbering monster who defeats Godzilla on the basketball court. His latest ad has him telling parents: "I'm not a role model. I'm not paid to raise your children."

He's right, of course. I haven't heard anybody ask that chump to raise their kids. I know I haven't; I'm my boy's role model. But is it too much to ask Barkley — and all those skirt-wearing brothers — to be a man?

May 17, 1993

Tina Turner movie bashes not just black men, but all men

Silly me. Here I was, thinking critics loved the movie "What's Love Got To Do With It" because it degrades black men worse than anything since "The Color Purple" — or since that handkerchief-head Uncle Tom Clarence Thomas crawled from under his rock.

Turns out they don't love Tina Turner's supposedly autobiographical film because it's against black men. They love it because it's against any men.

That's right: The movie's message has found a receptive ear among women of all races. There were black, white and Asian women in the theater where I saw the movie — a rainbow coalition, if you will — all testifying to the veracity of Tina's depiction of men.

That's why I now know the movie's male-bashing sentiment isn't a black thing. It's a man thing. Period.

Siskel and Ebert effusively praised the movie, giving it "two thumbs up ... way up." I figured they'd extol the virtues of anything portraying black men as violent, sex-crazed, manipulative animals.

Personally, I gave Siskel, Ebert and the film itself the finger — and not my thumb.

Yet while women all over America are lauding Tina for striking a blow against wife abusers with her "realistic, brutally honest" depiction of her former husband, Ike, they're also giving a V for victory — or could that be scissors — to the Virginia woman who cut off her husband's penis after, she says, he raped her.

Tina and that woman have a lot in common. Only difference is, Tina didn't use a knife.

I feel sorry for that soon-to-be-ex-husband in Virginia. But he should be able to pass his days in anguished anonymity, hanging around the park feeding the pigeons, his identity known only to the police and the doctors who performed his reconstructive surgery.

Not so for poor Ike.

I'm writing this within minutes of leaving — no, fleeing — Tina's movie. The last sound I heard as I stormed out halfway through it were Tina's anguished sobs and the two women seated behind me talking about what a mean, vicious snake Ike was.

I pity Ike if he should wander into the grocery store and find himself in the checkout line in front of some mad housewife reading this week's Newsweek cover story on his life with Tina. He's liable to get a zucchini shoved in his ear.

I'd better say right now that I do not condone violence: I've never hit a woman in anger, although a few have hit me. And if Ike actually did treat Tina as she says, something really bad should happen to him — like being forced to listen to that thievin' Michael Bolton re-record "Proud Mary." (Heck, didn't he do that already?)

You ought to be able to accept the premise that life with Ike was no day in Carolina while still being skeptical of Tina's version of herself as Coke-drinking, gullible Anna Mae Bullock married to coke-snorting, bell-bottom-wearing Ike from St. Louis.

The movie is being touted as one woman's struggle for liberation. But it is actually just a paean to pain — "The Color Purple" with a funky blues beat.

I'm not saying Tina is mischaracterizing her life with Ike — well, maybe I am — but it's hard not to question the credibility of a woman from Tennessee who now speaks with an accent that sounds like she's been having tea and crumpets with the Queen of England. In Rockingham, they call that puttin' on.

Thanks to Hollywood, you can even include "Jurassic Park," the biggest movie of the season in this summer of men's discontent. Even the dinosaurs are politically correct: They eat dark meat. They eat white meat. But they eat no children or women — just men. And guess who was the appetizer, the first man on their menu?

You guessed it: a brother.

July 01, 1993

Keep those unsightly, crime-deterring orange jumpers

The Durham County Jail is about to scrap what I consider one of the greatest crime-fighting weapons authorities have: those loud orange jumpsuits inmates wear to court.

Neither lawyers nor judges like the garish jumpsuits. And no self-respecting inmate looks forward to standing in what's derisively known as the courtroom "pumpkin line."

Lawyers, fearing that the jumpers stigmatize their clients, regard the brightly colored outfits as the latter-day equivalent of the scarlet letters that criminals wore in days of yore.

Speaking as someone who has stood in a police lineup or two, I agree. Whenever the guy next to me in the lineup had on prison-issue clothes, I knew I was home-free because his attire made even me look huggable by comparison. It's hard to look anything but guilty dressed in a baggy, untailored outfit that looks like it was rejected by Goodwill.

One good thing about the jumpsuit is that it makes the inmates easily identifiable. The last time I saw somebody walking down the street in a bright orange jumpsuit was in 1976, when I attended the "Pimp of the Year" contest in Baltimore. So unless the guy you see beating down the pavement has been rummaging through Iceberg Slim's garbage, chances are he's on the lam from the county slammer.

Of course, it's important to realize that many of the dudes standing before the judge are guilty of nothing more than being poor and unable to post bail. But it's not hard to imagine some judge, looking at a cat standing before him in the enormous, gaudy jumper, lowering the boom and finding the poor guy guilty of something — even if it's nothing but poor taste. People have done time for less.

Durham jail officials, apparently concluding that forcing inmates to wear orange jumpsuits constitutes cruel and unusual punishment, are now talking about replacing the jumpers with navy blue T-shirts and khakis.

Bad idea.

With the right shoes — say, a pair of Weejuns and no socks — inmates in the proposed new ensemble could look like they're en route to a frat party at Duke.

So, you ask, what makes me think the orange jumpers are a deterrent to crime? Well, just ask yourself: Would you risk stealing a car, selling a vial of crack or committing any other crime if you knew getting caught meant having to wear an orange jumpsuit — especially one that was uncuffed and had no belt or other accessories?

I didn't think so. It's no coincidence that inmates on television news — guys who have been charged with the most heinous crimes imaginable — are always covering their faces with their hands. Even accused sociopaths have pride, and they don't want anyone to see them in those clothes.

The current debate over inmate clothing gives me an idea to help solve another law enforcement problem — jail overcrowding. Instead of putting some bloke in the slammer for a misdemeanor, why not just make him wear an orange jumpsuit for six weeks?

The jumpers don't cost much — Bob Cote, Durham's director of detention, said he can get 30 for about $400. The county could even make money by renting out advertising space on the backs and sleeves the way tennis players do.

The spaces would be a definite hit with certain businesses, such as the makers of cigarettes, wine and beer.

And bail bondsmen.

July 05, 1993

Woe is the white man, tragic victim of racial injustice

Man, my knees hurt. I've been on them, praying for forgiveness for years of closed-mindedness and selfishness.

Here I've been complaining about the alleged racial injustices suffered by black men, while I was blinded to the plight of the real victims of discrimination — white men.

That's right. America's newest aggrieved minority is none other than white dudes. I reached that conclusion not by some mysterious message from on high. There was no burning bush or giant celestial golf club in the sky that spoke to me as I slept. I got the message from listening to, believe it or not, white guys.

It seems that after enduring centuries ... no, years ... OK, maybe days ... of discrimination, white men are rising up to demand full inclusion into the American way of life.

Stop giggling. I'm serious.

The News & Observer even had a story about how white men are preparing to deal with their new minority status in America. The story told of a new organization to help white guys get their due now that women and minorities are taking over. The group, the American Men's Resource Association, is based in Richmond, Va.

Then I read a column by Lewis Grizzard in which he lamented how the American Dream has turned into a "nightmare" for white males. He facetiously told one friend, who was crying that everybody hates him because he's a conservative, well-to-do white man, that he should give all his money to the "spotted owl people," quit working and sleep on the street. That way, he figured, maybe nobody will hate him anymore.

This phenomenon actually started last year. That's when I read a story in which a guy named Terry West, a historian with the U.S. Department of Agriculture, said, "White working-class males have been screwed. All I want is acknowledgment of our pain, acknowledgment of the price we've paid. Acknowledgment would go a long way toward healing the wounds."

Somebody hand me a handkerchief.

After reading their stories and hearing other white friends of mine tell how hard they have it, I've decided to dedicate my life — or at least the next 15 seconds — to the struggle for white male equality.

Ain't no doubt about it — there are certain advantages to being a black guy that I've been trying to keep secret. But after hearing of the pain of my white brethren, I feel compelled to share some of them.

For one thing, white guys will never know the thrill of always being a prime suspect, of being stopped by the police and frisked as you stroll hand-in-hand with your woman under a moonlit sky.

Nor will they know the omnipotence of never having to stand in line at the automatic teller cash-dispensing machine. Whenever I step up to one of those machines, everybody ahead of me suddenly remembers something more pressing he has to do and leaves me at the machine. Alone.

Want to know what else is fun? Always having elevator space because everybody jumps off the moment you step on. Man, that's a thrill that can't be experienced vicariously and is second only to the joyous sound of car doors locking for blocks around every time you walk down the street.

I don't mean to belittle white guy angst, and I'm willing to do anything I can to help them in their struggle for equality. OK, all together now: "We shall overcome..."

July 22, 1993

Something in common, from one minority to another

I got a call two days ago from this Asian-American dude. Said he wanted to complain about his people's status as "the forgotten minority" in America.

I thought the cat was joking.

I mean, when was the last time you saw Asian-Americans rummaging through garbage bins for dinner or panhandling on the corner or marching through the streets singing "We Shall Overcome"?

Indeed, I, like most people, thought Asian-Americans were doing pretty ... no, make that very ... well, having attained the American Dream while many other minorities have yet to awaken from a nightmare.

Billy Fan, a Taiwanese, is president of the Asian Students Association at the University of North Carolina at Chapel Hill. He thinks stereotypes about Asian-Americans are just as damaging as those saying all Jews are penurious or that all blacks are lazy or are good at basketball (I play with some cats everyday at Woollen Gym at UNC who disprove that theory).

"Everybody thinks Asians are all wealthy and smart and that we all drive big expensive cars," Fan told me during an interview at a Chapel Hill eatery. "At first I thought, 'Hey, this is cool.' But then, I realized that such a stereotype could be dangerous."

Fan is starting a newspaper in the Triangle to alter the erroneous perceptions of Asians and to allow second-generation Asian-Americans like himself to "speak up for our parents. For first-generation Asians in this country, maybe their English is not so good and they don't know about all the laws that are in place to help them. We have an obligation to protect their rights, to speak up, because they won't."

I admit that even I once viewed all Asians as being the same, not noting the difference between Taiwanese, Cambodians, Laotians, Vietnamese or Japanese. But that difference is profound, Fan said.

"I know Korean kids whose parents would disown them if they married a Japanese," he said.

The 1990 census shows there are 13,879 Asian-Americans in the Triangle, and Fan thinks that as more Asians move to this area — attracted by the hospitals and Research Triangle Park — anti-Asian violence and hostility could increase.

"That's been the trend in most sections of the country," he said.

The relationship between Asians, especially Koreans and Japanese, and blacks has not been a good one. The only Asians many blacks know own corner stores in our neighborhoods — Koreans — or are saying bad things about us in the newspapers — the Japanese.

For a while there, every time I looked in the paper, some high-ranking Japanese leader was saying something bad about blacks — comparing us to prostitutes, saying we don't pay our debts, etc. The insults from Japan were coming so hot and heavy at one point that I have vowed not to buy a Japanese car — and I love that Lexus — until Japan's prime minister or one of his associates calls me and apologizes.

One thing I learned when talking to Asians about this story was that blacks and Asians have more in common than I thought. You know how I'm always slamming black people who act as though they don't want to be black? I call them Oreos — black on the outside and white on the inside. Well, according to one Asian guy I met, it turns out Asians have names for other Asians who shun their culture.

"We call them 'Twinkies' or 'bananas' — yellow on the outside and white on the inside," he said. "They feel 'I don't owe my culture anything.' That is not true. They owe their culture a lot."

Right on.

August 12, 1993

Conspiracy theory misses meaning of Jordan's death

Damn, I'm hungry. Lost my lunch money today.

No, I don't have a hole in my pocket: I've got one in my head. Y'see, I actually bet a pal that it would take at least two days for Jesse Jackson to thrust himself into the middle of the James Jordan murder saga.

I was wrong. Quicker than you could say, "lead story, national news," three times, Jesse had usurped attention from the tragedy and focused it upon himself. Within hours of the discovery of the discovery of James Jordan's remains and his cremation, there was ol' Jesse on television DEMANDING an investigation into this "conspiracy."

Jesse, with no evidence but with his usual need to seem on top of things, said the rapid cremation — and the apparent "professional" hit on Jordan — stank to high heaven and pointed to a coverup.

What a piece of crap. Jesse is fast becoming a nonentity or, worse, a laughingstock among legitimate civil rights and political leaders. His willingness to shoot from the hip with such unsubstantiated jive will only further diminish him in the eyes of people who once viewed him as Dr. Martin Luther King Jr.'s heir. Even had the cat believed there was a coverup, he could have accomplished much more by calling one of his well-placed friends in government and suggesting an investigation. Uh-uh: Can't make the evening news like that.

If Jesse had wanted to know the truth, I could have told him the real deal behind the quick cremation. It wasn't a coverup that prompted Marlboro County Coroner Timothy Brown to incinerate Jordan's body before knowing who he was. To Brown, the body was merely that of an old black man with a gunshot to the chest. Nobody was asking about him, so no big deal. Now that's a crime, Jesse.

Upon hearing of the death of Michael Jordan's father I, like every black person who hears of some horrific crime, said to myself, "Man, I hope the killer ain't black." Not that I wanted him to be white, either, mind you, but it's just that we get blamed for so much anyway.

Now that two young men — one black and one Native American — have been arrested as suspects in Jordan's death, I wonder whether Jesse will sustain the same level of outrage he exhibited for the cameras when he thought there might be a coverup.

I hope so. I hope Jesse will find himself before he sinks into a sea of irrelevancy and dedicates himself to the most important dilemma confronting this country — finding a way to make a generation of alienated young black dudes feel they have a stake in this country.

When I go out into the communities and churches and bars in Durham and Raleigh and talk to black people about their fears, it ain't the Ku Klux Klan or skinheads they mention. Next to reactionary politicians like Jesse Helms and Orrin Hatch — people who would turn back the clock to slavery if they could — what frightens black people more than anything else are young, vicious, desperate black young people. The kind charged with killing James Jordan and then being stupid enough to make traceable calls from his cellular telephone.

But there's something else to be disgusted with in this tragedy: the way the media have tried to tarnish the image of James Jordan and his famous son. I threw a shoe at the TV set when some local blow-dried pretty boy sportscaster hinted — but didn't say — that Jordan's death was the result of either his gambling or his son's.

The death of any man diminishes each of us, but the senseless death of someone like James Jordan does even more so. I don't know about y'all, but I'm mourning James Jordan not because he raised a son who helped the University of North Carolina win a championship and who has become the greatest basketball player to ever pull on a jockstrap.

I'm mourning him because he represented what this country needs more of: strong, family-oriented men, black and white, who raise children who turn out like Michael Jordan and his siblings apparently have.

August 16, 1993

Amid health care crisis, Saudis get royal treatment at Duke

Hey, somebody hand me a tissue. Not for myself. For Duke University Medical Center administrators, so they can wipe that stuff off their noses.

High-ranking officials at Duke Med, displaying their usual restraint when they think there's an endowment on the horizon, shut down an entire wing of the hospital and posted heavily armed guards throughout the place so the Royal Queen Iffat bint Al Ahmed wouldn't have to be bothered by common people.

So naturally, the most common person I know — me — decided to stop by and see the queen. No, don't thank me. It was really no bother. I was already in the neighborhood, visiting an ailing co-worker, when my curiosity was aroused by the inconspicuous, natural-looking people in expensive suits who blended in so nicely with everyone else in the hospital's lobby — except that they were hiding behind potted plants and had wires running from their ears into their collars and had big bulges protruding from their waists through their coats.

These dudes were strapped and loaded for bear — or for anyone who might want to intrude upon the royal family's serenity. I wasn't afraid, though, because I had never seen a queen before — unless you count the rapper Queen Latifah at Gangsta' Rapfest '92 in Chicago.

I sauntered down the hall, past the fake mahogany tables and obscenely expensive floral arrangements and started rapping with a cute receptionist. I asked her all the normal come-on lines like: "Is your husband married," "What's your phone number" and "Can I see the queen?"

I thought I was making progress until she told me to do something with my notebook and pen that I assume would be physically impossible — or at least very painful. I saw my chance to sneak a peek at her highness when a Saudi gentleman, hooked to an IV stand, had trouble getting through the door to what I assumed was the queen wing. "Need some help there, Hoss?" I asked, rushing to his side.

He declined my offer, but smiling graciously, gave a burly security guard a knowing glance that seemed to say, "Shoot him."

Before he could ventilate me, though, a female security official in a red dress — with two wires coming from her ears — arrived. Now, I'll do anything a woman in red tells me — especially when she stands close enough for me to feel the warm, sensuous curve of a .357 Magnum under her jacket.

She grabbed me under my arm and gently led me out of there, all the while announcing through her walkie-talkie our arrival at each corridor, where we were joined by ever more security guards who helped her escort me all the way out of the hospital.

Let me tell you, that was a heady experience, having all that security behind little ol' me. I asked the woman in red whether they could accompany me to my car out in the garage.

Her baleful stare told me she was not amused.

Come to think of it, I don't think people associated with the medical center are amused by anything that doesn't promise an endowment. While every Saudi I encountered was kind and gracious — even the one who conveyed the "shoot" signal, every hospital and security official I met struck me as pretentious, pompous and humorless. Since they've never actually acknowledged that the royal family was even there, I guess we're to assume they carpeted the hallways and decorated the hospital for some retiree on a fixed income from Garner.

You'd think they'd be wary of sucking up to every person with a kingdom who comes along. Who can forget Duke's experience a few years back when Baron Maurice "Mo' Money" de Rothschild turned out to be "No Money" Mauro Cortez?

The answer to this country's health care crisis appears to be for everyone in need of health care to declare himself or herself king or queen of something — I've already crowned myself Exalted Supreme Ruler of Barryland — and then call Duke University Medical Center.

To be sure, they'll roll out the red carpet. But there's one danger: You may break a leg trying to step over all the bowing-and-scraping Duke officials.

August 23, 1993

Triangle can't beat Charlotte when it comes to leadership

I am sick — sick, I tell you — of hearing everybody dumping on Triangle civic and government officials just because they've stood mutely by and watched Charlotte leave us in the dust.

Oh sure, they deserve the scorn being heaped upon them by local residents and business people who look to the heavens and let loose this plaintive cry: "What's left for us, oh Lord, if our leaders stand passively by and let Charlotte have everything?"

Sure, Charlotte has a professional basketball team, a minor league baseball team whose stadium has a bar in center field, professional rasslin' — and is already selling tickets for its sought-after NFL franchise. But Triangle leaders can redeem themselves by beating Charlotte on what I'm predicting will be the next big thing of the '90s — badminton.

I'm serious. Since Charlotte has already beat us to the NBA, WCW and the NFL, obtaining a franchise in the WBL — World Badminton League — will allow us a chance to flip the birdie at Charlotte for a change. Instead of vice versa.

The Triangle beats Charlotte in everything that counts — except leadership. Money magazine, in its annual ranking of the country's most desirable places to live, ranked Raleigh-Durham fifth because of the quality of our schools, jobs, housing and income. Charlotte came in way behind — at 71st.

But one thing Charlotte has — besides a higher crime rate — is leadership with vision. The Greater Raleigh Chamber of Commerce recently invited a group of business, civic and government personages to a bacchanalia at an exclusive Pinehurst country club. Their purpose: to crystallize a vision of what we'll be doing here in 15 years.

Well, judging by the behavior of our leaders, we'll be eating a lot of barbecue ribs and consuming prodigious amounts of Chivas Regal scotch — some of it paid for from the public trough. That's what the assembled leaders did for two days — in addition to listening to a well-paid consultant tell them how wonderful everything is here.

Hell, if they'd paid me $65,000 — the fee the Independent Weekly says the group paid Henry Luke, its consultant — I'd tell them just what he told them: You're beautiful, babe. And make the check payable to "cash." You wouldn't expect the guy to say anything else, because at those prices they want a cheerleader, not someone to drop a fly in their barbecue sauce by presenting an unflinchingly honest appraisal of where we stand as a region — especially in comparison to the hated Queen City.

What Luke should have said is that the leaders are a bunch of provincial power-brokers who insist upon viewing Raleigh as the same small, southern town it was when Barney and Thelma Lou — yep, she'd come with him on the sly — would steal away from Mayberry and rent a corner room at the Y. In the meantime, Charlotte — a city whose leaders act as though its presence in North Carolina is a favor to the rest of us — is considered a world-class city.

It's not that the participants at the three-day Pinehurst powwow don't know what the problems are: They do. Raleigh's lame-duck mayor, Avery Upchurch, said: "We have to focus on specific projects and commit. We have enough generalities."

They got even more during the following 48 hours, as each panelist talked about the need for more and better schools, more jobs and improving the quality of life. Can't be much vaguer than that, huh?

There was also talk of the need for greater regional cooperation, yet no one from Durham was at the convention. "We were invited, but we have so much going on over here" was the response from someone in the Greater Durham Chamber of Commerce office.

Vernon Malone, chairman of the Wake County Board of Commissioners, made perhaps the best point at the conference. "We have to hold someone accountable for making this vision a reality," he said. Good luck, Vern.

Napoleon said he'd rather fight a battle with one bad general than two good ones, and I know where he's coming from. There are scores, possibly hundreds, of able, intelligent business, civic and government leaders in the Triangle, but so far none has been willing to come to the fore and exert his — or her — will the way George Shinn, Jerry Richardson or Bruton Smith did in Charlotte.

Governing or leading by committee absolves any individual of blame. But it also ensures that nothing grand — such as the Charlotte Hornets, the Charlotte Motor Speedway or possibly the Charlotte Panthers football team — occurs. No wonder the Triangle is consistently ranked among the best places on Earth, yet we're continually sucking Charlotte's exhaust fumes.

August 30, 1993

Michael Jackson's colorful life takes another strange turn

Back when Louisiana's governor, Edwin Edwards, was politically invulnerable, he said the only way he could lose was to be caught in bed with a dead girl or a live boy.

Edwin, say hello to Michael Jackson.

Jackson, the self-proclaimed "King of Pop," was riding as high as the Georgia pines — making millions every time he grabbed his pants, shook his chemically straightened locks and squeaked "Oooh" — until two weeks ago. That's when accusations arose that he went to bed with a live boy.

Only folks who spent the past two weeks in line trying to buy tickets to the Bulls' final game at Durham Athletic Park are unaware that the King of Poop is in deep doo-doo over allegations that his fondness for little boys extended beyond carrying "Webster" around and sitting him on his knee like a ventriloquist's dummy.

I, for one, was flabbergasted to learn that Jackson, a guy known to sleep in a hyperbaric oxygen chamber and ride a Ferris wheel while playing patty-cake with the Elephant Man's bones, might possibly have unnatural sexual proclivities. Who woulda thunk it?

Life is a trip, ain't it? I mean, just look at me. Here I sit: broke, busted and can't hardly be trusted, slipping and sliding in and out of my third-floor, barely furnished room, ducking the landlord. Yet I'm feeling sympathy for a guy with enough money to build a zoo with pet giraffes, elephants and llamas at his 27-room Hollywood mansion. Only one bed, apparently, but 27 rooms.

He has not been convicted of, or even charged with, any crime, but the picture that is coming into focus — sharper than the tip of his surgically altered nose — is of a troubled dude with more money than self-esteem.

Talent alone is not the reason for Michael's transcendent success. Heck, anybody — even I — can moonwalk. But it was Michael's Peter Pan quality — his ability to stay in touch with the kid within — that accounted for his unprecedented and unmatched acceptance across racial and gender lines. Now he's being accused of staying in touch not only with the kid within but with the kid next door as well.

I know people who actually believed Michael when he told Oprah a medical condition was causing his skin to turn opaque. I've heard of that condition: it's called negrophobia, a dread fear that people will notice that you're black.

But I reckon if members of the Durham school board can claim they don't actually vote along racial lines, then Michael can convince people of his cockamamie story about his skin.

Me? I'd rather drink a bucket of warm llama spit than watch Michael Jackson grab his crotch one more time. But still, I hope he's innocent, even though I've never bought into that jive about Michael being a goodwill ambassador to the world. I know too many people in Gary, Ind., who knew and helped him when he was black, then were later ignored.

Wouldn't it be painfully disillusioning for children who idolize this guy if we have to rename the King of Pop the "con of pop"? But even if that is the case, Michael shouldn't be held solely accountable — not until someone can tell me what kind of parents would allow their children to spend an unchaperoned night at the Beloved Gloved One's house in the first place.

Imagine it. Your doorbell rings and there stands a stringy-haired guy with skin the color of three-month-old cream of mushroom soup looking like an extra from "Friday the 13th." Then Junior comes bounding down the stairs with an overnight bag and says, "Mom, Dad: I'm going over to Michael's crib. Bye."

As a parent, I would ask just one question, and it wouldn't be, "Did you pack your toothbrush?" It would be: "Michael, where's that other glove?"

September 06, 1993

Gut check time: The sordid truth comes out of the closet

There comes a time when you realize you have to be honest — with yourself and with your friends.

But since I don't have any friends, I'll just be honest with you. Starting today, I'm coming out of the closet: I can no longer live a lie, as I have for the past 36 years.

No, I am not gay or a member of some secret cult that worships album covers of the late blues singer Z.Z. Hill. Worse: I've been passing as an NCE — a non-chitlin eater. For years, I have turned up my nose in mock disgust every time I was offered some of those malodorous yet delectable hog intestines. But turn your head, and I'd be wolfing down a fistful.

I hid my shameful secret because I wrongly assumed there was no dignified way to eat hog guts, and because they conjured up images a lot of people would rather forget. But I was forced to confront the reality — that I love them — when an irate reader called to excoriate me for referring to some of Raleigh's black leaders as "the kind of people who don't eat chitlins." She thought I meant that in a derogatory way: I assured her I did.

Next to Amway distributors, who were incensed that I said Gary Hart is now selling Amway, nobody got madder at my last column than black people who think we shouldn't eat — or even mention — chitlins in front of white folks.

Well dammit, I'm tired of living a lie.

I eat chitlins. I eat watermelon, too. And I no longer get them gift-wrapped when I leave the store so people won't know what I'm carrying. So, there!

Sure, chitlins stink and have about as much nutritional value as this newspaper sprinkled with salt. But they taste good. They also saved my life by giving me a clue that my first ex-wife wanted me to vacate the premises, on my own or feet first. I knew it was time to blow when I came home from the doctor and told her his concerns about my health. Her response: She cooked a 500-pound pot of chitlins.

"But baby," I said, "what about my high blood pressure?"

"Don't worry, Daddy," she said. "They're fat-free. Have another plate."

The sagest piece of advice I've ever received came from Mr. Pearlie, one of the wise old wineheads I used to hang out with growing up in Rockingham. The day before I packed all my clothes into a matchbox and headed off for St. Augustine's College, Pearlie handed me a bottle of MD 20/20 — well, half a bottle — put his hand on my shoulder and looked me straight in the eye. "Don't eat just anybody's chitlins," he said.

I've lived by those words ever since. I won't eat just anybody's chitlins, but I'll eat Sam's. Sam Dillard, owner of Dillard's Barbeque and Seafood in Durham, is probably the most knowledgeable person on chitlins I know. You could call him a chitlinologist, and if somebody ever endows a chair at Duke or UNC for the study of chitterlings, it'll be named for Sam.

Sam said it takes three to four hours to cook a chitlin — but that's only if you cook them "with love." It takes longer than that to clean them. Sam said, "You have to wash 'em, turn 'em, pull all the fat off and bleach 'em. Some people don't pull all the fat off 'coz they say you're pulling the taste off. Well, we think it's best to pull some of that taste off."

Sam still caters "chitlin struts" — parties featuring nothing but chitlins, coleslaw and corn bread. (Oooweee, man. Show me the way.) When I told him there are actually people who claim never to have eaten chitlins, he shook his head sadly and said, "Don't let 'em fool you. Just about everybody eats chitlins. If they don't it's because they've never tried 'em."

I'll never understand why the same people who swear they won't eat a chitlin will plunk down $20 for a plate of snails soaked in butter — as long as you call them escargots. So I figured we could change chitlins' image by coming up with a fancy French name for them too. Unfortunately, the French word for chitlins is — sit down, y'all — intes-tine.   *September 30, 1993*

A soul man is born again with help from the O'Jays

Whew! That was close. Thought for a minute I'd lost my soul — and I don't mean that metaphysical part of us that goes to heaven when we meet our Final Deadline.

I'm talking about the soul that aches when Sweet Thang stays out all night long and you hear Aretha singing about, "If you want a do-right woman you gotta be a do-right man" — or the soul that makes you smile at the mere thought of a meaty ham hock in a big pot of black-eyed peas. Have mercy.

First, Don Cornelius quit "Soul Train" after 23 years — and I didn't shed a tear. Then I went to church Sunday and couldn't even keep the beat when the choir and Rev. Vince started — to borrow a secular phrase — throwing down.

I knew my soul was in trouble. I mean, my clapping was off, I zigged when the rest of the church zagged and I couldn't even tap my foot in rhythm. I immediately rebuked myself for buying that "Barry Manilow's Greatest Hits" CD.

Any first-year resident at Duke could tell I was suffering from SDS — Soul Deficiency Syndrome. I've known other black folk afflicted with this ailment, but they are the kind of people who see nothing wrong with a world that produces Michael Bolton. They also consider Clarence Thomas to be a real soul brother, and they attend cocktail parties where they sip unpronounceable wines and say stuff like "Gosh darnit. Maybe Rodney King did resist arrest."

In other words, they're the kind of folks who make me puke.

It's too late in the semester to register at SSI —the School for the Soul-Impaired, so I did the next best thing: I went to see the O'Jays in Raleigh. (If you're black and your response was "Who?" it's too late for you, too.)

There ain't never been but four people in the world who could wear a mustard-colored double-breasted suit with shiny gold buttons. And one of them — country music fashion plate Conway Twitty — died just a few months ago. The other three were onstage in Raleigh last week.

Twitty was what country music is all about, and the O'Jays are what soul music is about. Soul has nothing — well, OK, very little — to do with being black or white. Shoot, I'll take one Sting, one Bonnie Raitt and an Eric Clapton over a roomful of Diana Rosses, Whoopi Goldbergs and Lionel Richies (since he left the Commodores, that is) any day.

You can tell a lot about a person by what they eat and listen to. Show me somebody, black or white, who's ever eaten a fried bologna sandwich for dinner — because that's what they wanted — or a can of sardines and saltines washed down by an Olde English 800, and I'll show you somebody who can be my friend. Especially if he's got an extra sandwich and can of OE8 on him.

Likewise, show me a brother or sister who doesn't like the O'Jays, and I'll show you somebody whose chitlins I would not eat for money.

I was in Charlotte when Luther Vandross — the king of bland, crossover, re-made pop music — was there. A haughty ticket agent proudly told me the people who like Vandross pay for their tickets with gold or platinum credit cards weeks in advance. They don't really care if the show is good. They just want to be able to say they were "in the house."

But people like me — and hundreds of others at the O'Jays show — buy our tickets with cash 15 minutes before showtime because hey, you never know, the dudes might get sick and cancel and you could use that moolah elsewhere.

Your ear would have to be in your foot to not realize lead singer Eddie Levert has the greatest soul-singing voice this side of Ray Charles. But even if he couldn't sing a lick, I'd like him anyway because — and I mean this in a good way — he's probably the only dude I know who would finish second to me in a two-man beauty contest.

October 14, 1993

COMING EVENTS

I've had some humiliating experiences in my life — like when I was 16 and ran away from home and nobody even noticed.

See, I'd hopped on a Greyhound bound for Chapel Hill, where I expected to find Dean Smith and impress him with my jump shot and ability to hit the open man on the give-and-go. Dean was out of town, but Walter Davis — then a basketball star for the Tar Heels — convinced me to go back home.

"Your family's probably worried sick about you, man," he told me.

Not exactly. The first question my brother asked when I staggered through the door after three days of wilderness living was, "Have you seen my Barry White 8-track tape? I've got a date tonight."

No tears, no joyous cries unto heaven for my safe return, nothing. I thought there could be nothing more humiliating than that.

I was wrong.

Want to know what could be worse? How about running into the first person you ever loved, a person you've thought about once a day — every day, just about all day long — and having her ask, "Who the hell are you?"

That's what happened to me a couple of weeks ago when, with head and heart filled with glee, I called up my very first girlfriend. I'd met her when we were both 18-year-old freshmen at St. Augustine's College in Raleigh, a school I attended for one semester. (I split when Coach Heartless — my nickname for the basketball coach — failed to appreciate my basketball genius and cut me from the team.)

Since she — I'll call her J — didn't, and doesn't, remember me, I never told her how much she'd meant to me or why she came to occupy such an exalted place in my life. But I'll tell y'all — if you keep it to yourselves. Before her, girls in my hometown of Rockingham gambled their reputations — and a good whomping from their parents — by being seen in my presence. If I caught an attractive girl looking at me, I automatically assumed she was a narc — or a hall monitor.

So, while waiting for J to answer the phone in her office at Duke University Medical Center the other day, I imagined all the profound yet witty things I'd say to her and how we'd laugh about the good — and innocent — times we'd shared.

Me: Hello, J...

J: Hello?

Me: Hi, this is Barry. Barry Saunders. From St. Aug's.

J: Uh, yes. May I help you?

You get the picture. I spent several minutes on the telephone trying to convince her I was not some pervert who'd found her recently lost wallet — and then several more minutes trying to regain some dignity. Man, by the time we'd finished talking, I felt like a rotten grape that had been squished on the supermarket floor of love. I even began to question, as she did, whether I'd ever known her or whether she was just a figment of my imagination.

Think about it: A man might forget a lot of things — the name of his first car or his second wife, for instance. If you're like me after my second bottle of M.D. 20/20 — taken for medicinal purposes only, I might add — you may not even always remember your own name. But breathes there any person with soul so dead they can't remember to whom they first said, "I love you"?

Lawd have mercy, I was in ag-o-ny!

I acted unconcerned, but I'm sure I gave myself away when I started hyperventilating and breathing into a paper bag. To be honest, there were some things I was glad she'd forgotten, like when I fainted the first time I kissed her because I didn't know you were supposed to keep breathing.

We met for lunch, where I hoped to discover she'd grown fat and

unattractive, unable to cope with the fact that I'd left St. Aug's to dribble on someone else's court. Yeah, that's it, I told myself, she hadn't forgotten at all, but was merely acting to hide her true feelings.

Not exactly. She was even more beautiful than when she was 18.
She was in a serious, satisfying relationship — and after an hour's lunch
she still had no idea who the hell I was. Oh, she tried to act as though
there was a flicker of recognition — and she did remember my roommate (Hmmm!) — but not me.

We parted friendly, but I would've felt a lot better if she hadn't
looked so good.

October 28, 1993

Children steal spotlight at special school's celebrity bash

Once in a lifetime, a song comes along that is so touching, so beauti-
fully haunting, that it tugs at your heartstrings and expresses the
essence of why we live. It can make you cry.

For me, that song was "I Like Trashy Women" and was sung by
Travis Butler. Oh man, I mean — it got me right (sob) here.

Of course, singing isn't Butler's real job: He works for Sprint/Carolina
Telephone. He — and several other people who won't be quitting their
"day" jobs to perform — sang at a luncheon to raise money for a marvelous school for mentally retarded children whose ages range from 3 to
7.

I can't lie: When Marvin Haller called and asked me to be a waiter for
a charity luncheon at the Marriott Hotel, I thought I'd get a chance to
meet Frankie Lymon — you know, from Frankie Lymon and the
Teenagers, the group that sang "Why Do Fools Fall In Love?"

When I got to the Marriott, though, I found out the luncheon was
actually for Frankie Lemmon, a Raleigh kid born with Down syndrome. In
1965, when Frankie was old enough to enter kindergarten, his father
could find none that would take a child afflicted by that congenital disease. So he started his own. Right in the basement of his church,
Hudson Memorial Presbyterian Church.

There were many celebrities in the joint Friday — and I'm not talking
about the television anchor who introduced us or the radio disc jockeys
who, like me, spilled food and wine all over people and collected donations for the school.

The real celebrities were a group of about 10 kids from the Frankie
Lemmon School and Development Center who came by to say "hi" and
sing — or, rather, shout — the alphabet. That might not seem like a big

deal to you, but some of those children couldn't even talk two years ago. To their parents and teachers, I'm sure, the kiddie cacophony sounded like angels singing.

Since its inception, the Lemmon Center has always been filled to its maximum enrollment of 25 students. And talk about your Rainbow Coalition: This year's class consists of 12 black students, 12 whites and a Kuwaiti. "We have to turn away as many as we enroll," said Martha Lee Ellis, executive director of the school.

But not only is the school's board of directors — one member of which, Dr. Burton Horwitz, came dressed as Elvis — considering expanding the enrollment, but it plans to integrate the retarded children into classes with those whose development is normal.

That would benefit both groups, Ellis said.

"Research shows that students we consider normal are more accepting of the disabled when they are in children's development programs together, and the normally developing children can serve as peer models for those who are mentally challenged." That's right in keeping with the school's state objective, which is to help mentally impaired children attain a certain level of independence.

Friday's luncheon, donations and auction raised $11,000 toward the school's $200,000 budget. The item that inspired the most intense bidding was a basketball signed by Dean Smith and the 1993 UNC Tar Heels. It went for $500, almost twice what Coach K's Duke-signed basketball went for.

Although the Lemmon Center has a contract with Wake Public Schools, fund-raisers such as the luncheon help offset additional costs. The state provides only $600 per month for each student, while some of them, because of their individual therapy and educational needs, require as much as $800 monthly.

Frankie Lemmon died just a couple of years after the school that was started to give him a place to learn was founded. But thanks to the dedication of people like Martha Lee Ellis and Marvin Haller — the board member who snared most of the waiters — and the generosity of people who contribute money and time, Frankie Lemmon won't be forgotten.

November 22, 1993

All a player needs for this Olympic event is a death wish

Anybody got Bill Campbell's phone number in Atlanta?

Campbell was just elected mayor of Atlanta, the site of the 1996 Olympics. Since Campbell is a homeboy — from Raleigh — I figured I'd give him a call and tell him about this terrific new sport I've thought of for the Olympics: the Black Dude Deathcathlon. It's a game in which contestants compete for medals to see how many black dudes they can croak.

Don't look at me like that: It's already a popular pastime in cities and towns across America. I realize the BDD is too macabre an idea to be embraced by the U.S. Olympic Committee, but if it were, you wouldn't have to be Jimmy the Greek to predict how the medal breakdown would look.

Bronze: The KKK. In its heyday, this group really knew how to throw a party — and a rope. Despite a centuries-long headstart, though, the KKK has seen its lead in the BDD eclipsed by the silver and gold medalists.

Silver medal: Liquor and drugs: 'nuff said.

Gold medal: The winner is ... drum roll, please, although there's no real suspense here ... black dudes. Somebody, usually a brother, is murdered in America every 24 minutes. The leading cause of death for black men in America isn't cancer, AIDS or TB. It's what Jesse Jackson calls the BBB — the big bad brother with a gun.

But not always. The Michael Seagroves manslaughter trial starts today in Durham, and that's what got me thinking about an Olympics event to call attention to the biggest crisis facing blacks since slavery: violence, usually blacks against blacks.

I can hardly wait to hear this white dude explain how he felt so threatened by a skinny, little 15-year-old boy who was running away from him — for God's sake — that he pumped at least two, possibly more bullets into him. Much of the black community was justifiably outraged by the shooting — although some, unbelievably, expressed agreement with Seagroves' action.

Yet, just last week, a 23-year-old black guy, Perry Jones, was shot to death in his apartment: There's hardly been any response at all. No deluge of telephone calls to radio talk shows, no preachers thundering from the pulpit against the evil of violence — as there was when Seagroves killed Jamal Elliott. If Perry Jones' killer is caught and turns out to be black, nobody outside the local media and the victim's family will give a rat's toenail about the outcome of that trial.

Now, back to my idea for the Olympics: Remember how Nike and Reebok fought over the right to outfit athletes in the 1992 Olympics in Barcelona? Well, undertakers and casket-makers could fight over the contract for Atlanta to see who gets to bury black guys who've been popped over a turf battle, for "dissing" someone or even for wearing their cap tilted to the wrong side.

Most dudes, black and white, are like me: law-abiding, peace-loving men who would kick a neighbor's cat only if no one was looking. But they're not the ones who have turned our neighborhoods into killing fields and who have 11-year-old boys in Washington planning their own funerals for when they meet what they consider their inevitably violent fate.

Nation of Islam minister Louis Farrakhan once suggested that the criminals who devastate our communities be beheaded and their heads placed on a pole in the middle of town as a warning to others. At the time, I thought Farrakhan was being unduly vicious, but my response now is, "Where's the pole?"

Of course, if we do that we'll find ourselves staring a judge in the face, facing 10 to 20 in prison. Yet, the fratricidal polecats who do the killing in the first place get two or three years in the joint or, if they're bad enough, a book contract when they get out.

On "60 Minutes" recently, a murderous black punk named Monster Kody bragged that he'd killed at least a dozen black men and raped scores of women. His punishment: six years in the joint and a $250,000 book contract to tell how he did it. One of the book's editors — white, of course — romanticized this thug on national television by calling his the "primary voice of the black experience."

Excuse me while I puke.

November 29, 1993

Cold beds and warm hearts on the Triangle's streets

I'm white," says the woman, huddled over the steam grate at the corner of Hargett and McDowell streets in downtown Raleigh. "I was raised by black people, but I'm white."

She says this in a matter-of-fact tone, as if it were the most obvious thing in the world, despite the fact her skin is blacker than mine. After talking to the woman, whom her male companion calls "Mom," I realize that many of her comments can be dismissed as the brain-addled ramblings of a woman who has lived on the streets — and slept on sidewalks — for too long.

But neither she nor any of the other people sleeping, living and dying on the streets of Durham and Raleigh can be so easily dismissed. I spent the night before Thanksgiving on Triangle streets talking to and hanging out with people who have been dealt — and who have dealt themselves — bad hands.

Mom's companion is a 37-year-old man named Grady who whispers to me, non-judgmentally, that Mom has spent a little time in Dorothea Dix Hospital. Grady himself has spent the past four years foraging through garbage cans for his meals and sleeping on the street. Yet he is still a handsome — almost regal-looking — dude. His neatly trimmed beard puts my scraggly effort to shame, and he has the lithe body of an athlete, which he was in a former life. Right now, it's about 2:30 in the morning and that body — along with Mom's — is huddled on the steam grate beneath some newspapers they use to shield themselves from the cold wind rushing around the corner.

Having spent a night or two on steam grates myself, I want to tell these people the steam is eventually going to condense and leave them chilled to the bone. But I figure they know more about life on the streets than I do and, besides, maybe someone has invented a newfangled steam grate since I involuntarily wandered the streets of Washington and Atlanta.

Grady says he was a high school basketball star in Wendell, but his dreams of pro stardom dissipated when "all my people started dyin' at one time and I quit school." When asked whether he thought his life would turn out as it has, he responds: "Shoot no, I didn't think I was going to be out on no street."

He once was a welder, he explains, but he drank so much that he became afraid of heights. Still, he hasn't given up. From beneath the newspapers with which he has covered himself, he pulls a book bag and offers me a book he's been reading — "Homelessness: A National Perspective" — along with several forms from the Wake County Mental Health Department and other government agencies. He says he has spent the past few days trying to help Mom negotiate the county's mental health bureaucratic maze and find a place to stay before "Hawkins" — homeless people's respectful term for cold weather, "the Hawk" — arrives. "Y'all got to get Mom off the street. I don't know how she survived last year," he says, his tone close to desperation.

Mom, though, prefers the freedom and uncertainty of the streets to shelters. "We walk the streets all day, having fun, talking to one another," she says.

Having fun while incessantly walking the streets might seem like a contradiction, but not to the people I met last week. In Durham earlier that night, some other guys and I shared some laughs and wine and talked about how they ended up on the street. They drank cheap wine and asked strangers for a hand, usually receiving only one finger — the middle one — in reply.

Ain't it funny how the people who have the least are the ones who laugh most often? And how they seem most willing to share? The guys I walked the streets with freely shared their food — mainly chicken they'd scrounged from behind a fast-food restaurant — and wine with me.

When one of our quartet scores a bottle of Night Train from a corner convenience store — no one asks how, although we know he was broke when he entered the store — everybody is jubilant. Or is it relieved?

Each takes a swallow and passes it down. When the bottle reaches me, I take a healthy swig without even wiping off the top of the bottle — that would have been a sign of disrespect — and ignore the half-chewed piece of chicken floating around.

Disturbing and familiar feelings start bubbling up. But I reach into my pocket, feel the key to my apartment and realize that I — unlike these guys — will eventually go home to a warm bed.

After a few more gulps and revelry, I forget about the meat inside the bottle and don't even notice when it disappears down someone's — I don't know whose — throat.

December 02, 1993

The appearance of justice may depend on the judged

I remember the last time my first ex-wife caught me in the middle of something I shouldn't have been doing.

I said: "Who're you gonna believe, Baby, me or your eyes?"

Unfortunately for me, she believed her eyes.

Unfortunately for America, some Simi Valley jurors refused to believe their eyes last year in a police brutality trial and acquitted four cops of beating Rodney King as if he'd said something bad about their mamas.

Well, the book was closed on that repulsive chapter of American history, and the ending was no surprise to me: A black guy goes into court, gets the book thrown at him and is slammed upside the head with it. The end.

Of course, that black dude — a most unsympathetic character named Damian "Football" Williams — had earlier slammed a brick upside the head of a white trucker who was pulled from his vehicle during widespread violence immediately after the King verdict. Williams got 10 years in the slammer and the prosecutor said she was sorry he didn't get more.

No question about it, Williams is supposed to do some hard time for what he did to Reginald Denny. The attack was cowardly and sickening. And if Denny were some kin to me, Williams would want to stay in prison because the streets wouldn't be safe for him. But although Williams received the maximum sentence and a stern lecture from the judge, the two cops convicted of taking batting practice with Rodney King's head got the minimum sentence — 30 months — and an apology from the federal judge who had to sentence them.

Television reporters blabbered away, trying to justify the disparate sentences by pointing out how unremorseful Williams seemed after the verdict — the way he smiled and gave the thumbs-up signal to his family. What's so surprising about that? If I were about to enter a prison full of hardened criminals — some of whom haven't seen a woman since Michael Jackson was black — I wouldn't enter the joint boo-hooing and saying "Oh, I'm so sorry" either. Even if I were.

But enough about Williams: Let's talk about me.

See, I'm scheduled to be in court in a couple of weeks myself — driving a little over the speed limit, the officer said — and I don't know what to wear. Now, to most of you, that's no big deal. You do as my "mouth" — that's street lingo for attorney — suggested and wear a dark suit and tie. "Try to look presentable, so the judge will know you don't have two heads and kick cats," she said.

"But I do kick cats," I said.

My next lawyer also suggested I wear a suit.

But I'm in a real quandary because dressing too well — you know, my lime-green leisure suit similar to the one Ron O'Neal wore in "Superfly's Revenge" — might lead the judge to think I'm loaded and he'll hit me with a big fine. On the other hand, if I go in looking down at the heels — "poor-mouthin'," as we used to call it in Rockingham — the judge is going to think I'm broke, busted and can't be trusted, and wonder where a broke man was going in such an all-fired hurry.

Being pulled over by the law isn't anyone's idea of fun. But every time it happens to me, I have visions of myself on television — against a backdrop of burning buildings, holding an ice bag up to my eye — saying something like, "Can't we all just get along?"

But I've got to admit, the state trooper who nabbed me, while not a warm, fuzzy type, treated me with dignity and respect. And I treated him the same way.

As he cautiously approached the car, hand on his holster, I remembered the first law smart brothers always observe upon being stopped: Keep your hands visibly and firmly on the steering wheel.

He had to use a crowbar to pry 'em loose, because I had no desire to be listed in the obituaries as a mistake. Nor did I want to be treated like a Rodney King.

December 09, 1993

Put the bankers before the lawyers on the hit list

Dick the Butcher was wrong, folks.

Dick, a character in Shakespeare's Henry VI, is remembered mainly for his quote, "The first thing we do, let's kill all the lawyers."

He no doubt said that before trying to withdraw some of his own shillings from his friendly medieval neighborhood bank. He would have added another scourge on society — bankers — to his hit list had he made a deposit on a Thursday afternoon and then been unable to withdraw a farthing of it before Saturday — and only then if he had an automated teller machine card.

As I write this, I'm sitting here broke, busted and can't be trusted, eating a seven-course meal: six sardines and a Coke with peanuts floating around in the bottom of the bottle. Even though I got paid yesterday and faithfully and immediately deposited my check in the bank, I'm as broke as a convict because the bank wouldn't give me a dime of my own moolah.

My banker, bless his heart, has a great sense of humor. When I told him I had an outstanding check that would come bouncing in any minute and that had to be covered, he actually offered to call the person and explain the situation with my account.

Thanks, but no thanks.

See, none of the people I know and owe — especially my first ex-wife and her attorney — accept excuses. And they don't accept American Express.

You know me: I'm nothing if not understanding. So I tried to give the bank the benefit of the doubt and convince myself there are good reasons why it takes almost 30 hours for a payroll check to clear and why banks should charge $20 when an exemplary customer of several years bounces a $2 check.

Yeah, and if you believe that, you'll also believe there's a good reason Whoopi Goldberg and Jim Belushi keep getting paid to make movies.

The final straw leading to my disenchantment with my bank was when it refused to accept a check for deposit.

Teller: Sorry. We can't accept that.

Me: What ... ?

Teller: Next customer, please.

I split when I saw her hand move to what I figured was the silent alarm for irate customers. I then went to the office of a bank dude in a starched white shirt who explained that, because I didn't have the amount for the personal check already in my account, they couldn't accept a check — not even for deposit. If they did, the teller had explained, "It'll take 10 days — maybe more, maybe less — before you get credit for it."

So I walked across the street, cashed the check at my bookie's ... er, associate's ... bank, and returned to my bank to deposit it. The teller was not amused when I asked: "Do y'all accept cash?"

There were no tears, no pleading, no gnashing of teeth from the bank's officials when I informed them I was closing my account and withdrawing my $23.72. As a matter of principle, I've decided to do as many Americans who lived through the Great Depression or the S&L scandal of 1990 did: I now put my money in a Mason jar.

I'm not saying all banks are as cold as a hired gun, nor that banks are the only institutions insensitive to their customers.

Monopolistic phone companies have a reserved spot in the Hall of Infamy for their treatment of customers, too. I went last week to straighten out my phone bill after my service was wrongly disconnected. Man, I was hot and about ready to turn the office into a car wash when a woman who was madder than I came into the GTE office in Durham.

"You mean to tell me," she asked incredulously, "that you cut my service off for $17?" She later told me she'd had phone service for 15 years and had never even been late paying.

She got the same excuse I got — a new computer system that's quick on the trigger, one that will drop a non-paying customer quicker than Pepsi dropped Michael Jackson.

The bank also blamed computers, leading me to conclude that Shakespeare and Dick the Butcher were wrong. Maybe the first thing we should do is unplug all the computers.

December 20, 1993

It's more than the disease of the month; it's a killer

I never had any friends later in life like the ones I had when I was 12. God, does anybody?"

That was the last line in a movie I saw the other night. It's also the story of my life. And probably yours.

Only problem is, the dude who was my best friend at 12 died of AIDS. And he didn't even tell me he was sick. From what I hear, he didn't tell anyone, not even his family. That's the kind of disease this is. Makes you withdraw just when you want to reach out.

I hadn't spoken to Kevin in several years, and because his life had been so much harder than mine since we were kids, I doubt he had the time or the inclination to sit back and reminisce about the mischief we used to get into just as easily as falling off a log.

I'll bet to the people who read his obituary — if, indeed, it made the papers in Washington — he was just a 37-year-old junkie who contracted the fatal disease from a dirty needle. To me, someone who knew him before the problems of his life forced him to seek solace in drugs, he was the friendliest boy in the world. I wish you could have known him.

I've been thinking about AIDS a lot lately, ever since last week when I attended the funeral of a brother who used to work at The N&O and who died from complications related to AIDS. His name was Kelly, he was 31, and he was a gentle, intelligent man who had a lot to contribute to the world. He wanted to be a playwright.

My friend Kevin, on the other hand, was a high school dropout who — truth be told — never succeeded at much after adolescence. He was, charitably, an average Joe. Not outstanding in anything, except being my friend when I needed one.

I'm not one of those people who try to glorify people in death beyond what they were in life, to say "Gee, what a swell guy" when in reality the dude might have been a jerk whom I couldn't stand.

But these two cats were swell guys. And my life was enriched by both of them.

It's sometimes easy to forget that AIDS is such a killer, that it's more than just another "disease of the month" to be turned into a television movie starring Farrah Fawcett and that guy who played John Boy Walton.

Sometimes, it's not until you're standing there, peering into a coffin, that you realize that this thing is — as the B-boys hanging on the corner say — "the real deal, Holyfield."

I mean, between Magic Johnson's beatific smile and Beautiful People celebrities wearing red ribbons just to be cool, you may forget that AIDS can take you away from here — will take you away from here.

Speaking of Magic: Neither Kevin nor Kelly was the kind of guy to complain about the hysteria — the national gnashing of teeth, actually — that greeted Johnson's announcement that he had AIDS. They were both too cool for that.

But I'm not. I — and scores of nameless, faceless dudes I've talked to who are afflicted with the ailment — resent that their condition elicited not a fraction of the concern or sympathy heaped upon Magic.

I wish somebody, anybody, would tell me why the world almost stops in mid-dribble when a famous basketball player contracts the disease, yet it takes little note when two decent guys — one of whom never did anything outstanding except be my best friend — die from it?

January 03, 1994

NAACP's image reflected in puzzling awards ceremony

Uh oh. Rap singer Tupac Shakur is arrested for shooting two cops and sexually assaulting a woman, so you know what that means, right?

Yep, an NAACP Image Award.

Fortunately, Sixpac ... uh, excuse me ... Tupac didn't win the image award for best actor: Denzel Washington did — for "Malcolm X." But the fact that the guy was even considered for an "image" award must have W.E.B. Dubois spinning in his grave. A New York congresswoman, among others, boycotted the awards ceremony, citing Tupac's misogynistic lyrics and his public image.

Face it, folks: the once-proud NAACP, an organization that has been at the forefront of black progress since 1909, has become a joke even to people who — like me — are beneficiaries of its good works.

I hate to say it, but if the NAACP — or at least its "Image Awards" — were a horse, I'd take it out back and shoot it to put it out of its misery.

We've got UZI-slinging black punks blowing innocent people away for such offenses as wearing their caps tilted to the wrong side, yet the NAACP is busy shilling for Michael Jackson — a chemically lightened guy who at every turn has run from his blackness the way I'd run from a buck-naked Whoopi Goldberg.

Remember when they were making a video for "Free Willy," a movie which I thought was about an imprisoned brother but was actually about a captive whale? Well, Michael requested — no, make that "demanded" — that he be portrayed in the video by a white kid.

Race had nothing to do with it, he insisted: "I just wanted the best dancer," he said. (At least he is helping destroy one stereotype: that we can all dance.)

The Beloathed Gloved One can have himself portrayed by an ambidextrous albino for all I care. That's his prerogative. But I was baffled, insulted, even nauseated by the spectacle of people at the NAACP Image Awards continually interrupting his pity-seeking speech the other night with standing ovations — as though Jackson were some prodigal son returning home.

I shouldn't have been surprised, though: this is the same organization that attacked the awful movie "The Color Purple" for its demeaning portrayal of black men, yet cried "racism" when the movie didn't win an Oscar.

And they wonder why membership and contributions are down!

What's important is finding an answer to the violence, teen pregnancy and illiteracy that leave too many kids unprepared for whatever opportunity presents itself to them. What's not important is going on television decrying the racism in the media's coverage of Michael Jackson. When it comes right down to it, I can't see a bucket of warm llama spit's difference between the media treatment accorded Jacko and the incestuous Woody Allen.

For the kids' sakes, I hope Jacko is innocent of the allegations against him. But I realize the impact of his guilt or innocence means nothing to people who are catching a different kind of hell every day — except, perhaps, his cellmate. It is folly to waste energy bemoaning the media's treatment of a guy who can afford the best lawyers in the world, when we've got dudes languishing in prison who can't even get the NAACP to accept a collect telephone call. I know: they call me after calling the organization.

Ever heard the quote "Patriotism is the last refuge of a scoundrel"? Actually, "race pride is the last refuge of a scoundrel."

In that regard, Michael has become the Vanessa Williams of the 1990s. Before she was defrocked as Miss America, Vanessa rarely gave an interview in which she didn't proudly point out that she never dated black guys or joined black organizations or hung out with black kids in school.

Once her sordid past was uncovered, though, 'Nessa played the race card at every opportunity, claiming racial persecution. The only thing she didn't do was wear an Afro and a dashiki, which I expect to see Jacko do while singing a crotch-grabbing rendition of "Say It Loud (I'm Black and I'm Proud — Now)."

I asked a representative at the NAACP's headquarters in Baltimore if last week's Image Awards show was the first Michael ever attended. His response: "Uh, well, I'm sure he must have been to one before, a long time ago. After all, we've been having them for 26 years."

If he has ever been to one, I'll bet it was before he got his first nose job.

January 10, 1994

Parting with gun brings no sweet sorrow — almost

Man, do I feel like a schmuck.

Just think: I could have had a brand new pair of Air Jordans — or at least a gift certificate for Toys R Expensive — if I'd only been a little slower about disarming myself.

Unless you've been cowering inside a bunker the past few weeks — and who could blame you, considering all the hot-tempered folks running around with guns — you know about the myriad of gun trade-ins going on around the country: guns for money, shoes, toys, licorice sticks.

Somebody came up with the brilliant idea that lives could be saved if people could be induced to part with their weapons. And thousands — ranging from grandmothers wanting some extra cash for Christmas to thugs looking for a down payment on a newer, deadlier model — turned in all kinds.

That's good. But the reason I feel so bad is that I got rid of mine just before all that mania hit.

Let me set the record straight before I proceed:

I developed no emotional attachment to my gun, an ugly little .380 that sounded like somebody bursting a paper bag when I fired it — which I did only in a shooting range.

Unlike some of my buddies, I never felt I was under-dressed unless I strapped on a shooting iron. And I have nothing in common with those Elmer Fudd clones who put bumper stickers on their pickups saying, "You can have my gun — when you pry it from my cold, dead fingers."

That is, however, the way I feel about my television remote control.

As much as I hated owning a gun, I must admit that having it saved my life once, possibly twice. But overall, it became more trouble than it was worth: Because it almost cost me my life twice, too.

The last time was about a month ago. I was coming home at about 3 in the morning after a wild night of — I swear — washing, drying and folding clothes at my apartment complex laundry. I had a giant bag of underwear in one hand and — apparently suffering a delusion that I was back in the Chicago area — my trusty sidearm in the other. Sorry, but some habits are hard to break.

So I'm getting out of the car, wondering how come my whites don't get as white as those on TV. But just as I rise, the moon gets blocked out by this big, muscular guy walking out from behind a Jeep. Although he was bigger than I, the only thing I saw was the shining, silver-plated gun in his right hand. I knew from watching Clint Eastwood movies that it was a .357 Magnum.

It took less than a second for me to recognize him — and him me.

It was my neighbor, the friendly, body-building guy from upstairs with a wife and two dogs. We talk daily, although usually unarmed, and he even volunteers to keep The Kid for me when I have to work late.

But in the split second before recognition set in, all I saw was a big white guy with a bigger gun, and all he saw was a big black dude with a bagful of drawers — and a gun.

After unleashing sighs that stirred the trees, we stood in the parking lot and talked for a few minutes. He explained that he works as a bar-tender-bouncer and encounters people who, shall we say, haven't been to finishing school and don't read "Miss Manners."

We were lucky: Neither of us became tragic, fatal accidents.

But it was close. That incident, plus continually having to make sure The Kid didn't stumble across it, made keeping the gun a losing proposition.

Most people I know say keeping a gun lets them sleep easier. Funny, but getting rid of mine lets me do the same thing.

I still wish I could have at least gotten a pair of shoes out of the deal, though.

January 24, 1994

State keeps bars on woman who straightened up her life

Shirley has done all the right things.

No, wait. First, she did all the wrong things.

But after four prison sentences, 10 years behind bars and being hooked on Boy — the street name for heroin — she got on the good foot. She went to college and set about making a better life for herself and her daughter.

Her daughter — who stood beside her mother even when she was behind bars — graduated from high school in Oxford within a month of the day Shirley received a degree in behavioral sciences from Shaw University. They looked forward, with something close to glee, to a life in which they — not a warden — held the key. Their destinies were in their own hands, and no matter what — Shirley figured — the nightmare was over.

Wrong! The nightmare of prison is over, but Shirley still finds herself imprisoned by her past. And the state still holds the key.

See, despite her impressive initiative, Shirley has to support herself and her daughter — plus pay back a college loan for a degree she now feels isn't worth the sheepskin it's written on — by working odd jobs: emptying bed pans, making upholstery for furniture, stuff like that.

At the same time Gov. Jim Hunt is touting a program to rehabilitate and educate prison inmates as part of his anti-crime package, directors for various state agencies keep slamming the door in the face of a woman who should be held up as a role model to everyone who has ever heard a cell door click shut and had their name replaced by a number.

Nobody's offered Shirley a job, but opponents of Hunt's anti-crime package want her to testify — in front of a special session of the House of Representatives — on her job-hunting frustrations.

Oh, people obligatorily call her in for interviews and tell her how proud they are of her, but in the end ... well, she gets it in the end.

The last rejection, and the one that makes her feel she can't stand another one, occurred just three weeks ago. Her resume and application for a job as a health care technician — even with the prominent admission that she had a criminal record — caught the attention of an administrator at Dorothea Dix Hospital. She called Shirley in for an interview.

"She asked me what kind of conviction I had and I was straight up with her: I told her it was felonious larceny. She made a telephone call and asked someone if there was a statute of limitations for a felony record ... When she hung up, she shook her head and said, 'Sorry.'

"Ooooh, I was just disgusted. Seeing my friends dying or getting killed — and then getting locked up — gave me the initiative to try to change my life, get a job and give something back to the community. That's what I want to do. The state is the one that's always preaching about an education, and then they won't even hire you when you have all the qualifications.

"Sometimes I feel that all the work I did was in vain," she said.

Shirley knows — and is frightened by the realization — that there is one job she can always go back to: stealing. Hell, that's how she supported herself when she was a dopehead. "I don't want to resort to that again, but it took care of my drug habit — so I know it'll pay my bills." She said as much to Judge Jerry Leonard in 1992 after being arrested for stealing clothes — which she planned to sell to pay rent — from Hecht's.

"I told the judge I had acquired an independence I didn't want to give up and that I couldn't get a job ... He said, 'Since you're trying to do something for yourself, I'll do something for you.'" He sentenced her to 45 hours of community service and gave her a stern warning not to come before him again.

She hasn't. But if she doesn't get a job soon, she will.

"One interview I went on for the state, the woman said she'd like to hire me but couldn't because of the stigma associated with ex-cons. I asked her 'How long is society going to stigmatize someone who has gone through their system and paid their debt?'"

January 27, 1994

Jamal Elliott's death creates enough blame to go around

I didn't have to spend $3.99 a minute to call Dionne Warwick and the Psychic Connection hotline to find out if Michael Seagroves would be found guilty or even retried for smoking Jamal Elliott.

I knew he'd skate the moment I saw Meribeth Seagroves on the stand dabbing her eyes while describing the havoc wrought in her husband's life by the events of March 18, 1993. I could almost hear the violins playing in the background during her testimony.

I was reaching for the Kleenex myself, especially after Seagroves' attorney started talking about how devastated "Mike" — did you notice how "Michael" became "Mike" whenever his attorney was talking? — was by the shootings. If you had shut your eyes for a minute and listened to William Thomas, you would have thought his client was the one shot in the back four times.

But my tears — at least those for the Seagroveses — dissipated as soon as I thought about another victim: Phyllis Elliott — Jamal's mom — seated at the end of a bench in the courtroom, hunched over and weeping after hearing that, from a legal standpoint anyway, no one was guilty of killing her son.

The ultimate victim, of course, was Jamal himself. From everything I've read about him, the dude was no Opie Taylor. If he and his running buddies — none of whom were strangers to police — had any ambition at all, it seemed to be to qualify for the "No-Good-Nik Olympics."

But one thing he had going for himself, something all the trigger-happy, law-and-order nuts who say he got what he deserved seem to forget, was youth: The dude was a kid. Fifteen years old. Who knows? Given a chance, he might have been able to contribute to something more than just the police blotter.

Ben Carson did. He, like Jamal, ran with a bad crowd and seemed destined for prison or Forest Lawn Cemetery at an early age. The only thing that saved him from prison was that the guy he stabbed in a Detroit gang fight wore a belt with a big buckle and Carson's knife didn't puncture anything vital.

Carson, 41, is still messing with knives, but now it's as chief of pediatric neurosurgery for Baltimore's Johns Hopkins Hospital. At 35, he performed the first successful separation of twins joined at the head.

I'm not saying Jamal would have become a world famous doctor or anything else. But he deserved a chance to find out. He sure didn't deserve to die in the middle of the street for trying to steal a motorcycle and some golf clubs.

I don't care what all those venom-filled folks who call Tom Joyner's radio talk show say: Somebody's guilty. You could blame the media for relentlessly portraying black males as vicious criminals and making poor Mike feel they were a threat even as they ran away. I don't know Seagroves, never even talked to him — since he hasn't returned any of my calls. But I doubt he or any other sane person would shoot somebody in the back if he thought they were only after his motorcycle and golf clubs. But because of the way the media portray black dudes, he probably looked upon them as threats even as they fled.

Hell, even Jesse Jackson, a professional black — not to be confused with a black professional — is trying to extricate his foot from his mouth after recently saying he breathes a sigh of relief when the footsteps coming up behind him on a darkened street turn out to be white and not black. We've all, unfortunately, been conditioned to think like that. So, if you don't want to blame Mike, which you don't — despite the four slugs in the back — blame the media. Or else, blame society for instilling a "shoot first, explain second" mentality.

But please, don't tell Phyllis Elliott nobody's to blame.

Listen here: Michael Seagroves had every right to defend his home and his young 'un. And as a father, I'll tell you something else: If the dudes had been coming at him with bad intentions while his baby lay defenseless upstairs ... well ... I'd have helped him pull the trigger.

But Elliott was shot in the back. Mike said he didn't aim but fired wildly. If he can shoot one guy in the back four times — and take off a piece of another's ear — without aiming, imagine what he could do if he aimed.

It's been two decades since I last broke into somebody's home. I quit after realizing the bootleggers in Rockingham had already robbed our intended victims, who were always drunk — and also after I found out that even drunk people can shoot straight.

I point out that lurid aspect of my past only to show that, if I or any of my partners in crime had ever been shot, it would have had to be in the back because we — like most every other criminal I've ever known — were punks who traveled the path of least resistance.

I feel sorry for Mike and Meribeth. Sure, I do. But I feel sorrier for Phyllis Elliott.

Most of all, I feel sorry for the people who see nothing wrong with shooting a 15-year-old kid in the back for trying to steal some golf clubs.

January 31, 1994

Councilman Skippy takes wrong turn on funeral escorts

It just so happened that when I first came here from Indiana to find a place to live last year, a cousin of mine had just been killed in a drug-related shooting in Rockingham — yes, Rockingham. A woman he was taxiing around got into a fight with her drug suppliers and they, after killing her, had to do him in to eliminate any witnesses.

I brought with me from Indiana a woman I was thinking of asking to become the next former Mrs. Saunders, but she — or I, I can't remember which — came to her senses and "I do" became "I go."

One of the more memorable — and few printable — exchanges between us occurred as we followed the procession to the cemetery for my cousin's funeral.

HER: Why are all those cars pulled over on the side of the road?

ME: Huh?

See, I was raised here in God's country, and it never occurred to me that there is a place where people don't pull over for funerals and turn off their car radios out of respect — unless a really good song is playing.

That, as much as coleslaw on barbecue sandwiches, Moon Pies and the State Fair, is a part of Southern tradition — a common courtesy you automatically show people in death even if, in life, you wouldn't have shared a plate of chitlins with them.

My girlfriend was even more amazed to see police officers standing at attention — hats over their hearts — along the route to the cemetery. It baffled her, but it gave me a warm feeling to know I was moving back to a state where even people killed in decidedly unheroic circumstances are accorded the same degree of official respect that a mayor would receive.

Now along comes Skip London, Durham City Council member, wanting to eliminate police funeral procession escorts — or charge citizens for them — because he considers escorts frivolous extravagances the city can't afford if we're going to put more cops downtown to make visitors to the Carolina Theatre feel safe.

Uh, excuse me Councilman Skip, but ain't that what taxes are for? To pay for municipal services? Hell, if you have to pay for a police escort for a funeral, you might as well live in Indiana.

If the council accepts Skippy's proposal to charge citizens for this basic right and police escorts become optional, funeral directors will be forced to schedule funerals for times when there's hardly any traffic on Durham's streets — like whenever Duke plays UNC. And preachers will have to alter their eulogies to something like:

Ashes to ashes, dust to dust

We're going to the cemetery,

but we gotta pay the cops first.

Councilman Skippy said it's "incredulous that six motorcycle officers spend a large part of their time providing funeral escorts" — as if that's the silliest thing he's ever heard.

Well, actually, something sillier was Skip, former mayor Harry Rodenhizer and others spending nearly $10,000 to go to Russia. I don't know about y'all, but I think the $50,000 or so the city spent last year to provide dignified police escorts for more than 1,000 funerals was better utilized than the nearly $10,000 they spent last May to seek world peace, to cheer Elvis impersonators named "Ivan" and to drink good vodka.

Skip must not realize that the police escorts are a very cost-effective use of time. Can you imagine the ensuing chaos if no cops directed traffic or how much time officers would spend investigating accidents caused by funeral processions running red lights just trying to keep up with a hearse?

Don't get me wrong. I think it is damned sporting of Skip to be concerned about how our tax dollars are spent. We need more elected officials with similar concerns.

But I'd like to make a suggestion: The next time he gets the urge to go to Russia, he can just watch Rocky and Bullwinkle on television, wait til Boris Badanov and Natasha come on screen, then raise his glass in a toast: "Za vasha zdarovye."

I'm not sure, but I think that means: "Sorry I couldn't come back, Boris, but Harry didn't win this year."

February 03, 1994

A disgusted dad admits it: Spanking begets spanking

I didn't want to hit him — really I didn't.

Ever since the last time my dad chased me with a two-by-four — for streaking through Rockingham in high school — I'd vowed to become one of those Ward Cleaver-type dads: get me a cardigan sweater to mow the grass in and never raise a hand at my son except to give a "high-five."

But then I became a dad. And last week, I became an angry, concerned dad who felt compelled to put his hands on The Kid in a less than loving manner.

Everybody remembers when your parents would make you go get a switch so they could whip you, right? Right? Man, no prisoner taking his final walk to the gas chamber was ever filled with such dread as I felt going to find a tree with just the right kind of switches.

And of course you were afraid to get a puny one because your parents might go out and chop down a whole hickory tree. Those whippings were usually preceded with "This is going to hurt me more than it hurts you." To which I'd reply — to myself, of course — "Yeah, but not in the same place."

I didn't use a switch last week — just my hand — but guess what? Your parents were right. It did hurt me more. The Kid recovered quickly — in about five minutes — although anybody alerted by his screams might've concluded I was killing him and dialed 911.

It took me considerably longer to get over it. Whoever said "violence begets violence" wasn't lying, but it also begets disgust. I mean, I was so disgusted — mainly with myself for having no more creative solution than violence — that I actually refused to watch WWF rasslin', even though Ravishing Rick Rude, my favorite villain, was fighting The Undertaker.

Over the years, I've interviewed dozens of battered women and the men who battered them, and there is one common thread in their stories: All the women said, "If he hits you once, he'll hit you again," and the men admitted the assaults became easier after the first time.

That frightens me, because I don't want it to become easier. I want it to make me feel as bad as I do now. You can bet I don't want to be like the guy who called me — after the Durham Department of Social Services knocked on his door — to adamantly defend his right to knock his kids around when they "need" it.

After the whipping, I did what I always do when I feel overwhelmed as a parent: I went to my library of self-help tapes: "The Cosby Show" and "The Andy Griffith Show."

I thumbed through my archives of Andy tapes — he had the tougher job because Cliff, the lucky devil, had Claire — to see how ol' Ange would have handled the situation. No luck: As far as I can tell, the closest Andy ever came to whipping Opie was when Opie said he'd gotten a quarter from a man named Mr. McBeevee who walked through the trees in the forest and wore silver, jangling spurs on his boots.

Andy was fixing to flog the boy for lying — or stealing a quarter, I couldn't figure out which — but turns out he wasn't lying: The dude walking around in the trees worked for Duke Power and was putting up some power lines trying to figure out how to charge more for electricity.

But my boy really lied — and put himself in danger at the same time. He was already on punishment ... er, we call it restricted privileges ... and won't be able to watch television or ride his bike until he's 29 — so that wasn't an option.

I have read Dr. Spock and T. Berry Brazelton and all those experts who contend spankings can scar a child for life. But I'll bet they've never been stared down by an obstinate five-year-old daring you to do something about it.

Like generations of parents, I found out that you can talk 'til you're blue in the face, but sooner or later you — just like Madonna — will have to say "Nothing'll work but a good spanking."   *February 07, 1994*

The man who won't Joe Jackson the Joe Jackson family

Gordon Keith of Gary, Ind., is the most famous man you've never heard of. He called me a few days ago — soon after Michael Jackson bought off the family of a little boy who was suing him for being a pervert.

If it weren't for Keith, the Jacksons — all but Tito, whose natural talents would have shone through anyway — would probably be working at Jiffy Lube, saying things like: "Do you want the 14-point treatment, sir?" Or wearing a headset at the drive-through, asking: "Would you like fries with that shake, ma'am?"

Don't believe me?

Just read Michael's autobiography, "Moonwalk." Even the Beloathed Gloved One himself admits that there'd be no Michael Jackson, superstar, without Gordon Keith. See, Papa Joe Jackson had despaired of ever breaking into big time show business. Club owners were telling him that children's groups were out of style, and he was about to throw all the instruments he'd bought for his boys into Lake Michigan.

Then Keith met the boys. It was Oct. 7, 1967. (He remembers the exact date. Wouldn't you?) He became their first manager, wrote and recorded a couple of songs on his Steeltown label and got them some big gigs. The rest, as they say, is a damn shame.

Keith refined the group, bought the guys clothes and food from his U.S. Steel paycheck, then watched helplessly as Berry Gordy of Motown came along and took them away.

That's when Gordon Keith realized the verbal agreement he had with Joe Jackson was worthless. But even though Joe Jackson discarded Keith like a wet foodstamp, he's not gloating, as I would, about the misfortune that has hit the Jackson family — the blistering TV miniseries, sex-abuse allegations against Michael, LaToya learning to write.

Indeed, the 6-foot-5, 240-pound gentle giant, whom I met as a reporter in Gary, called to tell me how sorry he felt for Michael and to talk about a new song he has written. It's called "Ain't That a Joe Jackson Way to Treat Somebody?" and it's the first hint of anger Keith has allowed himself to express publicly. But what he really wanted to talk about was Michael and how he'd like to help him!

And he wasn't kidding.

Gordon Keith is probably broker than I am — many were the nights we shared a bottle of apple juice while discussing a book he wants to write about his brush with fame and infamy — but he has more integrity than just about anybody I know. For years, he has refused the entreaties of sleazy shows like "Hard Copy," which have offered him big bucks to dish up some real dirt on the family. I know: They've called me and asked me to intervene on their behalf.

Settling the lawsuit, Gordon Keith said, prevented the little kid from being dragged through a lot of bad publicity. He's glad of that. "But I want to see the Jackson family get the help it needs," he said. "By just paying money, Michael is able to perpetuate the myth that they're the All-American family."

Bull.

I disagree with those music industry analysts who claim the public will forgive the King of Pop as soon as he has another hit. I think you can stick a fork in him because — as an entertainer — he's done.

Two guys I know — Reynaud Jones, a former bass player for the Jacksons, and Bob Smith, a Gary songwriter — would have no problem believing Jackson is guilty. They had a lawsuit against Jackson for nearly 10 years in which they sought money for two songs they say he took from them and never paid for. Jacko steadfastly refused — as a matter of principle, he claims — to settle that suit.

When his luck changed and the tide of the case began swinging their way, Jackson offered them a million bucks. They rejected it and subsequently lost the suit a couple of weeks ago.

But the pattern is crystal clear: When his ... ahem ... principles threaten his career, Michael is capable of changing them faster than he does those funny-looking, sequined coats with the epaulets.

Kind of makes you wonder, doesn't it?

February 14, 1994

The measurement of success depends on the yardstick

John Elliott is used to people looking down at him — and not just when he's kneeling to shine their shoes.

As a shoeshine man, Elliott makes his living at a job that elicits neither respect nor envy. To most of us, shining shoes ranks right up there on the pleasure scale with getting a tooth extracted or having to ask your first ex-wife for a favor — both of which are roads I will soon have to travel.

It's easy for people watching John walk along Durham's streets in jeans, an old coat and scraggly beard to consider him an unmotivated failure, someone whose fate should be avoided.

Until you talk to him. Then you realize he's a genuine entrepreneur who controls his own destiny and likes his life fine, thank you very much.

"People have a tendency to look down on you if you do what I do,"

Elliott said while taking me on a tour of Durham — both as it is now and as it used to be. As a Bull City resident for all his 47 years, he's qualified.

"That was the first Hardee's in Durham," he says, pointing to a building on University Drive next to a car dealership which he says is owned by one of his best friends.

He regales with tales of when the Hayti section thrived, when movie theaters bearing names like the Booker T. and the Regal and a hotel called the Biltmore existed, and you could go to a restaurant called Papa Jack's and buy a big bowl of pinto beans and a huge hunk of corn bread for $1.

He speaks wistfully of a period when black executives rushing to meetings in the Hayti business district — an area known around the world at one time as "the black Wall Street" — routinely left him big tips because they didn't have time to wait for their change.

"There were barbershops up and down that area," he says, the grin on his face finally breaking into a big laugh. "I racked up all along there. There was good money in those days."

A shoeshine was 10 cents when John started out in the late 1950s in the old Belk department store in downtown Durham.

"Man, you could get a shine and a meal — a hotdog and a soda — for a quarter," he says. "A shine now is $3, and some people consider that a lot. But it's not when you think about how much the stuff costs now and how important it is to have a pair of shined shoes. You can't put a price on that."

John comes across as something of an Ann Landers with a shoeshine box, dispensing advice along with spiffily shined shoes.

"Sometimes when people are down and have a problem, they need someone to liven them up. That's what I do. I mostly just listen, because it's important in my business to know when to keep your mouth shut so you don't talk yourself out of a tip.

"But sometimes I give advice. There was one guy who was gonna go get silly, go hurt somebody. I talked him out of it, gave him a Bible verse to read. He came back the next day and thanked me and gave me $20."

He says he has a steady clientele in downtown Durham's office buildings, but his goal to expand to the Research Triangle Park is being delayed while he fends off a hostile takeover.

"Competitors are trying to knock me out. They want my piece of the rock. But it's not going to happen," he said.

Unlike most career shoeshine men I've known, John doesn't have a bent back or dirty nails: He says he gets a manicure every so often when business has been particularly good. On a good day, he said, he can knock down $50 or $60.

So, go ahead, look down your noses and laugh at John and people who do the other jobs society reserves for the so-called uninspired. But I'm not laughing, because I just read philosopher Ralph Waldo Emerson's definition of success: to laugh often and love much.

Sounds to me like John has done a lot of both.

March 03, 1994

Durham lawyers may have to change gears — and diets

Squeeeeal! Squeeeeal!

That ain't the sound from the infamous male-bonding scene in "Deliverance." It's the sound of defense lawyers in Durham yelping over a rule change that will have some of them vacationing in Myrtle Beach instead of St. Croix, packing baloney sandwiches instead of lunching on crab cakes at Parizade and saying stuff to their spouses like, "Really, dear, the public schools aren't so bad."

Pardon me. I can hardly see the screen for the tears in my eyes, so broken up am I over this revolting development.

What development? Well, people charged with traffic violations in Durham can now be Monty Hall and play "Let's Make A Deal" in court — without having to hire an expensive, suit-wearing mouthpiece to do it for them.

See, in a switch from a rule that had been in effect in Durham for years, defendants in traffic court can now negotiate directly with prose-cutors in the DA's office instead of having to pay an attorney a couple of hundred bucks.

Like I did.

When the smoke had cleared and the tears had dried after my cameo appearance in court last month, I had paid more than $600 for an attorney to cop a plea for me. Oh, I'm not complaining — well, yes I am — but he gave it his all, a real Hollywood reading. Aided by a Southern drawl as thick as cold molasses — that's the reason I picked him — his performance in court would've shamed Atticus Finch in "To Kill a Mockingbird."

"Yo' honuh," he began. "My client is a really nice man ... raisin' his young 'un by hisself, and he sho'ly can't afford to be without a license for a whole year." (That gives you an indication of how fast I was — or how fast they say I was — going.)

While my high-paid mouth spoke, I stood humbly by, hat-in-hand, looking suitably remorseful and eyeing the exits, ready to run and leap through the window like the Cowardly Lion in "The Wizard of Oz."

I kept my license, but it cost so much I can't afford to go anywhere now.

Lawyers in Durham are battling a decades-long perception that they wield an undue amount of influence at the courthouse, and that the courthouse is run for their benefit — not the public's. I really can't figure out why people are so skeptical of lawyers. Just last month — when the temperature hovered near zero — I actually saw a lawyer with his hands in his own pockets.

Just kidding, guys.

If you're anything like me, you have a lot of trouble working up sympathy for lawyers, especially after hearing the inglorious way they're screaming like stuck pigs over the new policy.

If you believe the lawyers when they say they're only doing it to for us, you'll believe me if I say I've found an affordable house I'd like to sell you in Chapel Hill. Their self-righteous opposition to allowing defendants to speak directly to prosecutors reminds me of the practice, formerly condoned by the Catholic Church, wherein people paid indulgences to priests to talk to God for them. That practice was discarded in the Middle Ages — although I still ask the Rev. Gilchrist to speak to the Big Dude for me every time I go to Rockingham. He's never charged me a cent, though.

The lawyers point out, not very convincingly, that they're only fighting to preserve the sanctity of the prosecutor's office by trying to stop an insidious practice. How, they argue indignantly, can the DA represent the state by prosecuting alleged scofflaws and then offer advice to the scofflaws during negotiations?

The lawyers, altruism and civic-mindedness gushing from every pore, are livid, accusing District Attorney Jim Hardin Jr. of political grandstanding because of an anticipated tough election campaign. Hardin's prosecutors, they say, will be eating untutored, unaccompanied traffic court defendants for lunch.

The lawyers' real fear, if you ask me, is what they will be eating for lunch — baloney.

March 21, 1994

5 plays for 25 bring amazing rediscovery in country music

Now I know how Columbus felt.

Remember how Columbus "discovered" America? Well, I discovered a great country singer the other day.

But just as Columbus' discovery of America came centuries after people were already here, my discovery of Webb Pierce occurred about four decades after most country fans had already enshrined him in their memories and eventually in the Country Music Hall of Fame.

See, I was in Butner recently, talking to residents who worry the state wants to turn their town into one huge correctional center, when I stopped in a place called Bob's to grab some supper.

Whoever said that nothing is perfect lied. I can think of two things: Al Green singing "Let's Stay Together," and a restaurant featuring both an all-you-can-eat sign and a jukebox with old records.

Bob's had both.

I plopped in a quarter, pushed G-0 — "Lonely Blue Boy" by Conway Twitty — and turned to eat my lunch: four slices of pizza, a bowl of chili and a Diet Coke.

"You got fo' mo'," a voice said.

I confess that I've never been an overly religious person — except the time I considered becoming a Baptist minister — but when I realized the Bob's employee in an apron was telling me the jukebox offered five songs for a quarter, I could've sworn I had heard a multitude of celestial angels singing.

I pushed "Lonely Blue Boy" again. And in deference to the angels I was hearing, I also punched in a song called "Softly and Tenderly Jesus Is Calling" by some dude named Webb Pierce.

Oh lawdy. I couldn't even eat. So then I played Webb Pierce singing "If Jesus Came to Your House (What Would You Do)?"

This wasn't Travis Tritt — a country poseur making a few legitimate country tunes, then making a career of remaking pop songs. This wasn't Hank Williams Jr. ripping off his daddy's name and music. This, my friends, was country — the real deal. And I couldn't wait to find someone to tell about my amazing discovery.

The first country music-literate person I told of Webb Pierce — "a bad new country singer," I said — looked at me as if I'd just put ketchup in his chili. It was the same way I looked at a guy in Indiana two years ago when he came in, blabbering excitedly about a new singer he'd just discovered in the discount bin at a music store. It broke his heart when I told him that James Taylor's album "Sweet Baby James" was a classic.

I was just as ignorant of Webb Pierce. Only later did I find out that Pierce was country's "singer of the year" from 1952 to 1956 and from 1961 to 1963, that he drove a Cadillac decorated with a thousand silver dollars and that he built a $75,000 guitar-shaped swimming pool that was so tacky his Nashville neighbors tried to get a court order forcing him to move.

That's my kind of guy. It's also the kind of delightful tackiness country music sorely lacks now that Conway is dead and Porter Waggoner
has retired his neon, rhinestone suits.

I called Bob Thompson, owner of the restaurant, and asked if he's a
country music fan. His response made me want to sit down and drink a
cold one with him — although I doubt he drinks, judging by the stacks of
religious videotapes he was renting for $2. He said, "I went into country
music when I was separating from my first wife. That always turns people to country. I went out and bought every 'cryin'-in-your-beer' country
song I could find."

I welcomed him to the club.

Thompson also cited the British Invasion — primarily the Beatles —
for turning him into the kind of person who can hear something special in
the twang of a steel guitar. If anything is responsible for country's current resurgence — as if you'd need anything besides a broken heart and
a two-timing woman — I'd guess it would be rap music and Michael
Bolton.

Speaking of Columbus, a good friend of mine just got out of prison
last week. His offense: He discovered a Cadillac the same way Columbus
discovered America.

March 28, 1994

Knowing when it's time to stop and time to walk away

Before I tell you about my encounter with Duke basketball player
Grant Hill at South Square mall three days ago, I want to apologize to
three young cats I saw in Durham's Woodcroft neighborhood a week or
so earlier.

See, the dudes — all of whom appeared to be about 16 — were
walking down the street in the middle of a school day, talking loudly and
profanely but saying nothing, eating barbecued pork skins and guzzling
fortified malt liquor from a paper bag.

As I sat in my car, watching them through the rearview mirror —
waiting for them to get closer — I pictured myself jumping out and confronting them, impressing upon them the importance of an education
and taking them back to school. Forcibly, if necessary.

But as they got close enough for me to see the brand of malt liquor
they were drinking — I could smell it, it was so strong — and the type of
skins they were eating, I saw something else: a hardness and worldli-
ness in their eyes that made me step on the gas as soon as the light
turned green.

That's why I want to apologize to them — for not saying something.

Like too many people when confronted with a chance to do something, I punked out. I want to apologize to those kids for letting them continue, uninterrupted, down the street and down the path to ignorance and God only knows what else.

Remember that 1967 song by James Brown, the Godfather of Soul, called "Don't Be A Dropout"? It had a refrain that went, "Without an education you might as well be dead."

Godfather, you ain't never lied.

More than 80 percent of the people in state prisons across the country are high school dropouts, and you can bet many of their offenses were crimes of desperation — desperation spawned by being academically unprepared to compete in this society. You can also bet a lot of them would rather be dead.

That's why the Durham County commissioners should stop jiving around and give school Superintendent Owen "The Big 'O'" Phillips the money he wants to, among other things, pay for programs aimed at keeping kids in school. Oh sure, the commissioners are going to hem and haw and say they can't give him $16 million. Of course they can't. But they can give him some of it — like the $1.8 million he's seeking for dropout prevention. Considering what dropouts cost society, they can't afford not to.

Now, about Grant Hill. My boy and I were walking through the mall trying to find some shoes that light up or talk or something like that when we saw him. People came up to wish him luck, to get an autograph or just to touch the hem of his garment. He signed patiently and began walking away.

Then someone said: "Hey you, c'mere. C'mere."

Hill turned to see a kid, about 8, standing next to his mother and motioning for Hill to come back and sign a piece of paper he held. Hill walked away to continue shopping, leaving a disappointed boy and an angry mother in his wake. Moments later, though, when the kid approached and asked, "May I have your autograph, please?" Hill signed it. The kid, beaming, skipped away.

I hope that incident sticks with the kid the way I expect it will with me. If so, it'll teach him more about manners and respect — for himself and others — than any lecture Hill or anyone else could've given him.

Funny, ain't it?

Grant Hill did that kid a favor by turning away. I did those others a disservice by doing the same thing. Sorry dudes. I should've stopped.

So should you.

March 31, 1994

A message to blacks: Apathy is the ultimate denigration

Call me a sentimental old coot, but I long for the good ol' days of black exploitation movies when all black men were gun-strappin' super-studs with one — NO, two — things on their minds: All whites were evil and all the sisters stood flouncing on corners popping gum and going, "Hey, Sugah. Wanna party?"

Why? Because at least back then, you knew the person who'd written the movie and who was going to pocket the lion's share of the loot was white — and we could get unabashedly enraged and united against racism.

Now, though, the person most likely behind the new minstrel movies and television shows is black. And among many of us, it ain't cool to criticize another black who is "gettin' paid."

Even if he or she is denigrating the race.

Bull feathers.

How, I'd like to know, can people become righteously indignant when they think network news portrays us unfairly, yet sit back smugly humming "We Have Overcome" while erroneous examples of black life — as presented by a new breed of Stepin Fetchit like "Martin" and the folks on "In Living Color" — portray us as idiots.

I'm not as dumb as I look, so I know "Martin" and the other TV shows and movies are not the biggest threat to our existence. Martin Lawrence will have his 15 minutes of fame, get rich, then fade into well-deserved obscurity. But he has the potential to do a lot of harm meantime.

I reached that conclusion when I read an insightful editorial, "Amos 'n' Andy Ride Again," in The Carolinian. I realized this, too, when I talked to the mother of a 7-year-old who boasted of never missing an episode of "Martin" but who had never — ever — been to a PTA meeting at her son's school.

It was evident when I attended several Durham school board hearings at which parents were urged to voice their opinions about their children's education. At some of these meetings, there were fewer black folks than you'd find at a pep rally for the Duke University basketball team.

I've been doing some serious soul-searching since I blasted Durham School Superintendent Owen Phillips earlier this week for kowtowing to the whims of a vocal bunch of Chardonnay-sipping parents who wear sweaters around their necks and drive Volvos. Was I unfair to the Big "O"? Could I have been wrong?

Of course not.

But Phillips doesn't deserve all the blame. Hell, he'd probably say — if he were still speaking to me — that he was just acceding to the wishes of people who made clear what they wanted. That's true, because many black parents stayed home, displaying a plantation mentality — still prevalent among many blacks — that says "let massa handle it." Even when it involves their own children.

What'll it take to get blacks more involved in their children's education, especially when it's obvious others' agendas differ from theirs? I'll give Martin a buzz and see if he'll show up and tell some jokes at the next important meeting.

The Carolinian editorial aptly described the Martin character thusly: "a head-bobbing, slack-jawed, eye-rolling 'whussup, homeboy' caricature … totally ruled by his appetites." Yet many people — including the dude who called and threatened to do me bodily harm for criticizing Charlotte Hornet basketball player Larry Johnson for wearing a dress — think it's a sign of progress that you now see more blacks on television, regardless of what they're doing.

"So brag if you will," said The Carolinian piece, "about the abundance of opportunities for African-Americans in today's marketplace. But don't talk about how far we've come in our portrayal on TV."

Right on.

April 28, 1994

Stealing songs is a wonderful thing — until you get caught

I don't care how Oprah Winfrey feels about Michael Bolton: I think he's the anti-Christ with a microphone.

Bolton — the "Hair Club For Men" poster boy who is second in Oprah's heart only to Steadman, her fiancé-for-life — will be desecrating the hits live tomorrow night at Walnut Creek. As usual, he'll be employing his overwrought, pseudo-emotional, s'posed-to-be-soulful style.

Bolton, like rappers, represents what's wrong with music today: He takes somebody else's song and, with no creativity, claims it for his own. There ain't been but one remake worth listening to: Sam Moore and Conway Twitty singing "Rainy Night In Georgia." You're talking 'bout something good then, son.

But if I think Bolton is evil incarnate for what he's done to my favorite songs, the Isley Brothers probably think he's Santa Claus for what he did to one of theirs: He stole it.

A jury recently ruled that Bolton's song "Love Is A Wonderful Thing" sounded an awful lot like … Shoot, who are we kidding? It ruled his song was exactly the same in some parts as the Isley Brothers' song of the same name.

Bolton, with a straight face (well, I presume it was straight: It's hard to tell with that outdated Shirley Temple-in-a-rainstorm hairdo) said he'd never heard the Isleys' version and wrote his in a moment of inspiration. That was probably enough to convince the jury he was lying: Bolton has never had a moment of inspiration, unless it's while perusing the back pages of Jet magazine's weekly soul hits from 20 years ago and deciding "Hey, here's a classic I haven't ripped off yet."

But cheer up, Mikey. You're not the first person to get caught plagiarizing a tune. Someone very close to me — hell, it was me — got suspended from school for doing the same thing. Honest. It was in Mr. Webb's ninth-grade English class at Rockingham High School and I, having neglected to write an original poem as I was assigned to do, merely did a "Bolton." I cranked up the old Victrola and copied down "Just My Imagination" by The Temptations. Word for word.

I thought Mr. Webb was a very nice man, but a square. Figuring that no white teacher who wore a bow tie and wingtips and brought his lunch to school had ever heard of The Temptations, I stood proudly in front of the class to recite my poem and bask in the adulation.

Well, I'd barely finished the first line — "Each day through my window" — when Mr. Webb politely interrupted. "The Temptations are a talented group, aren't they?" he said. "That Eddie Kendricks sure can sing, huh?"

I slithered back to my desk, feeling lower than the price of chitlins in 1929, while the class howled delightedly at my predicament.

But I learned a valuable lesson that day. To always be honest?

No. I learned that if you're going to steal a song, steal one Mr. Webb's never heard of.

A mistake that cost me only classroom humiliation could conceivably cost Bolton millions. Good. The Isleys are a superb rhythm and blues group that rocks like Aerosmith when it wants to but specializes in the kind of bump-and-grind music that makes you turn the lights down low and start whispering stuff you'll undoubtedly regret later. They haven't received nearly enough credit for their versatility and longevity — they made "Twist and Shout" before the Beatles, "This Old Heart of Mine" before Rod Stewart and "Shout" before Otis Day & the Knights.

I couldn't reach Mikey for an interview, but he held a self-righteous news conference in which he said he lost the lawsuit because the jury of four blacks and four whites was racist. That's right: The same dude who has made millions picking over the stylistic bones of dead or forgotten black men and then serving up his offerings as something new on a white plate a la Pat Boone now claims to be a victim of racism.

Get hip, Mikey. The reason people deplore you and think you're a pompous, arrogant, nominally talented lounge singer has nothing to do with race. I know white people who puke when they hear you, just as I know black people who love Hall and Oates, Bonnie Raitt, Sting and other whites who can sing the blues but don't act as if they invented them.

Besides, who can take Oprah's opinions on anything seriously as long as she's wearing those green contact lenses?

May 19, 1994

Did you at least stop and take a look at the kid's flier?

Hurry, hurry. Step right up. Hear the saddest story in town for only 50 cents.

Hell, it won't even cost that much. Pull up a chair and check this out:

The kid standing at the Alston Avenue exit ramp of the Durham Freeway handing out fliers Saturday wasn't advertising a fingernail sculpting service, a two-for-one pizza deal or anything of the sort. Few people slowed down enough to take the 8-by-10 sheet of paper he thrust toward their cars. Others crumpled it up, without even reading it, and dropped it on the floorboard with the burger wrappers and apple cores.

Those who looked, though, were stunned at what the kid was trying to sell: himself.

See, the boy — I'll call him Andrew — is looking for a Big Brother to spend time with. Andrew's dad, like too many black fathers, hasn't been on the scene in years.

He used to specifically want a black man as his Big Brother. But after more than a year on the waiting list at Durham Companions, waiting for someone to care, he'll take anybody now. That's why he was handing out fliers indiscriminately, pleading for someone to "do fun activities" with.

A kid has to be pretty desperate to risk his life on a highway exit ramp, huh?

But if you think that's desperate, read the crudely written note he'd scrawled next to his picture: "Call Durham Companions at 477-4884. Now! Now! Operator standing by."

Luckily for Andrew, whose small frame makes him look 12 instead of 15, the person who stopped and picked him up was Matthew Bouchard, manager of the governor's One-on-One program for juveniles. Bouchard, who called his encounter with Andrew "a total coincidence, and terrifying," promised to help and warned Andrew of the streets' hazards.

Otherwise, our first introduction to Andrew could've been the same as it was to Jamal Elliott — another alumnus of Durham Companions who spent two years on the waiting list without a bite. You met Jamal, remember, in March 1993, after he was shot and killed while trying to steal a motorcycle and some golf clubs. Oh sure, you'd seen him before — along with thousands more like him. You just hadn't paid any attention until then.

Man, I still remember the wailing and gnashing of teeth that followed Jamal's death, the way radio call-in shows were overrun with calls from folks bemoaning their inability to do anything for him.

Alas, their concern must have been buried in Beechwood Cemetery along with Jamal, leaving Andrew and thousands of other boys wondering where all that concern went so quickly.

Of course, Andrew insists such a tragic fate will not befall him. He is, he says, "a good guy."

"I don't hang around bad people," he says. "I'm a friendly person."

If anything, that just makes it harder to understand why some people have made it their duty to make him cry. "I be wondering why they don't like me," he says of the Hillside High School classmates who ridicule him daily because his clothes are dirty and don't fit.

Breathes there a person with soul so dead that they've forgotten how badly such hallway humiliations hurt? I doubt it.

He has only one friend at school, a graduating senior. That's why Andrew frets that, "Next year, I might not have anybody to talk to."

Before taking to the streets — and posting fliers in the library — in search of a stranger to help fill the void in his life, Andrew tried to do it the right way: He wrote the Durham County Department of Social Services, asking them for a Big Brother. After all, the DSS got his 8-year-old sister a Big Sister. But so far, Santa's bag has been empty for Andrew.

"The social worker said not many men want to help out," he said without rancor.

Well, dammit, I've got some rancor — enough for two people. I know there are men out there who want to help boys like Andrew. I've heard from them, black and white. But saving boys like Andrew is not white men's duty: It is ours. Failing to do so reflects badly, don't you think?

There have to be more brothers out there like Keith Randleman, a Raleigh Boy Scout master whose selfless work awes me. Aren't there?

Where, I wonder, are all those big-shot black fraternity boys I know — the ones who drive their pretty cars and brag incessantly about their vacations to "the Islands" — when we need them? If you want to do something worth a damn, fellas, involve yourselves in the lives of these boys whose very existence is threatened, boys who may not live long enough to join a fraternity.

Oops, I forgot: Some of them have already joined fraternities. They call them by a different name, though: Gangs.

May 26,1994

Justice falls through the cracks in the war against drugs

This column is intended as a public service to area drug dealers, specifically the street corner entrepreneur who approached me a couple of nights ago inquiring if I wanted to "cop some rocks."

The short answer — if I had taken the time to answer instead of speeding off and running a red light — would have been "Hell no!"

The long answer is "Get smart, dude."

Far be it from me to try to pass moral judgments on how people earn their living. Truth be told, some might consider selling a little nose candy a more honorable way of making a living than writing a column. As it says in the drug dealers' bible: "Don't judge another person until you walk a mile in his Filas" — or was it " ... until you answer his cellular phone"?

For all I know, the dude out there dealing the other night has a sick mother and was simply trying to raise funds to buy her some medicine. Or a hospital. In the Bahamas.

As I said, I didn't hang around long enough to chat. But if I had, I'd have said, "That way lies madness, dude — and a longer prison term." See, even a square like me — whose mind-altering drug of choice is MD 20/20 wine or watching rasslin' on TV — knows that "rocks" is street lingo for crack.

I'm just guessing, but I'll bet the nocturnal narcotics dealer didn't read the editorial in The New York Times last week about the disparity in the sentences for selling crack as opposed to cocaine. If he had, he'd have known the penalty for dealing crack is literally 100 times worse than for dealing powder cocaine.

"But Dude," you say, "ain't crack and cocaine the same thing?"

Well, yes. Except in court. See, technically, the difference between crack and cocaine is the same as the difference between biscuits and a sack of flour — baking soda. All you do is add a little baking soda and ... oops, never mind. Don't want to give away any trade secrets.

But the penalties differ greatly. A first-time trafficker caught with five grams of crack gets a five-year mandatory minimum sentence. You'd have to get caught holding 500 grams of powder cocaine to get that much time.

I flunked math — many times — but even I know that's a 100 to 1 ratio.

Oh yeah: There is one other difference between crack and powder cocaine. Crack is the drug of choice primarily in inner cities and most of its users are black; powder cocaine users are predominantly white.

Don't look at me like that. I can hear you thinking, "Dadgummit. Here he goes again — bending over backward to find a racial angle in every-thing."

Well, you're wrong. As far as I'm concerned, all drug dealers are death merchants fit only to be strung up and forced to listen to Michael Bolton warble "Z.Z. Hill's Greatest Hits." Of course, the Supreme Court would rule that constitutes cruel and unusual punishment. Oh well. Just string 'em up, then.

As somebody who has seen more friends than I can remember lose their lives or — even worse — their minds and motivation to the ravages of crack and cocaine, I'd be the last person to advocate going easy on crack dealers just because they're black. If anything, I'm of the same mind as U.S. Rep. Bill McCollum, R-Fla., who says instead of lowering the penalty for crack, "we ought to be raising the penalties for the powder cocaine."

Quiz time: Who said, "Our prisons are full of black males who have used crack cocaine, and the more affluent white boys in the community who have used the powder cocaine are on probation"? Was it Farrakhan? Khallid Muhammad? Me?

OK, time's up. That statement was made by none other than our own U.S. Rep. Charlie Rose, a moderate lawmaker who nonetheless rec-ognizes that the racially skewered sentences are unfair and must be changed.

In the meantime, don't be surprised if smart drug dealers start pro-viding little packets of baking soda and do-it your-own-self kits with their cocaine. Of course, then we wouldn't be able to make biscuits.

June 06, 1994

Coming up: Song for a cross-dressing schlockmeister

Hey Phil, baby: I'm with you. I think the country — nay, the world — deserves to see David Lawson take the dirt nap, catch the vapors, whatever you want to call it.

Don't be discouraged by the N.C. Supreme Court and all those namby-pamby folks who claim they won't watch it. It's no coincidence that this country's unofficial motto is, "If you televise it, they will watch." How else can one explain Bob Newhart's ability to keep getting new shows?

I don't know about you, but I guarantee that if Lawson's date with the devil airs at any time other than 5 p.m. on a weekday — when "Sanford & Son" reruns are on — I'll be right there, with a six-pack in one hand and a bag of barbecue skins in the other. With nothing on the tube but "Full House" — and with the battery run down in my bug-zapper — I need some quality entertainment.

That's why I hope y'all will join me on the front steps of the Supreme Court building and sing with me — to the tune of the "Don't Mess With Bill" by the Marvelettes — the executioner's song. I call it "Don't Mess With Phil":

Phil is the guy who puts shlock in our eye
each day at 9 a.m.
But every time I turn the channel I turn right back to him
Hear what I say
Don't look away
Don't mess with Phil, no, no, no, no.
Now there's Sally, there's Geraldo and there's Oprah, too
Just to name a few.
But you've got Dave, Phil, and Dave's got you.
So, pass me another brew ...
Fourteen years they've waited
To see him 'sphyxiated.
Uh-huh. Don't mess with Phil.
Oprah says she'd never do it —
Claims she has too much class.
But Phil, you're being clobbered in the ratings
So please, just turn up the gas.
Your show could be saved
If you show Dave microwaved ...
Hear what I said
Don't turn your head.

Until he's dead.

I truly believe Donahue and Lawson when they say they want to televise the execution to educate people to the hazards of depression — which Lawson says caused him to rob Wayne Shinn's home and shoot Shinn and his daddy — and the horrors of capital punishment.

State Sen. Frank Ballance, a Democrat from Warren County, agrees. During the General Assembly's special crime session, he introduced a bill for public executions. Ballance, like that selfless public servant Phil, hopes the sight of someone strapped in the chair — writhing in agony, eyes bulging as the gas starts working on his nervous system — will shock people into capital opposition.

I'll give Ballance the benefit of the doubt for his motive because he, unlike Donahue, never hosts shows featuring dyslexic, midget mud rasslers or wears a miniskirt on national TV. (I reckon Phil would justify that by saying he was trying to sensitize us to the horror of knobby knees, eh?)

A lot of people argue that the death penalty is necessary for justice, not cheap entertainment. But hey, I figure if they can combine great taste in a light beer, they can combine anything.

And who says it has to be cheap? You could automatically lend class to the proceedings by getting one of those British dudes with the snooty, clipped accents to do the play by play. Me? I'd prefer John Madden: "Oooomph. There. You could see as the gas made penetration and ... "

To me, seeing a condemned man walking the last mile and taking the hot squat in Ol' Sparky makes far more compelling viewing than watching some guy sitting up in a chair being overcome by invisible fumes or receiving an injection as though he's being inoculated against the measles. But North Carolina doesn't use the electric chair. We're too humane for that.

I guess my great fear is that televised executions will soon become too commercialized, with companies fighting to get their products displayed. I can see it now: some smiling homemaker spraying Lysol in the gas chamber as soon as the body is wheeled away and saying, "If Lysol can clear a room of these noxious fumes only moments after a ghastly execution, just imagine what it can do for smelly tennis shoes and cigars."

Phil, you're all heart. But I think we'll pass on your offer this time — unless Bob Newhart is on.

June 09, 1994

Look out, Mr. Wrestling — here comes Bad News Barry

Here, Chief. Have a doughnut. Ha ha.

Boy, if Bruce "Mr. Wrestling" Newnam — the rasslin' police chief of Morrisville who is making such a big splash — even dreams of beating me, he'd better wake up and apologize.

I heard about how he defeated that great champion and statesman "Khan the Warlord" by using dirty tactics — smacking him upside the noggin with brass knuckles when the ref wasn't looking. Just like a cop, huh? But my name ain't Rodney King and I don't play that.

I tell you, if Mr. Wrestling ever meets me in the squared circle, he'd better pack a lunch, because it's going to take all day. That's right: I am challenging him to a no-holds-barred, steel-cage match. Any time, anywhere.

See, being a champion rassler is not only my goal, it's my destiny. Rasslin' and I go way back. I am a real man, you understand, not one of those Alan Alda-type, sensitive pantywaists. So don't hold your breath waiting to see me boohooing about anything.

But I wept like a cop who has dropped his last jelly doughnut — YEAH, I'M TALKING ABOUT YOU, MR. WRESTLING — the first time I saw Johnny Weaver and George Becker pull the masks off the Masked Assassins. And I was devastated the first time I saw Classy Freddie Blassie, the Hollywood Fashion Plate and rasslin' manager extraordinaire, wearing a clip-on bow tie.

True story: A few years ago — while publishing the late, lamented Richmond County North Star newspaper and running out of hiding places from my landlord, Watt Long — I contacted Jim Crockett Productions in Charlotte to see about rasslin' as Bad News Barry. But there was a slight snag in the negotiations: JCP never returned my calls, thus delaying the start of a great career.

But hey, Crockett's loss could be Southern Championship Wrestling's gain. The SCW is a new Triangle-based rasslin' outfit, and its promoter, Jack Cates, is the kind of representative any up-and-coming enterprise needs. I talked to him for more than an hour the other day, and the dude knows rasslin' like … well, like a cop knows Krispy Kreme. During our discussion of rasslin' greats like Wahoo McDaniels, Rip "The Profile" Hawk, Rufus R. "Freight Train" Jones — and his offensively named brother, Burrhead Jones — Cates said, "The only thing I know about rasslin' is that I like it. I know what looks good and what the fans like."

To me, that's all you need to know. With the World Wrestling Federation about to do a belly flop because of mass defections to World Championship Wrestling, Cates and his group are coming to the Triangle at the right time.

Ever since Charlotte bagged professional football and basketball franchises, Triangle leaders have been sucking the Queen City's exhaust fumes. But with the NFL and NBA on their last leg — (Quick: Who won the NBA title last week? See what I mean?) — rasslin' is just the thing we need to pile drive, drop kick and body slam Charlotte once and for all.

If you're interested in having someone gouge your eyes, yank your hair and say bad things about your mama — in a word, rasslin' — you can call Cates. The SCW needs a champ with charm, charisma and ring prowess: Here I am. Never lost a match in my life. Plus, at 6-foot-2, 220 pounds — well, all right, 240 pounds — I look good in those rasslin' tights.

Before I can ascend the throne, though, I need a name befitting someone of my stature. That's where y'all come in. I'll give an 8-by-10 autographed glossy of me in my rasslin' outfit to whoever comes up with the best name.

Second thing I need is a good manager. That big sissy The Undertaker is on hiatus, so his manager, Paul E. Bearer, may be available. If not, I'll call LaTonya Harding, who, I hear, is managing the American Love Handle ... er ... I mean Love Machine. (I know, I know: It's really Tonya. But if she wants to hitch her wagon to my star, it'll have to be LaTonya.)

I won't be on the card for the July 16 matches at Bethesda Athletic Center in Durham — so you can rest easy, Newnam. But I'm in training, and soon area rasslin' fans will be treated to the thrill of a lifetime: my ring debut.

So, Mr. Wrestling, you can run but you can't hide. And even if you do hide, I'll know where to find you: standing outside Dunkin' Donuts, waiting for a new batch of doughnut holes.

June 27, 1994

Group trying to get fathers back home and helping out

Ever tried to make a long-distance telephone call on Mother's Day? Chances are you couldn't get through, not with everyone trying to call their own dear, sweet Mom and thank her for the swell job she did of raising them — or at least for not telling Dad who really wrecked the car after trying to do a figure-8 like Starsky & Hutch.

Now, have you ever tried to make a long-distance call on Father's Day?

Probably not. And if you did, I'll bet my very last Ward Cleaver cardigan that you were not encumbered by a busy dial tone. Why? Because fathers, sadly, are the Rodney Kings of America: They don't get no respect.

Since the time when Ward, Jim Anderson on "Father Knows Best" and Andy Taylor roamed the Earth as three of the coolest, wisest, most unflappable white dudes you're ever going to see, men's stock has dropped faster than that in O.J. Simpson's restaurants. (See, I mentioned him.)

Oh sure, the image of the buffoonish dad with the mental capacity of a drunk armadillo was interrupted somewhat by an occasional wise dad like Bill Cosby, but for the most part, the media's standard-bearers for men have been people like John Wayne Bobbitt, Ike Turner and Joey Buttafuoco.

To measure the esteem in which dads are not held, all you have to do is drop a quarter in any decent jukebox. The songs about mamas are always loving, sweet, even reverential. Not so with dads. Along about 1969, before dad-bashing became a national pastime, one group made a song about a good daddy — "Color Him Father." I loved it, but it is on almost every list of worst songs ever made.

Think of a mommy song, and you get "I want a Gal (Just Like the Gal Who Married Dear Ol' Dad)" or "I'll Always Love My Mama." A daddy song? How 'bout "Papa Was a Rolling Stone"?

But fear not, all of y'all hairy-legged hardheads. A national organization is attempting to reverse the mind-set that regards you as superfluous. Jeff Rosenberg is a spokesman for the National Fatherhood Initiative, a five-month-old group that, he contends, is not seeking to put men at the head of the table. Instead, it just wants to get 'em back in the house.

"We're embarking on a long-term campaign to change the way this society and men think of fatherhood. ... We believe that all the big social problems we're facing in this country — crime, welfare dependency, teenage pregnancy — all share one common factor: father absence," Rosenberg said. "We're not going to be able to tackle those issues until we end the growing epidemic of father absence and convince all men to commit to being responsible fathers."

Pretty hard to argue with that — or with the data that show 70 percent of long-term prison inmates, 60 percent of rapists and 72 percent of adolescent murderers all grew up without fathers, huh?

Not if you're a feminist. Despite what to me seems like the best idea since toothpaste in a pump, Rosenberg said some women accuse the organization of launching a frontal assault on them and their gains. "The publisher of Working Woman magazine wrote in The New York Times that we're 'anti-women' and are trying to go back to the 1950s, when women stayed home and men were the heads of the household. That's not what we're saying at all."

Indeed, Rosenberg said, "if we're successful, women will be big winners, too, because the fathers of their children will be at home and involved in their lives."

Think of absentee fathers — or, in the current vernacular, "deadbeat dads" — and you conjure up an image of some hip-hop black dude who split the scene after knocking up Sweet Thang or some long-haired white dude who left Becky Sue and Junior to go drink longneck Buds and shoot pool with the guys at the Alibi Lounge.

But not Rosenberg. "Absentee fathers are in all social groups, and that's who we're talking to. We're speaking to the man who works 60 hours a week and spends all his spare time on the golf course, just as we are to the young urban black man who impregnates a woman and doesn't live up to his responsibilities. You're talking about emotional abandonment in both instances."

July 11, 1994

Don't go hunting reality in Janet Jackson's bellybutton

Somewhere near the end of her concert at Walnut Creek next week, the lights will go down and Janet Jackson will ask the audience to pray for, among other things, world peace and her brother Michael. She'll get so caught up in the lovely ballad she's singing that, near the end, she'll stop abruptly, put her hand to her chest as though startled and, through tears, say "Oops, excuse me" — as though she forgot she was baring her soul and, no doubt, her bellybutton — to 25,000 people.

At least that's what she's done in previous concerts.

It'll seem like a real, genuine moment. But like just about everything else about Janet — her nose, her tush, maybe even her famous navel — it's Memorex.

I don't know exactly what it is I dislike about Janet — well, yes I do. See, even though she can't help it that Michael is her brother, I reckon I'm just preternaturally disposed to dislike black people who, through the miracles of cosmetic surgery, try to look as unblack as they can. Especially when they use the money they make off black people to further distance themselves, cosmetically and philosophically, from them.

My buddy Jerome — or, as he prefers to pronounce it, Jayrome — was cursing the gods the other day, bemoaning his boss' refusal to let him off work to see Janet at the Creek. "Oh man, she is fine, my ideal woman," is how he put it.

And indeed, Janet has made just about everybody's Top 10 list of "most beautiful women." No surprise here. If she hadn't made the list, after all the work she's had done on her body — she even reportedly had a rib removed to elongate her abdomen — she should've requested a refund from her plastic surgeon. Hell, I'll bet even my last ex-fiancé would've looked good if she'd spent that kind of money redoing and undoing what nature had done to her.

Whenever I say something unflattering about any black woman — no matter how unblack she may be — I am invariably deluged with calls and letters from irate women calling me a sellout or questioning my blackness. Bull. Just because I get ill every time I hear the words "Whoopi" or "Tina Turner" — two negrophobic, self-hating women who flee their blackness the way a slug flees a salt shaker — says nothing about how I feel toward most sisters.

Hell, I love 'em — even though the sentiment is rarely reciprocated. I mean, I went ballistic a couple of years ago when, while watching "The Phil Donahue Show," I heard a black woman pleading with fashion designer Calvin Klein to make some clothes to obscure the size of her hips because, she said, "black women have a problem with big hips."

I — a dude who has never seen a hip that was too big or, if I did, has never had a problem with it — was on the phone in a flash, trying to set her straight.

Likewise, I jumped on the phone recently and called Janet's publicist, Susan Blond — I'm not joking: that's both her agent's name and the new color of her hair. Miss Blond imperiously informed me that "Miss Jackson isn't doing interviews." She told me to fax whatever questions I had and "We'll take care of them."

You reckon she thought I was calling for a date? Not to worry, ol' gal. I only wanted an interview. See, LaToya, in her much acclaimed auto-biography and in interviews on the Psychic Con Line or something, has already told me Janet isn't partial to — isn't partial hell, she detests — black men. Sorry, Jayrome.

Remember the forgettable movie "Poetic Justice" in which Janet tried to portray a typical, "around-the-way girl"? This ain't no lie: The movie's director had to actually hire some sistas from the 'hood to hang out with Janet to teach her how to act black and after the movie, she boasted of how she felt "at one" with the real sistas. Despite that, though, she was jaw-droppingly inept in playing a role which should've come naturally.

Unlike my pal Jayrome, Janet is not my ideal. I like women who already know how to act black. I don't care if she's waiting for a bus while wearing earrings the size of cable satellite dishes with two or three colors in her hair and on her fingernails. Those are what I lovingly refer to as "Shaniqua" or "Tonya from Uptown" sistas. God made 'em, and I love 'em. I don't even care if she's driving a BMW and wearing a conservative Donna Karan suit with discreet earrings.

The only thing that matters is that she be real.

Janet most definitely do not be real.

July 21, 1994

The cold of the North gives Southern hospitality a chill

Yankees go home.

That's right. Pack up your Louis Vuitton luggage, your Cuisinarts and Volvo station wagons, and head back up the road. And please, forget to write.

Everyone knows I always bend over backward to find something positive in any situation, person or group. And Northerners have certainly contributed much to our region. I don't know about you, but my life has been enhanced immeasurably since being introduced to sushi, bagels and Long Island iced tea.

But all of that largess is overshadowed by one Northern custom that's wreaking havoc on my neck and driving me mad, to boot — this custom of not speaking to people who speak to you. It had to come from the North, because I'd never noticed it until substantial numbers of Northerners arrived here.

Don't laugh. My chiropractor's secretary can now identify me by voice when I call, so often have my neck and shoulders been sore and misaligned from nodding to passers-by — passers-by who ignore me.

I tell you, nothing chills my chitlins faster than to flash my sincerest, downhomiest smile, nod and say "How y'all?" and have the recipients of my greeting look at me with the warmth one usually reserves for a zit on prom night.

While living — if you can call it that — in other parts of America and wishing I were back in North Carolina, nothing made me homesick faster than taking a simple stroll down city streets where the mere act of speaking to a stranger made you the subject of skeptical, hostile glares.

"They wouldn't treat me like this if I were home," I'd say to myself, home being anywhere that people look reverently heavenward when saying the name "Dean Smith."

When I left North Carolina for the last time — at least, I hope it was the last time — in 1986, the quickest way to have people in Rockingham say something bad about you was to not speak. Remember how distraught Aunt Bea became whenever she'd pass Clara Edwards on a Mayberry street and Clara would snatch her head away with a violent "hummmph" — usually after Bea had stolen her pickle recipe or usurped the affections of some new man? Wasn't that the saddest thing you've ever seen?

What's the deal, folks? Won't somebody please tell me their theory on why North Carolinians — or, more likely, people in North Carolina — have become such an inhospitable lot? If people were just not speaking to me, I wouldn't be concerned. Indeed, that would be understandable because, quite frankly, I sometimes can't stand my own self.

But others have noticed and commented on this unpleasant phenomenon — a phenomenon that transcends racial boundaries. I've discovered that a black homeboy is now no more likely to speak while washing his car right next to mine than the white housewife on the other side.

For instance, a few weeks ago, I pulled up beside two dudes at a red light. The passenger dude looked at me. "Yo, man. What's up?" I said. He warily looked me straight in the eyes — and turned his head. Not even a faint nod and an "Alright, now."

Dammit, that did it for me. From now on, for the sake of my neck and sanity, I ain't speaking to nobody else unless they speak to me. So there.

It may sound silly, but I ache and yearn for the days when people spoke for the same reason people climb mountains: because you — and it — are there.

I am not one of those William Faulkner-type apologists who is incapable of objectivity when it comes to the South. As much as I love it, I know that the region's legendary hospitality can — and often does — mask true feelings of indifference, contempt, even hostility.

Indeed, one of the nicest greetings I've received lately was from a guy who immediately identified himself as a member of the Raleigh Ku Klux Klan. Oh sure, he said he wished I would die a slow, torturous death or return to Africa on the ship I came on. But before that, he graciously inquired about my health.

"Hey, how're ya' doin?" he asked, seemingly genuinely interested.

"Why, I'm fine, thank you," I responded. "How can I help you?"

He proceeded, unfortunately, to tell me.

July 25, 1994

Looking up to a big league 'thinker' instead of 'stinker'

In the first "Rocky" movie — the only one I saw and, from what I hear, the only one worth seeing — a reporter asked heavyweight boxing champion Apollo Creed what advice he'd give his young fans.

"Be a thinker, not a stinker," he said, urging them to eschew a career in sports in favor of one using their brains.

Hell, that's easier said than done, especially when a kid can make more than the gross national product of many countries simply by slamming a ball through a hoop.

The situation is made even worse when the only role models held up for kids, especially black boys, are athletes who — like Col. Sanders — do one thing well. In an annual ritual as predictable as the mating of the wildebeest, colleges virtually back up a big truck to black communities each fall and haul away thousands of young kids by offering enticing visions of professional sports stardom.

Now, most of these fellas have about as much chance of becoming the next Charles Barkley or Larry Johnson as I do. But with the right priorities, they could use their athletic prowess to become the next Maceo Sloan.

In fact, just listen to this: Rrrrrrriiiipppp.

That's me ripping off my wall all those pictures of testosterone-laden, one-dimensional athletes like Barkley and Johnson and replacing them with pictures of Sloan. Despite appearances, he is not a small forward for the Los Angeles Lakers — although at 6 feet 7 he looks like he could be.

What he is is president of NCM Capital, a financial management company with offices on Wall Street and headquarters in Durham. He chose Durham over the city that never sleeps because he likes its small-town charm and "phone lines work just as well in Durham as they do on Wall Street."

And they seem to work especially well at his offices because he is, as the cats on the block say, "gettin' paid." As of July, NCM Capital managed assets in the neighborhood of $3 billion. Not a bad neighborhood to be in, eh?

Sloan is a capitalist to the bone. Nothing wrong with that. He loves making moolah, but that isn't all he wants to make. He also wants to make a difference in the lives of Durham's black children by "letting them know they can be successful without having to be a professional athlete or an entertainer or a drug dealer." His company's executive vice president, Justin Beckett, was a founder of the successful Realistic Executive Exposure Program — REEP — which exposes Durham high school students to the world of work and teaches them how to dress and act on the job while earning a paycheck.

I hope they don't revoke my NAACP membership for saying this, but I think Sloan and people like him have more of a claim to the mantle of leadership than bellicose spokesmen running around tilting at windmills — or flags, as is presently occurring in South Carolina — because he and they provide something tangible: jobs and training.

His latest enterprise, New Africa Advisers, is an investment company in South Africa that has 15 employees in Johannesburg and here. But again, money is not the only thing he is making in a country that for centuries was synonymous with racial oppression and violence and, Sloan said, whose "townships make our ghettoes look like palaces."

His company, he said, "has the only racially integrated investment staff in South Africa. ... We had a party with blacks and whites in Johannesburg recently, and for many of them, it was the first time they'd ever socialized with people of other races."

Booker T. Washington might have been right when he said, in 1895, that the races could be as united as a hand when it comes to business but as separate as the fingers socially. As a businessman today, though, Booker T. would starve with that philosophy, because more business is conducted on the golf course or over martinis and a plate of barbecue than in the executive suites.

When the media, but more importantly black parents, start holding up people like Sloan as role models rather than some dude with hyperactive pituitary glands — thinkers, not stinkers — we'll all be better off, don't you think?

August 01, 1994

Oh, Elvis: First heresy from Ray Charles, now this

Elvis is dead, and I ain't feeling too good myself.

OK, OK. I know that's sort of the title of a book. But honestly, neither the King nor I am doing too great after hearing about the one story that, mercifully, gave us a brief respite from O.J.

Unless you spent the past two weeks watching the Goodwill Games, you know that Elvis' daughter married King of Pop Michael Jackson last month.

For a minute there, I was miffed that I wasn't invited — until I heard that Tito wasn't, either.

Acquaintances of mine, mostly women — including one who pledged her undying love to Michael when both were teenagers and he was still black — refuse to admit that the world's least eligible bachelor is now even less so.

Not me. I knew it was imminent even before CNN confirmed it. And it didn't cost me a dime calling Dionne and her psychic friends. All it took was common sense. Think about it. If you're a single man being investigated for messing with little boys — and you've just paid one kid $20 million not to tell something you swear didn't happen anyway — what would you do?

Me, too. I'd find me a woman willing to marry me and moonwalk her down the aisle at warp speed. If she just happened to be the daughter of the King of Rock 'n' Roll, so much the better.

It's the King for whom I really feel sorry. Whether he's dead or alive, I'll bet he's all shook up now.

For someone supposedly dead 17 years — Tuesday is the anniversary of his death — the past month has not been kind. First Ray Charles questioned — questioned, hell, he lampooned — Elvis' title as the King of Rock 'n' Roll. Now his li'l girl ups and marries a guy whose most recent constant companions were pre-adolescent boys, a chimpanzee and the Elephant Man's bones.

The marriage is a boon for Michael, quelling — at least momentarily — questions about his sexuality. And Lisa Marie, asserting to the extreme her individuality and independence, seems happy. For now. I'd just love to see how the King of Pop reacts when his marriage faces its first crisis, which'll probably be when Lisa Marie issues the ultimate ultimatum: "Look Michael, it's either me or these bones, but one of us has to go."

As much as I like Elvis — I still get misty-eyed every time I hear him sing "In the Ghettoooo," and I get a lump in my throat whenever I eat his favorite meal, a peanut butter and banana sandwich deep-fried in lard — I agree with Charles. Said Ray, "I guess I'm going to lose at least a third of my fans, but to say that Elvis was so outstanding — the king — I don't think of Elvis like that because I know too many artists that were far greater. Black people been goin' out shakin' their behind for centuries. What the hell's unusual about that?"

To view Elvis as just another white boy who could shake his butt — hell, Tom Jones did that, too, but you don't see anybody making a pilgrimage to his home twice a year — is to miss the essence of the pre-Vegas, pre-gaudy jumpsuit man.

See, it is not cool for blacks to admit, in 1994, they once liked Elvis during a period when the only thing black in music was the color of the record and people like Pat Boone and the Andrews Sisters made millions performing tepid versions of blues songs. (I'll bet Pat Boone — the

Michael Bolton of the 1950s — would scuff his white bucks if he knew what Etta James was really singing about in "Roll With Me Henry." He did a sanitized version called "Rock With Me Harry" or some such nonsense that sounded like something you could sing at a church social.)

In my own Holy Triumvirate of the rock pantheon, Elvis ranks no higher than third — behind Chuck Berry and Little Richard and just ahead of Bo Diddley.

Any true Elvis fan knows that, during performances when the King and his band were really cooking, Elvis would turn to the band and say "TCB, baby, TCB" — take care o' business.

Considering all the poor man's been through lately, though, all I can say is "R.I.P., Elvis, R.I.P."

August 15, 1994

Some strategies for weathering this storm of approval

After reading the recent Money magazine story rating the Triangle as the top place to live in America, I did what every other person who loves this region did: I sat down and cried like a baby.

Don't get me wrong, now. I — like you — appreciate having the place in which I reside affirmed as a swell spot to raise younguns, to work and to play. Or acknowledged as a "a hip, high-tech college center with a low-cost, laid-back lifestyle," which is how Money put it. Makes me feel good to know I made a wise choice.

But as somebody who would one day like to live in a home in which strangers aren't stomping above my head all night, I think there are few things worse than the national recognition that comes from such a rating.

For one thing, if you haven't bought a home here yet — it's too late, Nate. It was just last year that various publications raved about what a great place the Triangle is for business and for living. As far as I can tell, the main result of that has been a hefty increase in the cost of houses that makes it impossible for anyone but Saudi royalty or Duke Hospital administrators to afford one.

You know all those $80,000 homes that started selling for $115,000 after Money ranked us fifth last year? Well, now they'll be selling for $135,000. Unbridled joy, indeed.

After the magazine hits the stands nationally, hordes of folks living in regions they consider too hot, too cold, too black or too white will descend upon the Triangle — trampling our crape myrtles, making left turns on red and serving unsweetened tea in restaurants. I've never read Gibbon's "Decline and Fall of the Roman Empire," but I'll bet the decline started with a waitress inquiring, "Do you want that sweetened or unsweetened?"

How do you think Charlotte got the way it is? Yup, a proliferation of fern-bearing restaurants with unpronounceable names serving unsweetened tea.

But have no fear. We Triangle-ites are a resourceful lot, and there are a couple of ways to slow the inevitable influx.

See, my plan — admittedly a long shot — involves buying up all the September issues of Money so people in other areas can't see the story. That's why I want everyone within the sound of my voice to send me $3.71 so my secretary, the lovely and talented Miss Blue, and I can travel the breadth and scope of this country buying up all the magazines.

I'd like to take credit for this marvelous strategy, but I can't. Remember the time Opie heard Andy talking about how boring Rev. Hobart Tucker's sermons were? Like any good reporter, Opie wrote it up in the school newspaper — prompting Aunt Bee and Andy to go door-to-door frantically scooping up the offending issues before Rev. Tucker read the story and cast a pox on them.

Since this country is a lot bigger than Mayberry and this is a daunting challenge, it'll require a lot of cash. But even if my strategy fails, at least one person would be able to afford a home in Cary afterward: ME!

Another strategy, one I cooked up, involves "puttin' on" — a Southern term that, roughly translated, means acting like something you're not. Everybody has a cousin or someone who spent a week in New York and came back speaking with an accent so proper you'd have thought they had just had tea and crumpets with Queen Elizabeth at Buckingham Palace, right?

Well, in this case, everybody in the Triangle could "put on" the other way — acting like the snuff-dipping, intrafamily-marrying hayseeds we were thought to be. Before Money, that is. One way to do that would be for everyone to put "Rush is right" or "Run, Jesse, run — Helms that is" bumper stickers on their cars.

If the first settlers from other parts of the country encounter a gas station attendant who makes Gomer look like a nuclear physicist — and who solemnly introduces the woman standing beside him as his sister and his wife — I guarantee you they'll jump back in their minivan and burn rubber. Best of all, they'll warn all their friends and neighbors. And they'll probably cancel their subscription to Money magazine.

August 18, 1994

Tim Malloy was found innocent of rape, but he's still not free

Nobody, least of all Tim Malloy, thinks Malloy deserved a medal for what he did — which was have sex with a drunken, stranded stranger who staggered into his workplace at 2:30 in the morning seeking a ride home.

But fortunately for him, nobody — well, at least not the 12 people who mattered — thought he deserved two life sentences for it either, after the woman told police Malloy raped her: the jury acquitted him of all charges.

End of story, the dude is happy and free to get on with his life, right?

Not exactly.

He is definitely not happy, and is free only of the penitentiary, not of the whispers or suspicious looks from people who recognize his name from television and newspapers. And while he kept his freedom, he lost two jobs — as a prison guard and at the service station where the incident occurred — and a girlfriend.

He's trying to regain his job at the Guess Road prison, but his woman is long gone. "I could see the pain in her face when she came and got me out of jail," Malloy said. "I knew it wouldn't be long before she gave me my walking papers."

Neither Malloy nor his accuser dispute that they had sex — or something approximating it — in a filthy back room of the Phillips 66 service station on Hillsborough Road. They differ only on why: she said she was persuaded not by his rap — which consisted of a less-than-romantic "I can get you home, but you gotta do something for me" — but by the gun she said Malloy drew on her.

He denied having a gun and said he bartered sex from her in exchange for the promise of a ride home after her friends left her at a nightclub.

The jury, swayed by medical evidence, inconsistencies in the woman's story — and, sadly, the fact that she said she was gay — ruled Malloy was guilty only of being stupid, a verdict he agrees with. "I wish I'd kept my mouth shut" instead of propositioning the woman, he says now.

Malloy spent almost two years sweating out the trial, no doubt turning over in his mind the greeting that awaited him in prison once other inmates discovered they had a former turnkey in their midst. That's why the first thing he did upon hearing the verdict was heave a huge sigh of relief.

The second thing he did was set about repairing his damaged reputation.

"I know you've heard about my case," he said when he called me shortly after the trial ended. His voice sounded angry and desperate. "They put my name in the newspaper, man. They said she was the victim, but I was the victim. I'm not an angel, but I didn't do that," he said.

In addition to his jobs and his girlfriend, Malloy says he lost something else, something maybe even more irretrievable than the woman with whom he once lived and planned to marry: his confidence in the judicial system. "The detective who sounded like he was so understanding at first, the one who kept telling me he didn't want to see an innocent man go to jail — he got on the stand and lied about what I'd told him. I was so disgusted that all I could do was shake my head. ... I think that bothered me more than what the woman was accusing me of.

"And the judge — man, he looked disappointed when the 'not guilty' verdict came in," Malloy said.

Instead of turning his back on the system, though, Malloy now wants to become a part of it — as a probation officer. "I think my experience will make me more sensitive to what other people are going through. I know all cops aren't bad, all lawyers aren't bad, all judges aren't bad. But something like this will sure make you wonder how many innocent people have gone to prison."

August 22, 1994

Trend of trying youths as adults is an admission of failure

See y'all later. I'm quitting the newspaper business.

Before you start celebrating too much, though, let me just say — "Gotcha!"

See, I'm not really quitting, but if I were of an entrepreneurial mind, I'd start me a new business making — get ready for this, folks — little bitty electric chairs.

Go ahead and laugh. I'm sure they laughed at Henry Ford, the Wright brothers and whoever came up with the idea for a purple dinosaur, too. So while y'all are laughing, I'll just be positioning myself at the forefront of what I confidently predict will be THE NEXT BIG THING.

You see, now that North Carolina has decided that it might treat some 13-year-old criminals like adults, I figure it's only a matter of time before an adolescent is sentenced to take the hot squat. But since most 13-year-olds haven't had that final spurt of growth which would allow their wrists and tushes to fit comfortably in an adult-sized electric chair, custom-made, smaller chairs seem to represent an industry with exciting growth potential.

The dubious distinction of being the first 13-year-old in North Carolina tried as an adult might belong to Andre Green, a Fuquay-Varina kid who last week was charged with beating and raping his neighbor. Andre is big for his age and, if his crime were a capital offense, would pose no problem for the executioner dude responsible for strapping him into Ol' Sparky or onto the gurney or whatever instrument of death the state uses.

But what about when the condemned 13-year-old is a little ol' thing — not much bigger than a typical 12-year-old?

Ah ha. Now, that's when my business would start sizzling and my telephone ringing. Because of the disturbing trend in North Carolina to routinely bump juveniles up to adult court — Durham's District Attorney Jim Hardin, for instance, has already recommended that course for more juveniles through the first six months of 1994 than he did for all of 1993 — demand for my smaller, kid-friendly electric chairs will be great. Why, I'll probably have to get two phone lines — or at least call-waiting — to handle all the calls.

District attorneys' increasing willingness to try ever-younger adolescents as adults is a political response to people's frustration with crime. But it is more. It is also an admission that institutions such as the juvenile court system and training schools are failing to provide successful alternatives. Before the state sanctions killing 13-year-olds, though, the governor should first try fine-tuning — or even overhauling — those institutions. There must surely be room for improvement in a system that so easily admits defeat when confronted with a 13-year-old who — despite being accused of a vicious crime — has no other criminal history.

I predict that as society's lust for retribution grows and its tolerance for crime diminishes, the age limit will be dropped even further — to 12, 11, maybe even 10.

We North Carolinians are not barbarians, you understand, and we certainly don't condone killing kids — at least not in the same old musty, foreboding chair we use to kill older convicts. That's why my "For Kids' Sake" electric chairs will come in a variety of lively colors that kids love — Drop Dead Red, Serene Green, Big Bird Yellow.

It's not hard to imagine the state's masked executioner — the guy who pulls the lever, pushes the button or drops the cyanide pellets — as a coldhearted type who chuckles when he hears grizzled, old condemned convicts scream for their mommies at the moment of reckoning.

But I wonder how he'll respond when a condemned convict's request for his final dinner is a McDonald's Happy Meal.

August 29, 1994

Let the mugging of Rosa Parks ignite another movement

I drove away shaking my head. Had an attitude, too.

You see, it was close to 90 degrees, the two old ladies pulling a grocery cart along a Durham street appeared on the verge of melting and here I was trying be a good Samaritan.

But when I offered them a ride, they turned me down. Cold.

"We don't know you, and we don't accept no ride with strangers," one said firmly, in a tone that conveyed she was insulted that I'd even ask if they wanted to ride with me.

Well, I was insulted, too, insulted that two women who looked like somebody's grandmother — mine, to be precise — would think they had something to fear from me.

"But lady," I wanted to say, "I'm one of the good guys." I drove away thinking "Who could harm some old ladies like that?"

Two days later, I saw where Rosa Parks was mugged in her own home.

Police have charged a 28-year-old punk with beating up the mother of the modern civil rights era. Because if Rosa Parks hadn't refused an order to give up her seat and go to the back of the bus in Montgomery, there's no telling how long it would've been before someone else with her combination of courage and moral rectitude had come along. And Clarence Thomas, who thinks he's the only black person who never benefited from the movement, might still be a shoeshine boy or mud farmer in Georgia.

Ah, you say of Parks' attack, but that was in Detroit. Nothing like that would happen here.

Don't think so? Just ask Inez Florence Williams. Oops, can't ask her. That Durham grandmother died late last year after being mortally wounded — while asleep in bed — by some pistol-packin' punks.

Well, then, just ask the old folks in Durham's Few Gardens housing complex, folks whose vulnerability actually makes them welcome the ominous black metal bars that surround their apartment buildings. Sure, the bars make the complex look like a prison, but they also make it tougher for the crack addicts to get to and carry off their televisions, sofas and other near-valuables.

Not much makes me queasy. I've been locked in a holding cell where other thugs were busy making a fellow inmate their girlfriend. I kept right on eating some runny grits and drinking lukewarm milk.

I've seen up close the damage a sawed-off shotgun fired into three people from two feet away can do. Unmoved by that carnage, I interviewed the police detectives and went back and wrote a story.

But when I heard that some human toe jam had robbed and beaten Parks ... well ... damn. All I could do was hang my head and cry.

Well-meaning but misguided sociologists and civil rights leaders are going to tell us how the drug-addled suspect, Joseph Skipper, was as much a victim as Parks was. We're going to hear sad stories of how he was victimized by racism, by an inferior public school education, even, maybe, that his mama didn't breast-feed him enough when he was a baby. You can almost hear the mournful sound of violins accompanying his supposed-to-be woeful tale.

Well, dammit, I don't want to hear no violins. All I want to hear is a funeral dirge when this disgusting piece of filth is scraped off the bottom of society's shoe once and for all and buried. But not before being subjected to a slow and exceedingly painful and dehumanizing death. Unfortunately, robbing and beating an 81-year-old woman — even one who's an icon — is not a capital offense. Not in the eyes of the law, anyway.

By simply saying, "I'm not moving, I'm tired," this now-frail woman in faltering health became the catalyst for a movement that allowed succeeding generations of blacks and whites to ride in dignity. (Oh, you thought racism was hell only on us, huh?)

In a sad way, her victimization last week could make her the catalyst for a movement that will allow others to walk in safety. I mean, does anything more reprehensible have to happen before the good people in our nation's inner cities tighten up and say "Enough"?

As a race, we have made tremendous progress, economically and politically, in the 39 years since Parks took a stand and remained seated. But what does it profit a race to gain the world only to lose its soul? If we continue to allow this crap to continue, some may say we already have.

September 05, 1994

Renters find 'Shaft' more than a character in this sorry drama

As if the Triangle isn't getting enough attention, what with all manner of magazines touting it as the best place to live and work, just wait until all those Hollywood types start showing up en masse to begin filming the new movie to be set in Durham.

Oh, y'all hadn't heard? It's a Cecil B. De Mille-like epic called "Home Improvement" and stars Chester "Shaft" Jenkins and the Rev. Lorenzo "Hallowed Be Thy Rent" Lynch.

They play a pair of property owners who travel the city buying up ramshackle, dilapidated houses and making them livable, more or less. Naturally, news that Chet and Lo are buying houses in a neighborhood sends residents streaming joyously into the streets and property values through the roof. (Which ain't easy, since many of Lynch's houses have no roofs).

As an indefatigable defender of the underdog, I feel compelled to protect the gentlemen from the venomous slander being hurled at them. Hey, can't two dudes own buildings that druggies call home — or plop down houses that are little more than glorified, crime-breeding lean-tos in the middle of otherwise decent neighborhoods — without folks calling them slumlords?

I ask you, would City Manager Orville Powell have appointed a slumlord to serve as the handsomely paid director — he pulls in $56,730 a year — of the Durham Human Relations Commission, which is responsible for, among other things, enforcing fair housing laws?

And would Lynch be the respected pastor of one of Durham's largest black churches if he were really a slumlord? (Oops, that was last year: that church has since given him the old heave-ho, in large part because of his inability to distinguish between "The Slumlord's Prayer" and the "The Lord's Prayer.")

When asked about his myriad condemned and soon-to-be-condemned properties throughout Durham, Lynch went lunar.

"I'm like the folks who tried to get to the moon — I wasn't able to meet my schedule" to fix them, he said.

Lynch's detractors call him a profiteer; he sees himself as a misunderstood environmentalist with "a love for recycling houses." Hence, the nickname by which Lynch, an acclaimed rapper, is known throughout the land: Grandmaster Recyclin' Lo. Remember his smash rap hit from last year, "Give 'em Shelter"?:

I own 18 houses, five don't have roofs.
I'll get to 'em directly, and that's the truth.
I'm just like the dudes goin' to the moon/ I'll fix up those cribs (but it
won't be soon.)
Word up.

Jenkins also has an interest in the space program. So many folks have gotten high at his 425 Pilot St. building that it is known — or could be — in law enforcement and drug circles as "the launching pad." Durham police have risked their lives countless times busting the same drug dealers and addicts at properties owned by Jenkins, who earns more than any beat cop on the force. Each time the cops write him letters informing him of problems. The next time Chester responds will be the first.

He did, however, once tell a News & Observer reporter that "I am not responsible for crime that goes on in Durham. That is a police problem." How's that for civic involvement?

The proposed movie, I suspect, will do for Chester and Lorenzo what Kevin Costner and "Bull Durham" did for the Bull City's baseball team. Remember how folks from all over the world came to see the DAP after that movie? If Reyn Bowman, the city's tourism honcho is smart, he'll capitalize off Durham's affiliation with the big screen's most notorious duo since Butch and Sundance and organize tours of Lorenzo's various run-down houses on otherwise solid, working-class streets the same way.

The tour bus driver won't even have to point out Lorenzo's houses because they'll be so easy to spot: they're the ones without roofs or with weeds tall enough to hide an elephant.

On second thought, when the movie on Chester "Shaft" Jenkins and Grandmaster Recyclin' Lo is made, a better name for it might be "Nightmare on Any Street."

September 08, 1994

Marion Barry a man of the cloth — the kente cloth

Kente cloth, not patriotism, is now the last refuge of a scoundrel.

I reached that conclusion while watching the world's most famous crack smoker, Marion Barry, get re-elected mayor of Washington after being booted out with a crack pipe in his hand four years ago.

How'd he do it? Why, by draping himself in kente cloth and self-righteousness.

Seems like every time a black public official gets into trouble, justified or not, he grabs a piece of kente out of the closet, clinches his fist and starts referring to everybody as "brother" or "sister" — whether they're kin or not.

Take me, for instance. When the state trooper who recently stopped me for exceeding — make that allegedly exceeding — the speed limit turned out to be black, my spirits soared. Briefly.

Me: Hey, what's up, bro'?

Him: Do I look like your $%$#@#$% brother?

Me: Uh ... no, sir.

Ticket, please.

Kente, for those of you who don't know, is the brightly colored cloth

from Africa. It has become, like the Afro hairstyle in the 1960s, the lit-
mus test of one's blackness. If you wear kente, the reasoning goes, you
must be down with the cause — a righteous dude who takes no crap
from The Man. Same with the Afro.

Of course, we all know that was baloney. I swear, one guy told me
he went to Africa in the 1960s and didn't see a single Afro, making me
believe the hairstyle was merely a marketing gimmick to sell hair products.

History is replete with dudes with big Afros who were also Uncle
Toms. Heck, I've seen pictures of Clarence Thomas — who raised Uncle
Tomism to a fine art — with an Afro, which is all the evidence I need to
determine that a hairstyle provides no insight into one's racial or social
consciousness.

When Barry was in Durham a few months ago for a forum on the
extinction of black men, I asked if he planned to run for mayor. The question was superfluous, because anyone who saw him standing there in full
regalia — a kente-trimmed blue suit — knew his name would be on the
ballot come September.

Now I'd be the last person to dispute someone's claim of redemption. Barry, as a Washington columnist wrote after the election, might be
just the man to get D.C. cracking. And let us not forget the Book of Fred
— Fred Sanford, that is — in which it is written "let he who is without sin
pick up some."

Cynics among you might say that when Barry, in his recent acceptance speech, cautioned young people against the evils of drugs, his
main goal was to ensure that there'd be enough for him. I, on the other
hand, think the cat is more qualified than anyone to warn folks against
the evils of crack.

Shoot, hearing the late Elder James Turner of Rockingham, one of
the most righteous — which is not to be confused with self-righteous —
men I've ever known, talk about his fondness for liquor and women
before finding The Way is what convinced me there was hope for a
wretch like me.

We Americans pride ourselves on the power of personal redemption.
There is a whole industry that allows celebrities — many of whom have
tooted enough cocaine to line Carter-Finley Stadium — to tell about the
sordid details of their lifestyles. For pay.

But now that blacks have elected someone who is less than pristine,
redemption seems not to be a good thing. Newt Gingrich, the Republican
senator from Georgia, called Barry's election "a tragic moment for this
country."

Yeah, Newt, like you wouldn't have voted for Tricky Dick Nixon if he'd been successful in revising history — as he attempted to do until the minute he departed for that big polling booth in the sky.

September 26, 1994

Good manners can take you far — and save your face

Did I ever tell y'all about the time my Aunt Lottie shot me?

Well, at least I thought she had.

See, she was from up North — Washington — and was visiting us, her country relations in Rockingham, for the summer. Somehow she got it into her head that she'd teach my 9-year-old self proper etiquette — the correct knife and fork to use, how not to eat with your elbows and feet on the table, how to sip soup without slurping.

On this fateful day, I was hunched over, elbows on the table guarding the plate the way you've seen inmates do in a million prison movies. (Me, I can usually tell if a fellow has been a guest of the state just by watching him eat.)

I admit my creamed corn was perched perilously close to the edge of the plate, about to fall off. I saw it, but before I could push it to the center — POW! — she got me. I heard the blow before I felt it, since it took a few minutes for the feeling to return to the right side of my face.

Then I started laughing. No, she hadn't knocked me senseless. I was just so glad to be alive after that horrific sock on the jaw. For the longest time afterward, I would duck every time she entered a room. And I haven't been crazy about creamed corn since.

But I'll tell you one thing: Whether or not she was in the room (room, hell, the state is more like it), I never let my food get near the edge of a plate again.

No way am I championing better etiquette through child abuse, but it is obvious some people could benefit from having an Aunt Lottie or somebody who was interested in teaching them proper table manners.

Poor table manners, folks, is a national crisis. But you don't have to take my word for it. Oprah, that national arbiter of what's important and what ain't, had a whole show dedicated to good and bad manners.

Now, I am no Miss Manners or Letitia Baldrige, a couple of prissy busybodies who spend their days worrying about whether the napkin should be placed in your collar or on your lap. I've never given such inanities a second thought. Shoot, I used to think a person was putting on airs if he just wiped off the top of the wine bottle before passing it on.

But I've changed in my old age. Now I know there has to be a special place reserved in hell — or at least on the front row of a Michael Bolton concert — for people who talk with their mouths full of a half-chewed piece of pork chop, which they invariably spray onto your plate. Or who use their forks to spear a piece of roast beef from the serving platter or to slice butter or dip gravy. In fact, I think the bell that opens the gate to hell is not a bell after all, but a loud, obnoxious burp.

A businessman once gave me some good advice, after I'd asked for a loan: Never let anyone know you're broke, and you can go far with impeccable table manners. Accidents will happen, though. Like when I dropped my spoon and splashed soup on the folks sitting next to me at lunch after hearing that my pal, WTVD-11 sportscaster Dwayne Ballen, is leaving the station.

There are three things I can think of that should be done in privacy. Modesty prevents me from mentioning two of them. The third, though, is picking your teeth. It used to be that only the most common, low-born person would even think of employing a toothpick — or the straw from a broom — to publicly dislodge meat that got stuck in his or her teeth. Now restaurants actually encourage the abominable practice by providing toothpicks. Or brooms.

Which got me thinking: What is the proper way to get rid of a piece of already-been-chewed pork chop stuck in your teeth? Do you swallow it? Spit it out? Ask for a doggie bag and take it home for a midnight snack?

I went to dinner at a pricey restaurant recently with a very rich businessman whose table manners would make Ernest T. Bass look polished by comparison. Right about the time he cut loose with a belch that sounded like the foghorn on an ocean liner, I vowed never to be seen in public with him again. But when the waiter arrived, my companion did something that changed my mind — briefly. He reached for the check.

Unfortunately, he only wanted to tear off a piece to dislodge some chicken from his teeth.

October 13, 1994

The last thing we need now is another Billy Graham

I know South Africa wants U.S. imports, but not this kind. Yet whoops — there it was: The first thing I saw after stepping off the plane in Cape Town was a poster announcing a revival crusade by Weepin' Jimmy Swaggart.

That, I remember thinking, is the last thing these folks need — unless they're experiencing a drought and need someone to cry up a storm on demand. But after reading newspaper accounts and listening to radio talk shows discussing the Rev. "Forgive Me, For I Have Sinned —

A Lot" Swaggart, I concluded that he is exactly what they need: comic relief. And true enough, many South Africans with whom I spoke regarded Swaggart as a joke.

But just because y'all were spared Jimmy's crying, hollering and, of course, crying, you're in no position to adopt a luckier than thou attitude.

Why? Because as South Africans were being subjected to the tears of a clown, y'all were being visited by the Rev. Billy Graham's boy, Franklin. I heard about young Graham's crusade at Walnut Creek Amphitheatre and saw a picture of him in this newspaper just as I was leaving the country. Thousands turned out, no doubt to see if Franklin was a chip off the old block.

God, I hope not. No blasphemy intended, but the last thing we need here in the latter part of the 20th century is a Billy Graham in fashionable blue jeans — someone preaching about the horrors of hell after death while ignoring the conditions that make people's lives hell before death.

I'm not impugning Graham's preaching. Nor am I, as 2nd District congressional candidate David Funderburk did, calling him a communist agent. Graham can certainly preach up a storm. But if the ability to preach a rousing sermon were all it took to be a leader, Jesse Jackson would be king and we'd all be pledging allegiance to Jerry Falwell.

No, it is in the area of true leadership that Graham, despite all his fame and media adoration, has been weighed in the balance and found wanting.

At least by me. See, the Rev. Graham and I go way back. I have vivid recollections of having my favorite television shows pre-empted by a week of his televised crusades. I even watched, right alongside my grandma, who was as much of a "Billy Grimm" supporter as I can imagine anyone being.

Indeed, my grandma and people like her are the reason I think Graham's reputation as God's main man is a bunch of hooey. I don't dislike the Rev. Graham, but I am saddened that he didn't do more with what he had. And what he had was the eye and the ear and the conscience of the nation.

Race relations in America have improved a whole lot since the 1960s, when my grandmother was a maid and the Rev. Billy, Ethel Waters, George Beverly Shea — (his version of "How Great Thou Art" still gets me right here, but it would've been even better if he could've gotten Miss Nora Dumas of Providence First Baptist Church in Rockingham to accompany him on her magic organ) — and others were on TV regularly.

But during a period when this country was undergoing social upheaval every bit as turbulent as South Africa is now, Graham never entered the fray. Never once said "racism is wrong" or "y'all white folks treat your colored maids nice." Nothing. The Rev. Dr. Martin Luther King Jr. responded to religious criticism of his civil rights involvement by writing the famous "Letter from a Birmingham jail." As far as I can tell, Graham never even sent a postcard.

Graham, like Forrest Gump, lived right smack dab in the middle of the turbulent events of the 1960s but emerged untouched by them. While America was on the verge of being destroyed by racial and anti-war conflicts, Graham remained content to preach his hellfire-and-damnation, "get y'all's pie in the sky by and by when you die" doctrine. Syndicated columnist Chuck Stone, a professor at UNC, called him a "magnificent phony" during that period after Graham, in response to a question on how America should deal with its racial problem, simply said we should "take it to the foot of Jesus."

Unassailable advice. But I'll tell you what: The folks in South Africa had better be glad Bishop Desmond Tutu didn't respond to their anguished cries for deliverance from apartheid with "take it to the foot of Jesus."

I read Graham's biography back when I thought I was being called to preach. Couldn't get beyond the first chapter, though. That's how long it took me to read about how the girl Billy loved and was preparing to marry called him up out of the blue and told him to take a hike. Scram. Get lost.

Did he pull a Willie Nelson and go sailing down a whiskey river for at least one night? Did young William even cry?

No. As best I can remember, according to the book the dude didn't blink an eye. Didn't even ask for an explanation. Just shrugged his shoulders and said something like, "That's the way God wanted it."

I confess, I couldn't read beyond that. Why? Because that was right around the time my first ex-fiancé called me up and told me to get lost. Let's just say I don't remember taking it nearly as well as young Billy did.

I do remember going down to the banks of the Pee Dee River and thinking about jumping in. I would have, too — if the water hadn't been so cold.

October 17, 1994

Ready, aim, fire — at yourselves, not innocent little girls

Because I know the punks who need to read this column won't — or can't — I'm asking y'all to do me a favor: Pass it on and interpret it for them. Use sign language if you have to. Just make sure they get the message.

The first rule of the street — any street — is that "a bullet ain't got no name on it." It cares not a whit who or what it hits.

Now I don't know, nor do I care, what Antonio "Noogie" Smith did to the person who came gunning for him in Durham's Few Gardens last Saturday night. But whatever it was, it wasn't worth killing somebody. Well, maybe it was — but certainly not a 2-year-old girl playing on a porch.

A lady who was outside her apartment seconds before the shooting said a dude dressed in black walked hurriedly past her and a group of other residents and asked, "Y'all seen Noogie?"

The second rule of the street, as enunciated ungrammatically but eloquently by another Few Gardens resident is, "You don't tell where nobody at. Because nine times out of 10 they're looking for 'em to do somethin' to 'em."

Police have charged Tony Lamont Johnson with doing something to 2-year-old Shaquona Atwater — shooting her — while firing at Smith.

Sure, Johnson — or somebody — shot Smith, all right. Just didn't kill him.

Killed Shaquona, though. She died right there on top of a washing machine, gasping for air, calling for her mama. Man, oh man. I hope for his sake Johnson, 24, isn't guilty. I saw his picture in the paper, and I can tell you, the dudes in the joint love big ol' chubby-cheeked, collard green-eating bad guys who kill 2-year-old girls. Love 'em.

Everyone has already said all there is to say about how horrible it is that these young black guys keep killing each other. I myself have talked about it until I'm blue in the face — and I'm not saying another word. Y'all can kill the hell out of one another if you want to.

Somebody looks at you the wrong way? Shoot 'em.

Some punk sells you a gram of crack cut with baking soda? Shoot 'em.

Some clown wears his hair parted on the wrong side? Blow him away.

Just don't shoot innocent little 2-year-old girls who are playing on the porch. You know those signs you see in men's toilets: "We aim to please — so you aim, too. Please"? That's my plea to the trigger-happy thugs who turn playgrounds into killing fields: Y'all aim, too. Pleeease.

There used to be honor even among thugs. Time was, if somebody dissed you and you wanted to take 'em out, you'd get close enough to kiss 'em, close enough to smell the fear on their breath, before blasting. No longer. Now the punks who are fleeing are afraid, and the ones with the guns are glad of it.

A couple of days after the shooting, I was at a meeting in Few Gardens during which residents of the perennially bad-mouthed public housing complex expressed their rage. At the little girl's killer. At society for looking down on them just for living in a place like Few Gardens. And at themselves — or, more precisely, at those like themselves — for allowing vicious punks to turn their community, as one lady said, into a "cesspool."

Ask anybody, even the police, and they'll tell you that much of the crime in Few Gardens and other public housing complexes is imported by people from outside. That doesn't mean the development doesn't have its share of thugs or thug accomplices: It does, just like any other community.

But most of the people I know in Few Gardens are just like you and me — law-abiding folks who worry about the same things I worry about: their children's education, safety and whether or not they're wearing clean socks when you take them to buy shoes.

Bye, now. I've got to go to a little girl's funeral.

October 27, 1994

Turning a dollar on a depressingly American reaction

Psssst. Can I come out yet?

I've been in hiding the past several days — surviving on Nabs and RC Colas — ever since that national manhunt began for a black man who kidnapped two white children down in Union, S.C.

Turns out, though, there was no black man — just a white woman who knew which red hot buttons to push to elicit sympathy and lend instant credibility to an incredible story.

OK, I confess. I haven't really been in hiding — but only because Susan Smith's story was fraught with such gaping inconsistencies from the get-go that Ray Charles could have driven through them without hitting a fact.

I can't lie: I feel relief that nobody black was involved in this tragedy, but I take absolutely no joy in seeing the lie explode in Smith's face. My heart is sick over the two little boys whose mama — apparently trying to snare a rich boyfriend who wanted no kids — killed them.

I don't know about you, but I went to bed the night Susan Smith's farce came unraveled thinking of the bewildered, deer-caught-in-the-headlights look on her husband's face as he tried to deny — at least to himself — that he had been married to a monster.

I also remembered the pained looks of those Union, S.C., folks —

black and white — when they realized the evil thing that had been done to the kids and, yes, to them. Those folks couldn't have been more devastated if the kids had been their own. Remember the gasp that went up from the crowd when the sheriff said the mama was being charged with killing her boys? That pain was real, Hoss.

Smith cost the state of South Carolina hundreds of thousands of dollars in manpower and resources spent searching for her kids, and more than that in bad publicity. And who can calculate the ulcers she probably gave to every black man from here to Kalamazoo who drives a red car and has a couple of light-skinned kids?

The South Carolina cops, to their credit, didn't emulate their counterparts in Boston who, a few years ago, trampled the Constitution in their zeal to catch the black man who'd shot and killed a pregnant woman and injured her husband as they returned from a birthing class. Those cops, up there in the enlightened North, strip-searched black men on the streets and even arrested one fellow for the shootings.

In that case, too, though, there was no black man — just a greedy, heartless husband after some insurance loot.

Whatever else one might say about Smith and the cat in Boston who killed his wife, they were at least smart enough to know that, in America, the bogeyman is always black. Not in reality, mind you, but in media-inspired perceptions. Judging solely from the calls and letters I get, one could conclude that ol' Beelzebub himself wears an Afro and subscribes to Ebony magazine. One earnest caller has bet me $100 that she can prove black men commit 95 percent of the crime in America.

She's wrong, of course, and I'm going to use that $100 to start my own business, the inspiration for which I can thank Susan Smith. It's called "Blame a Black Man" and I envision a whole chain of them. I'll rent out brothers who will provide you with excuses for any occasion every time you screw up. Call 1-800-A-Bro-Didit today for franchise information.

Say, for instance, you stay at Thee Doll House all night looking at Miss Four-Wheel Drive and an important work assignment slips your mind. Don't sweat it, Hoss. Just call Blame a Black Man and we'll furnish you with a brother to snatch your briefcase and pawn it for a rock of crack cocaine.

You: "J.B., I'd done a bang-up job on the Throckmorton account — stayed up till 3 this morning working on it — but a black man burst into the living room and took it."

J.B.: "OK. Want a raise?"

Man, I will be rolling in dough, and no longer will you have to rely on those lame, worn-out excuses guaranteed to engender skepticism, such as the dog — or the computer — ate your homework.

We'll even provide you with a realistic composite drawing suitable for framing or hanging up in the local post office — not one of those generic drawings like Smith gave South Carolina authorities of a black man who looked like Kunta Kinte wearing a toboggan.

On second thought, maybe I'll just use that $100 for some flowers for two little boys whose mama drove them to a watery grave, still strapped in their protective car seats.

November 07, 1994

A plaintive refrain from the NAACP to Ben Chavis

Don't be surprised if, in the next couple of weeks, we learn that the Rev. Ben Chavis started the Chicago Fire, assassinated Abe Lincoln and was hanging out in a Dallas book depository on Nov. 22, 1963.

Just think about it: Chavis' former employer, the NAACP, has accused the poor dude of just about everything else, so why not hang those heinous offenses on him, too?

The organization's national officials just laid off 100 workers due to, they contend, Chavis' extravagant spending and high living. Not only are they angry at him for paying $300,000 to settle a sexual discrimination suit, but they are also seeing white over Chavis' fondness for leasing Lincoln Continentals and staying in fine hotels.

I could be wrong — although that, as you know, is quite unlikely — but I doubt the NAACP would have been any more effective in dealing with the vexing problems confronting blacks if Chavis had driven a Yugo and stayed at the Hideaway Motor Inn in Rockingham, where — if Linda Kay is working the late shift and knows you — you can get a room for $12 for a half-hour.

With minimal ceremony, the NAACP executive board kicked Chavis to the curb after reaching a financial agreement that'll pay him the paltry sum of about $7,000 and a free subscription to Ebony magazine. If spent wisely, that should keep Chavis in those crisp, starched clerical collars he loves for about a year.

As if the chump-change settlement weren't insulting enough, the NAACP's general counsel last month ordered Chavis — a member of the NAACP since he was old enough to sing "We Shall Overcome" — to "cease and desist" with plans to present an NAACP award named after himself by himself.

Oh death, where is thy sting, now that I know I can never receive a prestigious Benjamin F. Chavis Jr. Award? The horror, the horror.

Chavis is a genuinely decent man, but after all the Oxford native has been put through in recent months, I'm sure he's in need of a friend. Do y'all remember that touching love song Michael Jackson sang about a boy and his pet rat named Ben? For some inexplicable reason, nobody wanted to play with the disgusting, disease-spreading vermin.

Ben Chavis, no doubt, must be feeling sort of like that rat. So I've written an updated version of "Ben" — sung with a reggae beat — from the NAACP to Chavis.

I hope this will cheer ol' Ben up. Maestro, hit it:

Ben, the two of us need talk no more.
We both know what you were looking for.
Some cash to pay for all your fun.
We thought you were the one
but we had to think again
when we realized we'd been
had by Ben.
Ben, here's some cash, now go away.
We won't listen to a word you say.
We've got better things to do
than fool around with you... ...
You have spent up all our dough
and left our cupboards po'.
We haven't got a cent;
it's time for you to went.
So take this seven thou
and hit the road right now —
but you can leave the Lincoln here.
And we hope this check will clear.
And you, my Ben we see
You're no friend of the NAACP.

Of course, blaming Ben Chavis for the moribundity and ineffectiveness of the NAACP is like blaming some guy who left his bathroom faucet running for the floods that devastated Texas last month.

There was a time when I would have rather drunk muddy water and slept in a hollow log than say something negative about the nation's premier civil rights organization. But its current state of irrelevancy saddens me. This is, after all, the organization that nominated outlaw gangsta rapper Tupac Shakur for its "Image Award," for chrissakes.

Several other stunts of that nature make me, a beneficiary of its good works, wonder: Is it just me, or do the folks running this once-proud organization no longer know their butt from apple butter?

November 14, 1994

A Volvo and a $3 thrift store coat make some folks see red

To me, the great moral debate of our time has nothing to do with abortion, prayer in school or which form of punishment — hanging, firing squad or being forced to listen to himself sing — Michael Bolton should face for messing up so many wonderful songs.

No, the great issue of life in the latter part of the 20th century is whether I am — as some folks say — the vilest piece of toe jam since Jeb Bush simply because I have, very infrequently, bought clothes from the Salvation Army thrift store.

Go ahead. Turn away from me in shame and refuse to look upon me. I'm used to comments like this, from a former friend: "It's a shame. My thinking is, if you can afford to drive a Volvo with heated seats, you should be able to pay more than $3 for a coat." But before you condemn me, you should walk a mile in my used shoes.

I do not think I am depriving poor people of quality clothes at a nominal price just because I occasionally browse in a thrift store and sometimes find something I can wear. On the contrary, I think I am providing a service for poor people by supporting an institution that provides essential services such as job training — and clothing — for them.

Upon learning that my favorite tweed coat — a handsome brown thing, not unlike me — cost $3 at a Salvation Army thrift store, most people act as though I went out and tore it off the back of some now-shivering homeless person. Instead of reveling in my good fortune, they act as though I am the Anti-Shopper and the nation's economy will collapse unless I rush out and buy some over-priced shirt with Calvin's or Ralph's name stenciled onto it.

Think I'm exaggerating? Hardly. I know people who are so cheap 11 months of the year that they use the same piece of aluminum foil to wrap their Vienna sausage sandwiches in all week. Yet, because the media designated Friday as the BIGGEST SHOPPING DAY OF THE YEAR, they were out at the malls using their elbows to gain inside positions at sales tables with the same ferocity — and lack of subtlety — as Eric Montross going after a rebound.

I went to two Durham malls the day after Thanksgiving, and believe me, I came away feeling abused. Why, I had more hand prints on me than Miss Four-Wheel Drive after 75-cent beer night at Thee Doll House. I was treated most rudely by a couple of umbrella-wielding old ladies after I foolishly blocked — very briefly — their path to a table marked "clearance." They, like many of the shoppers who apparently think spending tons of cash is the accepted way of remembering Christ's birth, were in a spending frenzy. After I got tired of being jostled and receiving dirty looks — apparently because I only purchased three Moon Pies that I found on sale at the drug store — I left the mall for the relative tranquility of a Salvation Army thrift store, where it's always a "blue-light special."

If you think I'm a cheapskate, you're wrong. You know my fluorescent lime-green, reversible polyester leisure suit — similar to the one Isaac Hayes wore in the sequel to "Truck Turner"? Well, I've actually got a guy who makes those for me. He isn't cheap, either. Honestly, it was only by accident that I discovered thrift stores even sell clothes: initially, they were simply the only place besides ex-hippies' yard sales where I could find Bobby Goldsboro eight-track cassettes.

In honor of the harried shoppers at the malls, I have written this poem called "Twas the Month Before Christmas" or "Pardon Me, Mona, But Can I Get an Extension on My Visa?":

Twas the month before Christmas and all through the mall
the people were desperate — yeah, I'm talkin' 'bout y'all.
The women were shoving, seeking the best deals they could find
Those who couldn't keep up were just left behind.
Little ol' ladies from North Raleigh, their backs might be bent
But they aren't leaving Crabtree 'til they've spent every cent.
"See that cashmere shawl, how much you want for it?
"Sure I'll buy it, wear it once and then I'll ignore it.
"But I've just got to have it, so give it to me.
"Or someone else'll get it — and that can't be."
They're wielding parasols in South Square, elbows at North Gate
There's a sale going on, they refuse to be late.
Throughout the Triangle they're looking for deals.
Oops, someone just found one — I can tell by the squeals.
"Get outta the way, I saw it first, Sonny.
"The mall's almost closed and I've still got some money."

Well, you get the idea of how it was in the Triangle on the BIGGEST SHOPPING DAY OF THE YEAR. Oh yeah. This is for those two old ladies with the umbrellas: If I ever catch you on a basketball court, you're mine.

November 28, 1994

He won't go gently into night

OK, I'm walking down the street one night, minding my own business, when out of the corner of my eye I see a reflection in a store window. It's of a large, slightly stooped figure hobbling on a cane.

I can't lie: It scares the hell out of me at first. But when I look closer, it brings a tear — not to my eye, but to my heart.

For you see, the old man on the cane, having obvious difficulty getting around, is me.

"Oh God, how can this be?" I scream inside. That doddering old dude can't be me.

I'm still young — aren't I? I play basketball regularly, take stairs two at a time, even find "Sesame Street" and Bugs Bunny genuinely amusing. I admit my face isn't going to make women forget Denzel Washington — on a scale of 10 I'd give me a 7 — but I take good care of myself. In short, to quote that great 20th century philosopher, Fred G. Sanford, everything's working and nothing's hurting.

Well, nothing was hurting until I pulled a hamstring muscle recently while lunging to intercept a ball at the Durham "Y" on Chapel Hill Road. Oh, agony!

The pain, while intense, was nothing compared to the mental anguish Dr. Stewart inflicted when he passed sentence on me: no basketball for six weeks, maybe more.

Now, there are lots of things I can do without for six weeks, maybe more, but basketball is not one of them.

Still, even that pain paled in comparison to that inflicted by the condescending attitudes of people who acted like they'd never seen a man on a cane before.

"You'd better quit trying to play basketball before you kill yourself," they admonished. I'm sure — or at least I think — they meant well. But I told them all, emphatically, where they could stick their opinion.

Even my doctor, while sewing up the chin I busted diving for a loose ball some months ago, felt compelled to say, "I know what the charts say, but how the hell old are you again?" — as if no 37-year-old man in his right mind would be diving for a basketball in a game with nothing at stake except bragging rights.

I'm luckier than most people because I know the exact moment Father Time reached out and ran his old gray fingers through my hair, making me old. For me, the trouble started a couple of months ago, on a Saturday. I know it was a Saturday because I was watching those sweet young thangs on "Soul Train." Only this time, I was shaking my head disapprovingly when I heard myself say "Those dresses are too short."

Oy vey. Next thing you know, I'm listening to and singing along with Barry Manilow, The Carpenters and David Gates and Bread songs on the radio.

The surest sign, though, was when the main topics of our courtside or locker room conversations changed from lying about sexual conquests to lying about how much weight we'd lost or discussing whether Hooked on Phonics actually helped our kids read better.

I am not some Peter Pan wannabe — you know, some guy who thinks he'll be young forever — pining away for lost youth. But I, like the poet Dylan Thomas, am determined to "not go gentle into that good night."

Thank God I'm not the only one. A co-worker at a newspaper in Indiana lamented bitterly that her husband was so addicted to golf that he'd shovel snow off the course in their back yard and hit buckets full of balls. Another said she broke off her engagement when her fiancé turned down a much higher-paying job because he didn't want to leave his company softball team.

"What kind of man is he?" she asked me incredulously.

The kind I'd love to sit down and listen to some Barry Manilow with, that's what kind.

January 30, 1995

Neighbor's keeper? Hardly

Hey, wait a minute," I started to shout at the 12 jury members as they left the courtroom to consider Isaac Stroud's fate Friday, "y'all are forgetting somebody."

The somebody they neglected to include in their deliberations were the neighbors who say they heard the all-night beating and berating of Jocelyn Mitchell two years ago and never lifted a telephone receiver to help her.

Of course, after the paramedics had carted her cold, lifeless body to the morgue and Stroud's to jail, charged with murder — those neighbors bravely ventured forth with tales of frequent "fights" between the couple. Couldn't have been much of a fight, seeing as Stroud is 6-foot-5, 200 pounds and Jocelyn Mitchell was 5-foot-6, 130.

Some neighbors, emboldened by the fact that Stroud could be sentenced to death, even testified in Durham Superior Court about the last beating on May 1, 1993, which prosecutors contend was a marathon battering session that left the Durham High teacher dead from her injuries.

You know me — I just had to see what kind of people could sit back and not do something to help while a woman's agonizing yet ever-weakening screams echoed in their ears.

So I went to the Garrett Square apartments. Nobody I asked knew a thing about the case, they claimed. On the stand, though, others recounted how they ignored the documented and frequent violence coming from the apartment above, below or beside their own. On the night Jocelyn died, one told of turning over to try to sleep, even when it sounded as though someone was being thrown through an adjoining wall.

Save your damn tears, I said upon hearing how one dude blubberingly explained that he didn't call 911 because he didn't want to get involved.

Save your tears. They're not helping anyone now. Oh, perhaps they'll help him feel a little better, sleep a little sounder by allowing him to delude himself that he is a sensitive soul. God, I hope not.

Neither he nor anyone else who heard what happened in Apartment J-27 for several months deserves the least bit of solace — not in this life, probably not in the next. Certainly not the woman who said she was awakened at 1:28 a.m. that day by a loud bang and cursing. She turned over and, I suspect after fluffing up her pillow, went back to sleep. When she left for work about 6 a.m., she said, she heard Mitchell's pitiful whimpering and a man still yelling. She got in her car and went to work.

When she returned, though, she saw the yellow police tape that told her maybe, just maybe, she should have gotten involved.

After sitting through that tale of viciousness and indifference, I went into a courthouse bathroom to splash some water on my face, hoping to disguise the tears. There was another guy, who said Jocelyn Mitchell got his daughter interested in track, doing the same thing. "What kind of people could ignore something like that?" I asked, although not in those exact words.

"I don't know, but I'm glad they don't live near me," he answered, not in those exact words, either.

I could be wrong — although you know that's unlikely — but I'll bet you a nickel to a nail that if those same people had heard a dog being beaten the way District Attorney Jim Hardin says Stroud beat Mitchell, they would have called someone.

Sadly, Hardin told me, there is no law against refusing to help someone in distress — unless you're a doctor or nurse.

Well, damn, how about if you're a human being?

February 06, 1995

The AWM: a curious case study

You hear so much these days about creatures called Angry White Males — they're the ones, we're told, responsible for the Democratic massacre last November — that I just had to go out and find me one.

So, like Marlin Perkins did for so many years on Mutual of Omaha's "Wild Kingdom," I went looking for them to find out where they habitate, what they eat, just what makes them tick.

As a light snow fell on the Triangle last Friday, I donned my pith helmet and, armed only with my AWM field guide and a compass — my trusty sidekick and translator Chuck was on vacation — I trudged off alone in search of the elusive creature.

From studying the species, I knew they like to eat about noon. As luck would have it, I spotted one standing outside a Durham feeding hole — called a restaurant — about that time.

"What are you angry about?" I asked Merritt Mulman of Durham.

"I'm not an angry guy," he smiled. I was disappointed, but as he searched for something to be angry about, he was joined by a friend, Chuck Solomon of Raleigh. Unfortunately, Solomon wasn't angry about anything, either. "But I'll be angry Sunday," he said helpfully, motioning toward the falling snow. "I'll be angry when I get ready to go skiing and find that all the roads are closed."

Hmmmm, an interesting trait, I thought to myself. AWMs can get angry at whim, even predict when they're going to be angry. I made a notation in my journal and sloshed on.

Because it was feeding time, few others were willing to talk and met my questions with hostile stares. So I dialed up an AWM who'd called me once. Rob Pearson, who moved here from the Northeast, said, "I'm angry at being discriminated against just because I'm a white male and having to prove myself more so than others. ... I've had companies tell recruiters they like me, but they had to select a minority female."

Yes! Now here was the real deal, the genuine article. I got my notebook and started scribbling furiously. Pearson didn't deny there's been discrimination against blacks and women, but he says, "Two wrongs don't make a right. Why should the white male pay for something that was done in the past?"

All right, stop that laughing, y'all. No, seriously. Stop it.

Pearson said white males as a class had been "slam-dunked" by recent news stories.

As he talked, I thought back to when I used to see my upstairs neighbor, a just-married, friendly young white dude, sitting forlornly on the steps or playing listlessly with his dog. I knew he was frustrated at being unable to find work, so I thought, "You know, Barry, maybe you're wrong; maybe white guys don't have it made." After all, my neighbor — I'll call him Rob, because that was his name — is a bright guy who, I assumed from the despair etched in his face, must have been pounding the pavement for years, only to have jobs handed to unqualified minorities.

Being the kind of guy I am, I felt sympathetic — until I talked to him. Turns out Rob had just graduated college and had been job-hunting for — sit down for this, Margo — TWO MONTHS!

That made me angry, and I wanted to hold him down and make him listen, really listen, to B.B. King sing "Why I Sing the Blues." But then I realized he and I are from two different worlds, a point made crystal clear soon after our conversation — about the time he started receiving so many job offers that he didn't even bother to unpack his bags. Needless to say, he is now gainfully — very gainfully — employed.

February 13, 1995

See there? Money ruined us

I love to say "I told you so," so I'll say it loud: "I TOLD YOU SO."

Remember a few months ago when Money magazine named the Triangle the best place to live in America?

Well, while everybody else was popping champagne corks — and buttons on their prideful chests — it was little ol' me who had the lone voice of reason in this entire region. I'm the one who warned that the sound of those corks and buttons was actually the death knell for the good life most of us associate with North Carolina.

Not only did I shout out about the invariable influx of obnoxious Northerners who pluck our crape myrtles right off the side of the highway and then complain about our lack of culture, but I also warned that housing prices in the Triangle would go so high that only Duke Hospital administrators would be able to afford one.

I began my own search for a house B.M. — Before Money — and it continues A.M. — After Money. So I have seen firsthand what the magazine's rating hath wrought. Remember that little bitty, cramped house that listed for $65,000 that you and Sweet Thang thought would be a perfect first house? Well, now it's a "cozy little bungalow" — or a "charming cottage" — that'll set you back six figures.

What about that big ol' ramshackle thing that looked like something Gomez and Morticia Addams wouldn't be caught alive in? Last year, it seemed to beckon only the wrecker's ball. Now, it's listed as a fixer-upper or handyman's delight with a price that beckons anyone willing to mortgage their first born.

One real estate agent, who obviously mistook me for Sammy Sausagehead, said — without laughing — that the magazine's rating had no impact on the price of houses locally. Any cost increase, he said, occurred because "there are fewer houses ... ... and your tastes probably increased." Houses, he said, are a better value than ever.

He seemed blissfully ignorant of the recent N&O and USA Today reports contradicting everything he said. Anyone who has been house-hunting here knew without being told by the National Association of Realtors that the cost of homes rose 15 percent — the biggest increase in the country — since Money gave the Triangle the kiss of wealth. The average home here now costs $124,000.

In "War," that classic anti-war soul song from the 1960s, we were told that war had just one friend -- the undertaker. Does that mean the only people happy about this very real war between home sellers and prospective home buyers are real estate agents?

Not to hear them tell it. Most agents with whom I spoke were poor-mouthing so bad that I had to wonder, "Who's selling all those 1,000-square-foot lean-tos for $105,995?"

While admitting that good brokers prosper even during the worst of times, David Berry, a Century 21 broker in Raleigh, said none were getting rich because of Money's ranking.

Susie Clemons, also with Century 21, said the magazine caused her and some other agents more headaches than anything else. "It brought truckloads of people into Raleigh, and many of us Realtors ended up spending weekends with people who weren't even thinking of relocating. They were only interested in finding out what the number one rating was all about."

Well, I could've told them what it's all about. It's about me — and I'm sure I'm not the only one — trudging wearily each night up to my little third-floor room, feeling like a homeboy instead of a homeowner because I can't afford a place to call my own.

But hey, it's a real fixer-upper with a great view of the interstate — if you're interested.

February 16, 1995

No slaves to history, these Sons

Don't know much about a science book. Don't know much about the French I took.... ... Don't know squat about the Middle Ages. Look at the pictures and I turn the pages.

Those lyrics to an old Sam Cooke song applied to me and most subjects taught at Richmond Senior High School in Rockingham: I didn't know much, but I did know a little bit about the Civil War.

Or at least I thought I did -- until I received a flier from the Sons of Confederate Veterans observing Black History Month and an application inviting me to join the group.

"Whoa, Nellie. What in tarnation is goin' on here, hoss?" I asked myself. "Black men fighting for the Confederacy? Wearing those ugly gray uniforms? Singing 'Dixie'?"

Say it ain't so, Stonewall.

I was, to say the least, taken aback by this possibility. So I called up Frank Powell III, commander of the North Carolina Division of the Sons of Confederate Veterans, and asked if this were some premature April Fool's joke or something.

"Uh, Frank," I asked earnestly, "weren't y'all the bad guys and if you'd won, there'd be no Black History Month, Week or even Hour?"

Silly me.

The Civil War, Powell said, setting me straight, had nothing to do with slavery. "That was just a political ploy Abe Lincoln used to keep England and France from joining the war on the side of the Confederacy. [The war] was over states' rights, not slavery.

"Most people don't realize slavery would've died a natural death by the 1870s anyway, because it was not economically feasible.... ... It was cheaper to pay someone a wage than to take care of their every need."

I was unmoved, even insulted, that Powell made the era of slavery seem as if it was merely a time when blacks had full employment, paid vacations and were allowed sick leave. So, being of an inquisitive and warped mind, I decided to call those sons of... er... ... Sons of Confederate Veterans at their national headquarters in Tennessee.

I found the toll-free telephone number — 1-800-MY-DIXIE — on the application that someone sent me in the mail. I only got an answering machine, so I called Powell again. He was most obliging, although he quickly corrected me when I referred to his group as "the Sons of the Confederacy." That, he said, "is a Klan group, and they've caused us nothing but trouble.... ...

"We want to make the public more aware of the role blacks performed during the war," Powell said. "They always hear about the black Union troops. We want to tell them about the black Confederate troops. They didn't just serve as cooks and laborers, but by taking up arms."

At that, I pictured a whole battalion of Clarence Thomas-like soldiers fighting to their last breath to remain enslaved. "Freedom? We don't want no stinkin' freedom," I imagined them saying as they fought off the advancing Yankee soldiers. But then, I remembered a relative of mine — a great-uncle — about whom family members spoke only in hushed, shameful tones.

Seems this relative, Col. Beauregard Saunders, did indeed fight on the side of the Confederacy for a short while. See, he mistakenly assumed the crossed-rifle insignia on Confederate caps was the "X" sign for Malcolm X.

The Rebs kicked him out of their army — legend has it — because, after learning the truth, he persisted in blowing reveille each morning to the tune of B.B. King's "Why I Sing the Blues."

Hard to believe, huh?

Well, not as hard to believe as some of the other theories being peddled about the war.

February 23, 1995

Loving to hold the line

Most of the time, I'm just about the humblest dude you'd ever want to meet. Of course, as anyone who knows me can attest — and usually does — I have a lot to be humble about.

But in the past couple of days, you might have noticed an extra bounce to my step. It seems — you'd better sit down for this, Gladys — that I am being wooed.

No, the party constantly dialing my telephone number isn't some sweet young thang just dying to check out the view atop Mount Barrymore: It's the phone company. Two of them. Let me explain.

See, I was sitting at home the other night, sopping up the last of a jar of molasses with a pan of hot biscuits -- and watching a "Roc" rerun on BET -- when the telephone rang. I answered in my usual cheerful tone.

"WHAT?"

The soft, pretty voice on the other end was unflustered by my harshness.

"Hi Barry, I'm Cynthia from [a certain international long-distance telephone company]. Are you satisfied with your current long-distance service?"

Now, I was disappointed the call was not of a more personal nature, but it was still refreshing to hear a soft voice that wasn't yelling something at me like, "Get away from that window, you pervert!"

Truth be told, I was pretty satisfied with my long-distance service — but I figured I could keep Cynthia on the line if I said I wasn't. Her voice set my heart aflutter and she offered all kinds of inducements to get me to switch companies. Besides, she sounded like she really liked me, like I wasn't just some nameless schmo whose name she'd gotten from a computer. I figured that since she was trying so hard to get me to come over to her company, why not try to get her to come over — to my place? Bad move: She only laughed when I, in my best Barry White voice, asked if she'd like to share a biscuit and some molasses to sop it in.

I was stung by her rejection, but I signed with her company anyway.

A week later the phone rang again, and this time it was my old international long-distance carrier — sounding uncomfortably similar to a spurned lover. "Barry," a female voice cooed, "I see you have changed your long-distance service. Were you unhappy with us?"

Uh-oh. I hated to admit to such a lovely sounding voice that I, like some heartless mercenary, had sold out to the highest bidder. So I lied. "Yes."

I then cooked up some cockamamie story about how I blamed her company that I hadn't won two tickets to Hawaii in a radio station contest.

"The phone line stayed busy, and I couldn't get through, even though I knew the correct answer was 'Got My Mojo Workin' by Muddy Waters," I said.

She then offered me essentially the same deal as the other company — plus $15 cash. Being not quite as dumb as I look, I took the deal and apologized for ever doubting her. I also promised I'd never leave her again.

Man, I was flattered by all this unsolicited attention and tried to make the most of it. Indeed, when the phone rings now, I actually find myself hoping it's the phone company.

It's been a few days since I went back to my original company, and I still haven't heard from that woman who first tempted my tummy with a lower rate.

Call me cynical, but I think companies intentionally have honey-voiced women call lonely old men at home, at night, to sell them things. After all, it is an inscrutable law of nature that women can get men named Barry to buy anything.

But in the case of the phone companies, I ask just one thing: "Put it in writing."

March 16, 1995

Seeing red over blacks and blues

I can't lie. I left home one recent night to see and hear Koko Taylor, the queen of the blues, at the Cat's Cradle in Carrboro. But for a brief minute there, I thought I'd stumbled into a Led Zeppelin concert by mistake.

Nothing, not even that seventh Old Milwaukee, could explain such a wrong turn. I mean, there I was, ready to pitch a wang dang doodle in the joint, when I found myself surrounded by tie-dyed T-shirts, white wine and white people.

But before I could check my ticket stub and split the scene, I heard that familiar blues guitar riff I'd heard so often at the beginning of Koko's shows on Chicago's South Side — while I was serving my 6 1/2-year sentence in the Midwest and leaving half my paycheck in some of those dangerous, no-name blues joints.

Of course, the only danger I faced in the Cradle that night was having my corns stepped on by the big dude from Zebulon who danced the entire night in front of me and who shattered one of the few poignantly silent moments of the whole night by snorting — literally — and shouting, "I'm a hog for your love, Koko."

Anybody who knows me knows I try to keep an open mind about things, but nothing prepared me for the sight my bloodshot eyes beheld that night. Longhair, grunge-attired college kids who looked like they were seeking Nirvana — both the band and the state of being — rocked right alongside silver-haired or balding college professors.

They were joined by yuppies in full yuppie regalia: chinos, Weejuns on sockless feet and sweaters tied around their necks while they sipped white wine. (I don't care what Letitia Baldrige or other society mavens say, but I think sipping white wine at a blues concert is an unpardonable social faux pas. Save it for Kenny G., folks.)

What impressed me about the crowd at the Cradle was its lack of pretense. These folks seemed to really enjoy the show and to know as much about the blues as I — which ain't easy, considering that I wake up some mornings with my head feeling so bad that I could swear I invented them.

Once the show got rolling, I didn't pay much attention to who was or wasn't there. Because by the time Miss Taylor started singing "I'd Rather Go Blind (than see you walk away from me)," man, I got all choked up inside and just didn't want to be bothered.

It was only after the show that I reflected upon the weirdest aspect of what I'd seen that night. No, I'm not talking about Koko's wig, which invariably tilts to the side halfway through her show. I'm talking about the paucity of blacks at the show.

Speaking as someone whose lone regret in life is that I didn't get to shake Conway Twitty's hand for writing "Lonely Blue Boy," I realize that there are only two types of music — good and bad. But I swear, I don't want my boy reading in the history books 10 years from now that Eric

Clapton invented the blues. It would be easy to reach that conclusion by looking at MTV, because it seems that blacks are running from the blues and white dudes are the only ones playing anything close to them.

It's as if young blacks are ashamed of an integral part of our heritage. "I don't want to hear that old depressing music," is a phrase I've heard young so-called sophisticated blacks use often when I ask them if they listen to the blues. Few probably even have heard of Koko Taylor, yet, I'll bet they'll all be there to hear Luther Vandross, the crossover king of bland, watered-down pop, at Walnut Creek next month.

Remind me to miss that because, honestly — I'd rather go blind.

April 03, 1995

Time to shoot down crazy idea

Here, as a public service, is a tip to all criminals or criminal aspirants: When you can't tell a gun from a wad of money, it's time to get out of the crime business.

That's the predicament I found myself in one night when I was 16, and spending the summer in Washington. I saw this dude I intended to rob come out of the liquor store after thrusting a big wad of cash into his pocket.

I was big even then, and thought I'd just flash the little 5-inch knife I carried, overpower the slightly built guy, take his loot and run. But was the knot in his pocket really cash? Or a .38 pistol that he would use to blow what little brains I had all over the pavement?

As he got closer to the shadowy corner where I waited, I became less certain and more nervous. Then, when he was about 5 feet from where I planned to yoke him, a car shone its lights on me — taking away both my cover and my courage.

That, as far as I can remember, Your Honor, marked the beginning and the end of my violent crime career. Of course, I'd still break into the gym at Leak Street School in Rockingham to play basketball, or snatch a pack of Nabs from the counter in King's Grocery when no one was looking. And for at least another year, whenever the Rockingham cops said "Round up the usual suspects," they still usually meant me. But I became less of a menace to society after that night when I couldn't tell a bulging wad of money from a gun.

"Ah ha," backers of the current proposals to legalize concealed weapons in North Carolina will say. "See, we told you. Allowing people to carry concealed weapons really does cut down on crime by frightening punks with bad intentions."

Yeah, and if you believe that, I've got an affordable house to sell you — in Cary.

Sure, the prospect of being ventilated made me hesitate — and then abandon my plan to rob that guy that night. But I was only doing it in the first place out of boredom and some vague sense of teenage alienation. Had I been a more hardened, determined malefactor, a gun in my intended prey's pocket would have been no deterrent at all.

I'd have just shot him first, then rifled through his pockets and taken the cash. And his gun.

I predict that will happen a lot if any of four bills guaranteeing the right to carry a concealed weapon passes in the North Carolina legislature.

While part-time or criminal wannabes like I used to be will think twice before pulling a switchblade and demanding some hard-working schmo's money, others will just arm themselves more heavily. You don't have to be a criminal mastermind to realize that a switchblade looks pretty anemic compared to a .45. (Although a blade does have one advantage: As comedian Richard Pryor pointed out, a gun may misfire, but a razor will never miscut.)

But legalizing concealed weapons will have an insalubrious effect on law-abiding citizens as well. That pleasant, turn-the-other-cheek kind of guy who lives in the apartment upstairs may not be so meek after he has strapped on a .45 and downed a couple of 100-proofs at happy hour.

And that simple little fender-bender that caused $50 worth of damage could escalate into a life-or-death confrontation if the person who backed into you is armed with a gun and a quick temper — and fears you are, too.

The NRA is quick to come up with catchy little jingles espousing Americans' rights to blow one another away. "Guns don't kill people — people do" and "An armed nation is a polite nation" are just two of them.

Well, I've got one too, one which I fear will be adopted by increasing numbers of criminals and law-abiding citizens if any of these bills pass: "When in doubt, shoot first."

April 13, 1995

Self-made sexperts tell all

See, I told you Joe Willie was right.

Joe, you may recall, was an Army veteran and the house man at the local pool hall in Rockingham. But mainly, he was the slightly older guy who taught us everything we knew about sex in the days before schools assumed that responsibility.

So what if everything he told us was wrong: At least he was the first person to show us a real condom. And he only charged 25 cents.

Skeptics around Rockingham thought Joe Willie just pulled his theories about women out of thin air — like when he said wiggling your eyebrows while wearing a mixture of Hai Karate and vanilla extract would make us irresistible to women. But now it appears he got them from a reputable source — or at least from the same source that state Rep. Henry "The Juiceman" Aldridge got his.

Aldridge, a dentist and freshman Republican from Greenville, caused Tar Heels everywhere to lie "That's Greenville, South Carolina" after his outlandish comments about rape, incest and juice garnered national attention.

The controversy, which if we're lucky will catapult Aldridge out of the legislature and on to greater prominence, started innocently enough. Heck, he was only saying poor women shouldn't have the right to abortions, even if they are the victims of rape or incest. He was joined in his enlightened attitude toward poor women by Rep. Mike Decker, a Forsyth County Republican, who demanded that poor women who claim they've been raped or are the victims of incest put up or shut up: Name the person who did it or get no state-funded abortion.

Aldridge, quoting from the same medical textbooks Joe Willie no doubt used, said, "The facts show that people who are raped, who are truly raped, the juices don't flow, the body functions don't work, and they don't get pregnant."

Hmmm. With a single statement like that, I expect Aldridge will become a hero to every teenage boy trying to pressure his girlfriend into having sex.

Girl: "But Billy, I might get pregnant and you'll have to quit school, get a job at the 7-Eleven and move into the double-wide with my parents and Uncle Rudy."

Billy: "Don't worry 'bout it, girl. You can't git pregnant — s'long as you don't let yo' juices flow. 'Least, tha's what Dr. Aldridge says."

Girl: "Oh, alright. If Dr. Aldridge says it's OK ... He's my hero."

Billy: Mine too.

Lots of people, Democrats and Republicans, men and women, were enraged by Aldridge's comments and are demanding that House Speaker Harold Brubaker do something about them — such as spearheading an impeachment or, at the least, sending him to bed without dinner.

Nonsense. As Brubaker correctly pointed out, Aldridge is entitled to freedom of speech and was only speaking for himself. (And, I might add, for other NEWBs — Neanderthals Elected Without Brains.)

No, my friends, when it comes to Aldridge, we have nothing to fear. Why, any day now, I expect Henry will resign his legislative seat and move on to bigger and better things — such as a guest appearance on "Larry King Live" or at least "Saturday Night Live," a show that could use some real humor. And don't forget the "Dr. Love" book tour and possibly even his own show as a sex therapist. (Hey, it worked for Dr. Ruth, didn't it?)

Aldridge could call it "Say 'Ahhhh.'" As in "Say 'ahhh' and let me pull that foot out of my mouth."

April 24, 1995

Hidden perils of the lottery

Hey Dan, I'm with you on this one, Hoss.

State Rep. Dan Blue and I haven't always agreed on everything, but we agree that a lottery would not be good for Tar Heel residents. Mainly me.

The legislature is making noises about — imagine this! — letting voters decide for themselves whether we should have a lottery. Blue put up a good fight to keep that contemptible, satanic enterprise out of our state when he was House speaker, but if the issue goes to a referendum — who knows?

Blue and other lottery opponents envision a bleak future in which children go to bed hungry because Pa, instead of buying that bag of pinto beans and slab of fatback for dinner like Ma told him to, bet the family's last $2 on the futile hope that their baby sitter's boyfriend's cousin's address would hit.

Proponents say a lottery would help finance schools and prevent state residents from scurrying over to Virginia, where they spend $80 million a year playing the Wahoo lottery. Opponents agree a North Carolina lottery might stop some residents from going to Virginia, but fear it would send the whole state to Charlotte in a handbasket by hastening our moral decline.

My opposition, unlike Daniel's and the moralists', has nothing to do with morality. When it comes to morality, my view comes from the First Book of Fred (Fred Sanford, that is), where it says: "Let he who is without sin — pick up some."

No, my opposition is based on the fact that a sandwich once cost me $1,000. See, when I was in Washington a few years ago trying to publish a newspaper, I sought to augment my meager income by playing the lottery. Like most people who never hit, I had a guaranteed scientific system. It was called Dr. Lenny's Dream Book, which I consulted after dreaming two nights in a row that I was playing center field for the California Angels. Did I mention I was naked?

Any novice dream book reader knows the number for playing center field naked is "1-2-3." So each day for two weeks I faithfully and cheerfully put down $2 — which would've netted me a cool $1,000 — on that number.

One day, though, as I went to play my can't-miss number, I was less cheerful than usual because my stomach was growling louder than usual.

Stomach: Feed me.

Me: Huh? Who said that?

Stomach: I want me one of them Arby's sammitches. Now.

I tried to ignore it, but my stomach was persuasive. I stumbled in to the Arby's restaurant next door to the gas station where I played my numbers and bought a roast beef sandwich with my last $2.

I almost lost it — my mind and the sandwich —- a few hours later, when a pal who knew my lucky number called and said "Let me borrow $50. I know you got that number, didn't you?" He proceeded to tell me that my number had hit — straight.

Buying that sandwich ruined — no, make that changed — my life: A couple of weeks later, my first ex-fiancé, distressed over my poverty, called it quits. It didn't help when I asked to borrow $2 from her to play another number I'd dreamed up.

Later that year, though, after Cynthia was but a bitter — very, very bitter — memory, I did hit the lottery, in a sense. Or, more precisely, the lottery hit me — in the form of a car driven by a nurse with a suspended license who didn't want the accident to show up on her insurance.

She gave me mouth-to-mouth resuscitation — and a few big bills — to keep my mouth shut, thus enabling me to publish a few more issues of The North Star, my newspaper.

The moral of this story? Good things come to those who ate.

April 27, 1995

The danger of being convenient

You know how when you go into a store and buy something and the cashier gives you back change for a 20 when all you gave her was a 5?

What do you do? That's right. You say "thankyouverymuch" and split before she discovers her error.

That's sort of what I expected Walter Goldston and his attorneys to do after the jury rendered its decision in Goldston's first-degree murder trial Tuesday. What the jury did was give Goldston back more than he deserved — his life — after he'd been found guilty of blowing away General Wesley Cheek during a robbery 30 months ago.

Seems the jury couldn't determine whose bullets actually killed Cheek — Goldston's or those of his running buddy, Robert Louis Davis — so they benevolently imposed a life sentence instead of the death penalty.

But Goldston and his attorneys didn't humbly hightail it out of there as I would have, tumbling over each other in an attempt to get away before the jury realized its error.

Oh no. Perhaps emboldened that the gods — of Irony, perhaps — had smiled upon his client, Craig Brown informed the court he would appeal. In other words, he wasn't satisfied with the verdict.

Gertrude Cheek wasn't satisfied with it, either. But she has no appeal. Just sorrow. You see, she's the one who had to bury a son after Goldston and Davis pumped six bullets into him while he worked at his beloved B's Stop and Shop.

As owner of the convenience store on Roxboro Road, General Wesley Cheek knew the dangers he faced each morning he opened the store. That's why he kept the little .25-caliber semiautomatic behind the counter. But that was no match for the .38 and the .22 Davis and Goldston were packing. After they finished slinging lead across the counter, Cheek lay dead on the floor. His gun was found next to his bloodied body, beside the $190 in blood-stained cash that prompted Goldston's attorney to say, without laughing, "See, that's proof my client didn't rob him." Or words to that effect.

As a person of admittedly meager gifts, I have often had to work at the kinds of dangerous, unglamorous jobs teachers are always warning misbehaving students about. In the past 10 years, I've driven taxicabs, cleaned toilets in Kmart, removed asbestos from buildings for minimum wage. There isn't much I haven't done that's legal.

But working in a convenience store or gas station is a job that, for me, has all the appeal of sponge-bathing Roseanne or clipping Whoopi's toenails — with my teeth. And is even more dangerous.

A service station owner in Washington once offered me a job as an attendant, promising me $5 an hour and all the Slim Jims I could eat. My stomach was as wrinkled as a chitlin, but I told him, "Man, I ain't that hungry yet," and kept on stepping.

Honestly, I'd go on welfare first, and gladly endure the disapproving looks as I handed over a book of food stamps for a pack of neck bones and a bag of rice.

But fortunately for poor people whose neighborhoods have been abandoned by supermarkets, there are — or were — people like General Wesley Cheek who have not succumbed to the palpable fear and dread they must contend with each time a customer enters the store.

Of course, pistol-packin' punks could make such stores — and store owners — endangered species.

May 11, 1995

Thou shalt not peep

I swear, I was just about to feel sympathy for the Rev. Billy "Eyeball" Riggs after he was caught looking upon the wife of another in a covetous manner as she innocently caught some rays at the Electric Beach tanning salon.

He's only human, I figured. The dude erred and deserves forgiveness. As the Bible says, "All have sinned and fallen short of the glory of God." Or, as it says in the Book of Fred (Sanford, that is), "Let he who is without sin -- pick up some."

But all my compassion, I'm sad to say, vanished when Riggs blamed his reckless eyeballing on a sickness -- "my impulsive/compulsive behavior" is what he called it in court Monday. And just like every womanizer, manizer and anyone else caught with their drawers down this century, he will obligatorily enter therapy.

To use a biblical word: bull.

Somewhere in my gin-soaked past I might have peeped at a woman or two (I'm admitting nothing, since I don't know whether the statute of limitations has expired), but the only thing that compelled me was a desire for a cheap thrill, not some illness.

But regardless of what compelled Riggs to look, the charges against him signal a troubling trend in the ministry. No, not the fact that a man of the cloth gazed lustfully upon the wife of another: King David did that way before Jimmy Swaggart learned to cry, sing and beg forgiveness at the same time.

The troubling trend I'm talking about is ministers getting tans in order to cut a more dashing figure in the pulpit. Traditionalists, I know, will consider it unseemly for a pastor to waste time tanning his epidermis.

"He might have a nice tan, but he's goin' to hell if his soul ain't right," they'll say.

I myself have never been to a tanning salon, but when I think of people who have, I tend to picture some shallow, self-absorbed dude lurching through a midlife crisis in a leased red Corvette.

You don't think of a preacher. Or at least you didn't — until now.

Actually, one cannot underestimate the importance of a good tan in a profession such as the ministry: Regardless of how spiritually illuminating a sermon is, it would be like pearls cast before swine if the congregation was focused on the paleness of the preacher instead of the power of his words.

Still, some consider it unseemly for a minister to give two figs about his appearance.

Of course, such cynicism is unlikely at Crossroads Fellowship, Riggs' former church. For one thing, Crossroads is one of those churches where members take a vow not to speak disparagingly of it or its members. For another, Crossroads will soon be the largest house of worship in the state. It is described as a new-breed "megachurch" that teaches a fundamentalist version of Christianity tailored to the needs of busy, affluent yuppies.

Silly me. I thought yuppies had the same spiritual needs as the rest of us. I reckon their liturgy goes something like "thou shalt not covet thy neighbor's hard drive or Cuisinart, nor his BMW, and thou shalt drinketh not of wine that costs less than $22 a bottle, and if thou Volvo offendeth thee, trade that sucker in for a Lexus. Forever and ever, amen."

I truly hope the Rev. Riggs can find redemption, because not only does God use imperfect vessels, but I have always related well to ministers who have the same human frailties — but not as many — as I have.

How, I ask, can you preach against the evils of demon rum, loose women and such if you've never partaken of them?

But for Riggs to be redeemed, he's going to have to drop this "illness" nonsense and admit — as historical figures from King David on down have — "Oh Lawd, I done wrong."

May 18, 1995

Mother's woe is woe of a nation

I went to Rockingham a couple of days ago to see an old girlfriend. But we didn't sit around reminiscing about old times.

Heck, I didn't say much to her at all, except, "I'm so sorry."

She was in town, you see, to bury her only child — a 19-year-old son named Gregory. He was shot and killed on a Baltimore street corner last week for $3, a pair of sneakers and a watch.

Gregory and three of his pals were walking down the street at 8:30 p.m. when a punk with a gun ran up behind them, forced them to lie down on the sidewalk and robbed them. Baltimore police could describe the gunman only as a black man in his 20s.

My 19-year-old cousin, who was one of those forced to lie on the ground, told me what happened.

"We gave him our shoes and watches ... ... We could hear him backing up, so Greg started to raise his head up. The guy shot him in the temple."

He said Gregory tried to say something, but he died almost instantly. The gunman jumped into a waiting car and fled.

I'm not some wistful old geezer longing for the good ol' days when the skies were bluer, the grass was greener and the robbers were kinder. But you do have to wonder what would make a creep shoot a kid who's lying on the ground offering no resistance?

Maybe I've just been lucky: Of the three times I've been robbed, only once did the robber have a gun -- and he tossed some of my money onto the ground after I said, "C'mon, man. Gimme $20 to walk with."

Right around the time of the shooting last week, I saw something on television that angered me. Jesse Jackson was leading a march in Georgia — Newt Gingrich's home state — to protest planned Republican cuts in welfare and other social programs. And, of course, to gear up for his self-aggrandizing presidential campaign.

Some people are going to say that cutting social programs will lead to more senseless crimes by desperate people. But there is no problem in this country more pressing than the obscenely high number of young black men who are being killed by other young black men.

Funny — that's the same thing I heard Jesse say a few months ago. Before he moved on to his latest cause of the week.

The budget? Damn a budget. Social Security? Hell, most black men won't live long enough to collect it anyway.

Baltimore had 353 murders in 1993. Two hundred eighty-three of the victims were black men. As were most of those arrested for the murders.

Which explains why Jesse Jackson was in Georgia. Had the person who robbed and killed Gregory been some white dude who used a racial slur before pulling the trigger, Jesse and others would've been right there on the first thing smoking, smiling and profiling for the cameras and railing against this outrage.

Well, dammit, it is no less of an outrage that the punk who shot Gregory is black, as are the punks who hold many of our neighborhoods hostage.

Hey, I've got a great idea. Why don't we make murderers attend the funerals of their victims — so they can see and hear the pain and agony they've caused? Then we can pull the switch and send them to hell or wherever it is that coldblooded murderers go.

I didn't know the kid, but when I knew his mother, we were both around his age. The picture of him on the funeral program looked like she did then.

I had seen her only once in the past 15 years or so, but I remember her being loud and gregarious, just as lively as you'd want to be. At the funeral, though, she looked much older than she should have.

Of course, I imagine losing a child does that to you.

May 25, 1995

Fashioning a reasoned judgment

Hey out there, you groovy guys and gals, this is your deejay, Grand Master BS, with the stacks of wax you want to hear. Here's a special dedication going out from attorney Mary Mendini to Judge Susan Renfer.

It's Rod Stewart's disco classic "Do Ya' Think I'm Sexy?"

All right, already. I know disc jockeys no longer say "groovy" or "stacks of wax" — hell, they don't even play stacks of wax anymore. And Mendini, a Durham attorney, didn't actually dedicate that song to Judge Renfer. But if she had — or had even asked the judge "Do ya' think I'm sexy?" — the answer would have been a resounding "No."

Indeed, so unimpressed with Mendini's appearance was Renfer that she grabbed two handfuls of Mendini's blouse and forcefully tried to cover up her habeas corpus. The judge said she was "appalled and incensed" when Mendini entered her courtroom bearing not just law briefs, but baring her brassiere and breasts, too.

Unbeknownst to Mendini, Judge Renfer administers not just justice -— but fashion tips, as well — from her seat on the District Court bench. The judge angrily ordered Mendini into her chambers for a private fashion consultation where, Renfer admitted, she demonstrated the way the veteran attorney should wear her blouse by grasping the blouse by the lapels and firmly pulling them together.

Mendini was unimpressed with the judge's fashion statement and has decided to make a statement of her own — to the Judicial Standards Commission accusing the judge of assault.

Mendini swears she was not auditioning for an upcoming Playboy spread on "Women of the Law" or trying to catch the eye of some cute prosecutor when she entered court revealing her bra a la Madonna. She figures she must have lost a clasp on the white linen blouse en route to court that day and didn't even know it was undone.

Since the incident last week, colleagues and attorneys have come forth with their judgments — most of them unflattering — of Renfer. The consensus is that Her Honor is ornery, dictatorial and intemperate, and in interviews the portrait emerged of a judge so mean that I'm surprised she didn't give her ownself some time on slow days.

Renfer is one of the few District Court judges anywhere in the country before whom I have not had to cop a plea or say something like "I swear, Your Honor, I thought she was 21." In the event I ever do, though, I'd like to get on the good foot with her by offering a possible explanation for her bizarre behavior.

See, I don't think the revealing nature of Mendini's attire is what offended the judge. I think she was more offended by Mendini wearing white linen before Memorial Day. Laugh if you want, but that is a major fashion faux pas.

Even I — who learned all I know of fashion from rassler Classy Freddy Blassie, the Hollywood fashion plate — wouldn't be caught dead in a low-cut white linen blouse before ... oops. Never mind.

But anyway, society must put its foot down somewhere and Judge Renfer is that foot. Why, if she lets female attorneys wear white linen blouses before Memorial Day, the next thing you know, male attorneys will be wearing those clip-on suspenders — a crime in itself — and belts at the same time.

Even if Renfer is found guilty of assault, don't bet on her doing any hard time. Not because of what vengeful inmates might do to a cellmate who sentenced them to the slammer, but because it would constitute cruel and unusual punishment if the fashion-conscious judge had to trade in her stately black robe for one of those garish orange jumpsuits inmates wear.

June 01, 1995

Unjust justice sinks lower

Well, I did it again last night.

No, not that. I'm talking about this recurring dream. No fooling. In this dream, I'm at a service station pumping gas into the dudemobile and drinking from a gallon jug of ice water when Supreme Court Justice Clarence Thomas comes running down the street on fire. He stops and looks pleadingly at me. Being the kind of person I am, of course I offer him a sip — of premium.

Don't look at me like that. Have you seen the price of premium lately?

When I was younger, I thought that nothing too bad could happen to the good-looking high school guys I envied who were smooth with girls and wore argyle socks that matched. Now, I feel the same way about black Supreme Court justices who benefit from the blood, sweat and tears of blacks and then spend their entire lives attacking anything that might make their lives a tad easier.

That is exactly what Thomas has done. I thought the unjust justice had sunk as low as he could when he ruled that a busted-up inmate couldn't file suit against a vicious jailer unless the inmate could prove the jailer intended to cause serious injury when he beat and kicked him. He followed that appalling decision with votes to abolish black-majority voting districts and a school desegregation plan.

But then, just a couple of weeks ago he cast the deciding vote that landed a bolo punch to affirmative action and, consequently, to the legitimate aspirations of millions of Americans who aren't white males.

I swear, for a minute there, I thought the dude had forgotten how to talk. I mean, he's usually content to sit on the bench like a mute black-robed doll, voting an even 90 percent of the time whichever way the equally hateful Antonin Scalia votes.

But along comes an issue into which he can sink his self-hating teeth, and he attacks it like a rabid Rottweiler on a piece of undercooked rotisserie chicken. This son of a — uh — sharecropper was not content merely to cast the deciding vote sounding the death knell for something meant to level the playing field for blacks and women.

Oh noooo. He had to add vocal salt to the wound. His only regret, he said (and I swear I thought I saw Scalia's lips moving), was that "I can't do more to abolish affirmative action.... Government-sponsored discrimination is just as noxious as discrimination inspired by malicious prejudice."

Noxious this, Clarence.

Those comments are particularly noxious coming from a guy who, were it not for affirmative action, would be a servile waiter on somebody's veranda in Acworth, Ga., going, "Y'all want some mo' mint in dis heah julep?" You can bet he wouldn't be on the Supreme Court.

Some of y'all, especially you blacks who feel it is wrong to criticize another black, are going to come down hard on me for coming down hard on him. But what was it the rappers Public Enemy said? A brother ain't a brother just because of his color.

But the main reason I feel so strongly is that I was deceived. See, I'm usually a pretty good judge of character — except for when it comes to picking women. Unlike most people, I didn't lament Thomas' nomination, just because he appeared to be a Negrophobic assimilationist who had rejected his heritage so completely that he jettisoned his first wife for political expediency and now wanted nothing black but a Cadillac — if that. I thought he was just running a game until he secured that lifetime seat.

Once on the bench, I assumed, he'd become a staunch defender of minority rights and cut out all that shuffling and grinning.

I was wrong. He's still shuffling. And grinning.

Here Clarence. Have another sip.

July 10, 1995

Curse the tribulations of aging

You all know the kind of person I am: If I can't say something good, I keep my mouth shut.

But not this time. There's nothing good to say about an affliction — and I don't care what you say, it IS an affliction — that has jumped in the front seat of the car of life with me and won't get out and won't help with the gas.

I'm talking about old age. I know railing against old age does no good. To most people, it is as inevitable as Jim Belushi and Whoopi Goldberg making another movie -- and just as dreaded. But I dread it not as some Peter Pan-wannabe who refuses to grow up. I actually think I'll look cool and distinguished with a few flecks of gray in my beard. I've even stopped fretting excessively about the injuries I routinely suffer on the basketball court: Even athletes in their prime get hurt.

But no athlete in his prime ever suffered the indignity I just experienced — going into the 7-Eleven and asking, "Where's the 1 percent milk?" As far as fun experiences go, that one ranks right up there with rectal exams — something else I have to look forward to as I age. If you young whippersnappers think I'm overreacting, just wait until it happens to you. Today, 1 percent milk, Hoss; tomorrow, incontinence pads.

I wanted to tell the pimply faced kid behind the counter that the 1 percent milk was for an elderly neighbor or something, but to my relief, he hardly looked up from the computer magazine he was reading.

When I eyed myself in the security mirror slinking out of the store with a half-gallon of imitation milk, I almost fell apart.

The reason for my anguish was the realization that this once fine, proud body — a body which for years easily digested a gallon or more of WHOLE milk a day — can no longer even handle 2 percent milk without my stomach feeling like the War Between the States is being re-enacted inside it. With sound effects.

Oh death, where is thy sting when the simple act of buying milk for my Cap'n Crunch can wound me so deeply?

My doctor, Dr. LeRoy, said I may have lactose intolerance and recommended I try some kind of milk with something called lactase added to it. He tried to make me feel better by saying it was an inevitable consequence of the aging process. I thanked him, but told him nothing's going in my milk but Cocoa Puffs or whatever came out of the cow.

Don't y'all remember the angst you felt the first time you had to buy 2 percent milk? But you could rationalize it because at least 2 percent still tastes like real milk that came from a cow (and the label on the jug is the same color as Vitamin D whole milk — so unless the sweet young thang behind you in the checkout line looks real closely, she can't tell you're getting the fake stuff). One percent tastes — on a good day — as though a cow might have spit in it.

You know how you always see smiling old people on television, waxing ecstatic about the so-called joys of their twilight years? Well, I've listened to them, considered their point — tried to give them the benefit of the doubt.

But I have concluded, with all due respect, that they are full of lactose.

There once was an execrable TV show called "thirtysomething," better known as "whining yuppies." But anyway, one of the male thirtysomething characters uttered a classic line that the worst thing about getting older is that you become invisible to teenage girls. Well, they may not be able to see him, but if he drinks milk, chances are they'll sure hear him.

July 17, 1995

Minorities need friends like Rufus

I've always liked Rufus Edmisten. Never met him, but I've always liked him. I mean, his fondness for fun is legendary, and mutual acquaintances of ours tell me he, unlike many people in government's upper echelons, doesn't take himself too seriously.

I like him even more since a local television station and The N&O last week reported the secretary of state's friendship with a 23-year-old state employee, Miss Rosemary McBryde. Edmisten swears everything is on the up and up, that she is merely the daughter of a friend and that there is no hanky panky. I don't know about yours, but my own response is taken from the Bible: "Judge not, that ye be not judged." Or else from the Book of Fred (Fred G. Sanford, that is: the "G" stands for glory, glory), where it says, "Let he who is without sin — pick up some."

I, for one, am not casting any stones because, truthfully, I — like Rufus — would mow a 23-year-old woman's grass, too. (But hey, there are days when I prefer to mow a 46-year-old's.)

Despite the politically inspired outrage over Miss McBryde's relationship with Rufus, we, as a nation, owe the pair a huge debt for illustrating once and for all that blacks and women don't need affirmative action to get ahead in America. All they really need is a father who is best pals with the secretary of state.

Isn't it amusing the way Republicans are clamoring for Rufus' scalp over these alleged, unproven peccadilloes, as though they have a monopoly on righteousness — as though they don't have a Rep. Ken "Hey, sweet 16: You wanna come up and see my big legislative agenda?" Miller in their own party.

These are the same folks who had us believing that had Rufus become governor in 1984, North Carolina would've become Sodom, Gomorrah and Charlotte wrapped into one, people would be shagging all over the Capitol and the state song would now be "Get Down Tonight" by K.C. & the Sunshine Band. Or "My Baby Does the Hanky Panky."

If anything, Miss McBryde deserves our respect, not opprobrium. If the Republicans were smart, they'd tout her as a role model to blacks and women who want special treatment. After all, did she sit back waiting for some government handout to get herself started in a cushy state job?

Noooo! From the time she was a freshman at N.C. State, she showed admirable zeal and picked herself up by her own bootstraps. Of course, she also picked up the telephone:

Rosemary: Ohhh, Daddykins. Tuition here is ever so high and the food in the caf' is simply dreadful. Whatever shall I do?

Daddykins: Don't worry, Punkin'. Call my friend in Raleigh. He may be able to help you. I'll ask him to check in on you.

By all accounts, Rufus did. Records from his state-owned cellular telephone indicate he was a diligent surrogate parent, calling Miss McBryde frequently 'round midnight.

Rosemary: Hello?

Rufus: Rosemary, honey? This is Rufus. Just checking in to make sure you're all right. You know I told your daddy I'd keep an eye on you. Now, you turn off that television and go to sleep, because I've got a lot of work for you to do tomorrow. And don't forget to floss."

As Edmisten asked in response to insinuations about his relationship with Miss McBryde, "When in the world did it become a crime for somebody to help a friend of the family?"

When, indeed? I'm convinced that those folks calling for Rufus' resignation for helping his friend's daughter would be just as angry if he'd turned his back on her. I know I would be. Indeed, that's just one more thing to like about Rufus: his sense of loyalty to old friends.

Besides, how could I not like a white dude named Rufus?

August 07, 1995

A teacher's demand for respect

Parents, are you tired of seeing your male offspring walking around in pants big enough to cover Roseanne?

Don't think you can take reading "Fruit of the Loom" or "B.V.D." once more when he walks past en route to the refrigerator — where he'll invariably hold the door open 10 minutes before gulping milk directly from the carton?

Well, have I got news for you! You no longer have to threaten to take him to a Yanni concert or cut his allowance. All you have to do is tell him where that "fashion trend" started.

In prison. Yup. The joint. The hoosegow. The Big House.

Kenneth Cutler, a teacher at Durham's Hillside High School, told me he heard that theory from people who should know. The style, they say, originated among gay men in prison to signal their sexual preference and to provide — hmmm, how can I say this in a nice way? — easy access.

Makes sense to me, although the last time I was a guest of the state (it was just a misunderstanding: Honest) everybody's pants were hanging low: the cops had taken all our belts lest someone try to croak himself during a moment of lucidity.

My disgust with seeing kids with their pants riding low has little to do with moral outrage. No, the source of my anger is selfish: You see, as someone whose backside can best be described as "Rush Limbaughish" in size, I can never find britches big enough to fit me because some reed-thin pipsqueak just bought the last pair.

But Cutler, a physical science and biology teacher, said he thinks the oversize clothes — or, more precisely, the belligerence that often accompanies them — make doing his job difficult. "Once you get discipline, then you can teach," he said.

His next comment surprised me. "The students like discipline," he said. "I've found they want an authority figure. I spend the first week of each year getting to know the kids — letting them know why they are here and what I expect from them."

Too many people — and not just teachers — are afraid to tell kids what they expect from them. Indeed, it was with great trepidation that I said to a young but very big kid at the YMCA in brightly colored, but inappropriately displayed boxers, "Boy, pull those pants up."

I expected a fight, or at the least a string of epithets. Instead, he did a very strange thing: He pulled them up.

But Cutler is no mere fashion consultant. During a conversation a couple of days ago, he told me stuff that, with the beginning of school imminent, should help all teachers.

For instance, he told me how he got male students to take off their hats inside buildings. At Hillside, the student dress policy allows boys to wear hats inside the lobby. Not Cutler. He said, "I can't accept disrespect toward women ... ... Unfortunately, many black men have a problem with respecting our women.

"When they come in with their baseball caps on, I tell them that it is disrespectful to women, especially their mothers. Then I ask them to name one person who is not an athlete or entertainer who wears a baseball cap and makes over $40,000 a year: They can't."

And, you remember how in Miss Landers' class on "Leave It To Beaver" there was always a mad dash to the door the instant the bell rang? Not in Cutler's class. "When the bell rings, nobody moves," he said. "The ladies go first, then the men."

So, parents. Be sure to tell your sons where the droopy-pants style originated and what Cutler said: "There's only one kind of man I know who likes to show his butt to another man." See if that doesn't make them pull their trousers up.

Now, if we could just think of a way to make them close the refrigerator door.

August 14, 1995

The wait was forever for Donnie

Here, as a public service to kids out there who might find themselves held hostage by a mad gunman, is a health tip from Uncle Barry: When the cops ask how you're doing, you should ignore the gun pointed at you, speak clearly into the telephone, and tell the truth: "This dirty, rotten ????? is going to kill me."

But make sure you have just the right amount of hysteria in your voice — enough to let the cops know you're serious, but not enough to set off a deadly explosion in the wicked SOB who's standing there glaring at you with a hand cannon.

That last part is extremely important, because apparently, 14-year-old Donnie Morris didn't adequately convey the true terror of his situation to Raleigh police last week. That's why, even after the kid told cops his stepfather — stepfather, hell: his mother's boyfriend is all the dude was — had shot him, he bled to death from a gunshot wound to his belly while scores of cops waited outside.

Hold it, let me clarify that. Did I quote the kid as saying he'd been shot by Johnnie Bennett? He didn't. His exact words were, "I've been killed." OK, mouth those words to yourself. Now, put them in the mouth of a frightened little boy who has just been shot. Awful, huh?

But hey, like I said, neither those stark words alone — nor the gunman's admission 10 minutes earlier that he'd shot the boy — were enough to convince the cops of Donnie's true peril.

Police Capt. Dennis Ford sought to explain why police waited 10 hours after hearing three gunshots and Donnie's macabre message to storm the house and discover the murder-suicide. "We were hoping he wasn't shot, that it was just a ploy. I'm sorry that's the way it ended up."

Oh yeah? Sorry this, Captain. Unbelievably, the department seemed to blame the kid for his own death -- or at least for the cops' lack of response. Was anybody else as offended as I was when Ford stood before the television cameras afterward and said police had caught the kid in lies earlier during the stand-off, so they didn't know if he was being truthful this time?

Who wouldn't lie if an evil stepdude had the drop on them? I know I would. I'd tell the cops he was Mother Teresa if that's what he wanted.

I'm no psychologist or hostage negotiator, so somebody will have to tell me what motive Donnie, a big-eyed kid who looked like me when I was 14 — only cuter — and Bennett had for telling the cops Donnie had been shot if he hadn't been.

And shouldn't it have sent some kind of signal of Bennett's intention — or at least of his capability — when he freed his own biological children but held onto his girlfriend's son, whom neighbors say he treated badly?

Being a cop ain't easy. I saw the pain and despair etched in the cops' faces once they realized the evil that had been done inside 205 E. Bragg St. while they waited outside. They were in an untenable situation and faced criticism no matter what.

I'm also sure that, if given the chance, Capt. Ford or Chief Mitch Brown or whoever can explain to Donnie's little friends and everyone else why they waited. But they can never explain it to me.

Nor to Donnie.

September 07, 1995

Vengeance may be his at reunion

Scuse me, Lord, but this is one instance where vengeance is just too good to be left to You alone.

Blasphemous? Sure. But this is no ordinary instance. We're talking here about a 20-year class reunion, folks.

I've been waiting ... ... oh, about 20 years ... ... for this weekend, hoping to return — as a professional basketball player or rassler or brain surgeon — and turn up my nose at all those former classmates who turned up theirs at me so long ago, at all the girls who wouldn't go out with me.

Alas, things turned out differently than I planned on the career path. The NBA was an unattainable dream, and I didn't become a doctor because I hate the sight of other people's blood. I didn't become a rassler because I hate the sight of my own.

So, I need to ask y'all to do me a big favor: If anybody from Richmond County asks have you seen me, just say, "No."

Or, better yet, say something like, "Uh, Dr. Saunders was here a few minutes ago, but he just flew to Sweden to accept a Nobel Prize for dis-

covering the cure for the Heartbreak of Psoriasis. So he won't be attend-
ing your silly reunion. But he sends his warmest regards anyway."

I don't know if I'll bypass the reunion or not, but I do know it seems
silly for a grown man's blood to still boil with anger over slights — or presumed slights — from two decades ago. But I can't help it.

And if you're honest, I'll bet you can't either. Who among you wouldn't
like to do something about all those golden boys and girls you envied in
school, the ones who were better-looking, smarter and smoother with
members of the opposite sex than you were?

Remember Janis Ian's song, "At Seventeen"? She truly wrote my life
when she rhapsodized about "Those of us with ravaged faces/lacking in
the social graces." But you know what? The traits that made one popular then — good looks, a winning smile, being a mindless lick-spittle sucking up to teacher — won't get you a cup of coffee at Western Sizzlin'
Steak House, where, I'm delighted to say, one of my main high school
tormentors now works restocking the buffet table. I hope he comes to
the reunion. God, I hope he comes.

True, I haven't exactly set the world on fire myself, but I also admit
that for a dude everyone predicted would be in prison — or dead — by
18, I'm doing OK.

When I hear guys speaking wistfully 20 years later about memorable
nights spent in the backseats of cars petting or watching the stars with
someone special, I have no conception of what they're talking about. If
you ever saw me in a backseat then, chances are I was being escorted
to a police lineup.

That's why I'll compare my high school horror stories with anyone's.
In three years, I received two telephone calls from girls: one called to ask
for my buddy Ervin's telephone number; I never knew who the other one
was because I wasn't at home.

"I think it was Sharon," my aunt said when I returned.

So I vaulted to the phone to call her, my 16-year-old hands shaking
and voice quivering excitedly. "Hello, Sharon. This is Barry. Did you call
me?"

Twenty years later, her response still sends a serrated knife into my
heart and makes my face turn crimson. "Hell no. What would I call you
for?"

What for, indeed?

September 21, 1995

They just want to die honorably

The torture and kidnappings — even murders — that led pickets to grab signs and hit the street aren't taking place in some far-off country. They are occurring right here in the Triangle.

Not much touches me, but the story in The N&O had me fighting back tears and — like the protesters' leader, Dietrich von Haugwitz — truly ashamed of man's inhumanity to man.

Well, actually, of man's inhumanity to lobsters.

You see, von Haugwitz is not protesting the genocide occurring in Rwanda or Bosnia or even in some of the Triangle's housing developments. Nosiree. His ire is up over the fire that's under the succulent crustaceans that go for $15 a pound.

Stop that laughing. Von Haugwitz is serious, as are the 20 or so people who joined him outside Fishmonger's restaurant in Durham where they protested a lobster-eating fund-raiser for the Durham Symphony orchestra this past Sunday.

I'm not belittling von Hogwash's — er, Haugwitz's — commitment to his shell-backed friends or his earlier protests on behalf of goldfish, but I can't see how anyone can be so upset by the treatment of lobsters while innocent people are being subjected to Hootie & the Blowfish.

The arrogance of von Haugwitz and his merry band of pickets is what really has my blood — like the 250 or so lobsters consumed at the fund-raiser — boiling. Just because von and the gang would be screaming and writhing in agony if someone dropped them in a vat of 210-degree water, they assume lobsters would, too. Their attitude reminds me of people who try to housebreak their dogs by rubbing their pets' noses in poop: heck, dogs — for all we know — might actually relish and look forward to having their schnozzes dipped in that stuff.

Likewise, lobsters might view death by boiling and being gobbled up by tipsy businessmen on expense accounts — the only folks who can afford them — as the noblest way to go. Just think of poor Charlie Tuna. Remember the shame and ignominy he suffered when Starkist continually passed him by, despite his best efforts at self-improvement? I mean, the finny dude even learned to play Beethoven's Fifth on the piano. If a tuna can learn that without any hands, imagine what a lobster can do with two claws?

Speaking of claws, the most famous lobster lover — actress Mary Tyler Moore — said she has seen lobsters "flirt with one another, claw-in-claw" along the beach. Uh, pardon me, but is it safe to conclude that Mary has perhaps spent one evening too many with Ted Baxter?

I interviewed a lobster two days ago, and he was pretty upset over the humanoid meddling.

"Tell 'em to mind their own business," he said as he worked out on a treadmill to get in shape for the next seafood draft.

I admit I conducted the interview after a couple or 10 gin-and-tonics, so I might not be quoting him exactly right. But "Larry" [not his real name] confirmed my suspicions that lobsters actually aspire to being eaten.

"But only in fine restaurants," he said. "On the playgrounds, the cruelest insult you can hurl at another lobster is, 'Oh yeah, well, at least my dad wasn't eaten at Red Lobster.' Those are fighting words."

September 28, 1995

Once upon a (Light +) Time

Here is another installment of the inspirational story of "Young Tom Fetzer, Boy Mayor."

In our last episode two years ago, our hero Thomas had decided he was tired of running conservative political action committees but was still not quite ready to — for the first time in his life — get a real job.

"Therefore," he declared archly, "I shall cast my lot and run for office my own self."

Young Thomas was ... ... well ... ... young, and his face had that unlined, untroubled look of one whose greatest worry each day was "Hmm, should I watch 'Seinfeld' reruns or 'Jeopardy' tonight at 7 o'clock?" He had a full head of his own hair, and he was, though short, not difficult to look at. (In the latter part of the 20th century, that was often all one needed to be elected.)

So, armed with blessings and endorsements from people who felt that "that government's best that governs for me," he threw his hat into the political ring. Truth be told, he never wore hats, for fear they would mess up his carefully tousled hair.

No one gave Thomas much of a chance at first, but using the fundraising skills he learned at the knee of his mentor, "Uncle Jesse" Helms, he quickly proved adept at this most indispensable part of politics.

And even though Young Thomas was conservative and a chip off the ol' Jesse, he displayed surprising sensitivity toward residents of Raleigh's southeast section during his campaign — even venturing there for a "photo opportunity" with the mother of an innocent black man killed by police during a drug raid.

Giving the family his best "I-feel-your-pain" look, Young Thomas promised them he would "look into it" if elected. (He looked into it, all right, but then eagerly cast the deciding vote to deny the family compensation, an official apology or even an "oops.")

But before that, there was much rejoicing in the streets as Southeast Raleigh residents felt that, at last, they had a candidate who would not ignore them. "Young Tom Fetzer, he's our man/If he can't do it no one can./He's a Republican, and he's white/But we still think he'll do us right," they chanted. Jubilant residents killed some fatted calves, wrung the necks off some chickens and partied heartily.

Young Thomas triumphed, and there was real hope that the state's capital city would become a truly progressive city known as more than just "the place Barney comes to party."

Alas, all was not as it seemed. Behind the mask of the smooth, urbane politician that Young Thomas presented to the world was a dude with very old-fashioned ideas about what government should do to help a city and its citizens: nothing.

He set about cutting city services, closing libraries, opposing low-income housing. Indeed, Young Thomas accomplished so much during his first term that the most important issue he could find to focus his re-election campaign on was the huge Light + Time Tower art display on Capital Boulevard.

Think I'm kidding? Well, listen: one week before the election, Young Thomas had already spent $221,419 to tell Raleigh voters — ad nauseam — that his opponent, City Councilwoman Mary Watson Nooe, spent "your tax money" for the tower.

Oh, I tell you, he whined incessantly, "She supported the tower and I didn't, na-na-na-na-na," and kicked up such a fuss in hopes that residents would be blinded by the lights of the tower and not see that he was turning out the lights on the city.

The end.

October 05, 1995

A dream too cruel to continue

I'll be honest with you. Twenty years ago, I'd be ready to kick my own butt for what I'm about to say, especially with NBA training camps opening this week: America needs a moratorium on black basketball players.

That's right. No more Stackhouses, Jordans or Hills for at least 10 years. No, these aren't the insane rantings of a bitter old man whose jump shot left him stranded at the free throw line of life. Well, all right, maybe a little.

But the main reason I think we need fewer black ball players is that pro sports — especially basketball — have deluded too many black kids into thinking salvation lies in their ability to shoot jumpers or hit the open man on the give-and-go.

I know I'm going to catch pure hell from some black people who'll accuse me of airing our dirty laundry in public — as though everyone can't see that too many of our boys are more proficient at slam-dunking a basketball than conjugating a verb. But look in just about any high school or college yearbook: the sports teams have enough brothers to film a one-hour episode of "Sanford & Son," but when you get to the honor graduates, our presence in significant numbers is lacking. Go ahead and look: I'll wait.

There are just enough high-profile black athletes to keep the dream burning in the hearts and minds of millions of little black boys and their families, the dream that they alone will beat the staggering odds and land at point guard for the Charlotte Hornets and get paid millions to wear a dress and a big gold tooth like Larry Johnson. Believe me, that dream dies hard: Hell, after a couple of bottles of 90-proof Gatorade, I start looking for Pat Riley's phone number to see whether he needs someone to come and drill three-pointers for him.

But for most athletes, and for me, that call will never come. One of my buddies, a still-superb athlete who tried out with a couple of NFL teams, told me years ago through moistened eyes how he knew his dream of sports stardom was over: it was the first time he had to buy his own sweat socks instead of having them handed to him in bulk by some solicitous high school or college team manager.

By the time most guys have to buy their own sweat socks, they've used up all their college eligibility and find themselves possessing the best jump shot in the unemployment line but no other marketable skills.

Parents, too, have fallen victim to this cruel dream. I see many fathers, vicariously living out their own sports fantasies, steering their sons toward a sports career — and already plotting how to spend that first million-dollar signing bonus.

Yet, they allow their sons to neglect their school work while spending an inordinate amount of time mastering the intricacies of the crossover dribble.

Speaking of crossover dribbles, it was a picture of a young basketball player from a local university working on his dribbling that illustrated for me how all-consuming and devastating this sports dream has become. I refuse to mention his name or the school because fans of that wonderful institution have already called me everything but a Reuben sandwich for questioning the priorities of its football coach last month.

But anyway, the kid said he had to pass two summer courses or else pass up the U.S. Olympic Festival in Denver, and when I saw him dribbling on a court in Seattle I felt a surge of pride. "He passed," I thought.

Then I saw that one of the courses was strictly Mickey Mouse — Music Appreciation or something. I hate to break it to him, but knowing the difference between Isaac Hayes and Barry White is not exactly a career-enhancing bit of knowledge.

October 14, 1995

The reason so many marched

If I never see another bean pie this decade, it'll be too soon.

But, of course, I will, because I have 11 in my refrigerator right now. I bought them when vendors at the "Million Man or — depending upon whom you ask — 400,000 Man March" lowered the price.

Actually, they didn't have to do that for me, because my buddy Maurice and I were walking and driving through Washington at 3:30 a.m. the day before the march asking anyone who looked like a member of the Nation of Islam, "Yo, man. You got any bean pies?"

I, of all people, should've been more sensitive, since I get asked the same thing each time I wear a bow tie.

But man does not live by bean pie alone, and that's not what we went to Washington for. No, the nourishment we sought was spiritual and more elusive than anything we could've found on a vendor's table.

But we found it. At least I did. I guess you had to be there to understand why I felt as giddy as a school kid on prom night when I looked about me and saw regular old black dudes as far as I could see. Oh man, it was great.

I remember how I used to laugh when I heard people who went to Woodstock rhapsodizing about what a beautiful, cosmic experience that was. "Bull," I'd think. "That was just a bunch of white people frolicking in the mud and listening to rock music."

Thirty years — 30 years, my eye: 30 minutes — from now, I expect some people will look at the Million Man March I'm rhapsodizing about and say, "It was just a bunch of guys listening to a hate-monger."

To which I'll say, "Bull." I heard no hatred in Minister Louis Farrakhan's two-hour, 20-minute speech. I heard anger and disappointment, no question about that. But most of it was directed at the people standing before him. Sure, he talked about what slavery has done to us — and to whites — but he primarily chastised us for what we have done to ourselves and for our failure, in many instances, to live up to our obligations.

During one stretch when Farrakhan was really rolling, I closed my eyes and could've sworn I was listening to a Republican — that's how conservative his message was.

In a day of remarkable events, one that I vividly remember occurred hours before Farrakhan spoke. It was, admittedly, a little thing, something most white guys take for granted: It occurred when I turned and accidentally bumped into a guy. Hard. And do you know what happened? Nothing. He looked at me, I looked at him, we apologized and went on our way. That happened several times during the day, and the response was always the same.

That's no small thing when you're dealing with guys who feel their manhood is at stake in every confrontation, regardless of how minor. Just ask Kathy Patterson.

But not right now. Y'see, she's keeping vigil inside her son Alan's hospital room in Baltimore, where he was taken after being shot in Washington — where he'd gone for the march and to sightsee.

Alan, an N.C. State University student, is on a respirator and paralyzed and doesn't even know why. According to police, some punk just pulled up beside the Jeep in which Alan was riding, shot him in the neck and rode off into the night.

And you know what? That horrific incident wasn't even unusual.

And you know what else? That's why we marched.

October 18, 1995

Taking all the blame for David

Ladies and gentlemen, no more calls, please. We have a unanimous winner for the "Tammy Wynette Stand By Your Man" award.

Actually, our winner, Betty "But my friends call me 'Peanut' " Funderburk, wasn't standing — she was sitting — by her betrothed when he ran into trouble. In true "good ol' girl" fashion, Mrs. Funderburk was willing to sacrifice points on her driving record to protect the political career of her husband, U.S. Rep. David "Don't I look like JFK — sort of" Funderburk.

I invited Tammy to come and sing this song, but she, like many others, was afraid to drive in North Carolina — especially since both Funderburks still have driver's licenses.

So, I will sing it my ownself — as soon as I pull on these white cowgirl boots. Okay, maestro, hit it:

"Sometimes it's hard, to be a woman/ Taking all the blame and doing the work.

"He'll get in trouble, but he'll deny it/ Why? 'Cos his name is Funderburk...

But if you love him, you'll forgive him/ Even though responsibilities he sure shirks.

"So don't y'all crowd him, 'cos she's proud of him/ And she loves his Congresh'nal perks...

"Sit by yer man, tell the law it was you who was drivin'/ although you were on the passenger side...

"Never say that you lied."

By now, everyone is aware of the incident last weekend in which the Funderburks' car ran a van and another car off the road and kept going. Funderburk pleaded "no contest" to charges of driving left of center. "This does not mean that I accept guilt," Funderburk said as he accepted guilt.

Call me naive, but I believe him when he says, sure, y'all may have seen him outside his car after the incident, but he wasn't changing seats with his wife: He was merely checking the car for damage.

Say what? There was no collision? Not with another vehicle there wasn't, but have you seen the size of those mosquitoes in Harnett County?

I admit that I, like most people, was concerned when I heard the Funderburks didn't get out of their car to check on the condition of the injured people or use their car phone to call for help — until Betty Funderburk explained why. They were afraid, she said, of the "mob" — two people — who were "screaming at us and shaking their fingers."

I don't know about you, but where I come from, shaking your fingers at someone is a declaration of — well — something.

Friends say Funderburk wants people to think of him as Kennedyesque — with his Bob Forehead, parted-on-the-left hair style and his rep ties — but if he reminds folks of anyone right now, it's Michael Jackson. Remember when the Beloathed Gloved One denied molesting a little kid but paid the kid $15 million not to tell what he says never happened anyway?

As trifling and lowdown as I've been at various stages in my life, nothing is going to make me confess to something I didn't do. Likewise, if Funderburk wasn't driving that car, do you think there is any way in the world he would not go down swinging to the end, blaming a liberal media conspiracy and whatever else he could think of for his woes?

The main reason to believe him, though, is that I can't imagine the Republican Funderburk driving — or doing anything else — left-of-center. Can you?

November 02, 1995

No longer in 'Peanuts' gallery

I readily admit I was a rather dimwitted young 'un. That's why it took me so long to understand what the fable of "The Emperor's New Clothes" was all about.

Shoot, I thought Miss Watkins, my first-grade teacher at Leak Street School in Rockingham, was simply talking about some dude who was naked and the people he ruled who were afraid to tell him. I didn't realize until I became an adult that the story was a metaphor for life and was really about people who are so afraid of speaking out that no one will say what desperately needs to be said.

The story of the emperor goes like this: A slick tailor sold the emperor some "clothes" that were so groovy that only really hip people could dig them, and since everybody wanted to be hip, no one would confess that they didn't see them. Which suited the tailor just fine, since the clothes didn't really exist anyway. It took a little kid to finally shout, "Hey, that ol' dude ain't got no clothes on," or something to that effect before the ruse was uncovered.

Well, the latest episode of the emperor with no clothes on can be found in thousands of newspapers daily — on the comics pages — where Charles Schulz, creator of "Peanuts," has been naked for a couple of decades. But nobody bothered to tell him.

I know this is something no one wants to admit - that they don't "get" "Peanuts" any longer. To do so is like admitting we've lost a part of our inner child, the part that makes thirty-something adults cry when they hear the song "Puff the Magic Dragon" or when the Peanuts gang calls Charlie Brown a blockhead for dragging in that scraggly old Christmas tree.

But it's not you who has lost your innocence, dear reader: It's Schulz.

I have talked to a dozen comics readers, and every one of them agreed: "Peanuts" has lost its flavor, and Linus, Lucy and the rest of them should be sent to the old comic strips home.

"But, Saunders," I hear someone say while sopping up the Thanksgiving gravy with a cold biscuit, "with all the real problems facing the world — Bosnia, government shutdowns, Michael Bolton being spotted in a recording studio — why are you writing about cartoon characters?"

Good question. See, I long ago despaired of reading a funny or even amusing "Peanuts" strip. But when I heard that my favorite comic strip — "Calvin & Hobbes" — would cease publication Dec. 31, I couldn't hold in my contempt any longer.

"Calvin & Hobbes" is about a 6-year-old and his stuffed tiger — well, it's stuffed to everyone else, but very real to him — who see the world from a hilarious perspective. Bill Watterson, its creator, is hanging up his pen after nine years, at the peak of his popularity. He's walking away from millions a year at age 37 because he feels constrained by the limits of comic strips. Just last year, another wildly successful cartoonist, Gary Larson of "The Far Side," called it quits at 40.

Both guys are fabulously wealthy. But so is Schulz, who is ranked among Forbes magazine's 400 richest Americans. Maybe that's why he continues drawing his strip even though he's obviously lost interest, and why Snoopy is pimping for Met Life.

Once again, it took a little boy to point out that the emperor isn't wearing any clothes. Only this time, the boy's name is Calvin.

November 27, 1995

Boycott Santa? Bag that idea

I've always thought I was a bad dude, willing to take on anything and anybody. I have that luxury because I don't worry about losing my popularity: I've never had any to lose. And for the most part, I have great respect for others who refuse to kowtow to sacred cows.

But there is one icon even I won't take on: Santa Claus.

Not so Curtis Gatewood, president of the Durham chapter of the NAACP.

Gatewood made news recently by urging Durham's black residents to "boycott Santa" this holiday season. His goal, he said, is to "warn people ... about this pressure that's on to spend every penny we have to accommodate the tradition of pagan Santa Claus."

Viewed objectively and rationally, one can see many fine points in Gatewood's lamentations about the over-commercialization of Christmas and how the ostensible reason for the holiday — Christ's birth — is overshadowed by a mindless rush to get (and give) expensive gifts. I know many people, especially poor people, who go into crippling, yearlong debt just for the thrill of seeing their daughter's face light up when she unwraps a baby doll that cost more to deliver under the tree than the real young 'un cost to deliver from the hospital.

But even having acknowledged the wisdom of Gatewood's argument, I must ask him, as Fred Sanford used to ask Lamont each time he and Rollo did something stupid, "ARE YOU CRAZY?"

Gatewood, who is harder to contact than ol' St. Nick himself, said in an N&O interview that the NAACP may gather in front of Durham malls with placards urging people to rethink their Christmas shopping habits.

That, predictably, almost gave Durham Chamber of Commerce President Bob "It ain't Raleigh-Durham, it's Durham-Raleigh" Booth a stroke. "I think that would be counterproductive ... [and] would tick people off," Booth stammered.

Not only that, Bob, but just think what it would do to the psyches of little kids. Sure, most adults know Santa Claus is about as real as Whoopi Goldberg's blue eyes. But that's no reason to burst the bubble for children. Kids need fantasy. (Adults do, too, but that's a subject for a later column.) How many of you remember how you felt when you found out the truth about Santa? Me, I was so distraught, I came close to dropping out of college for a semester. But with the help of counseling and massive quantities of 90-proof eggnog, I pulled through that crisis.

Remember that song called "I saw Mommy Kissin' Santa Claus?" Well, in light of the recent attack on the little fat dude by Scrooge Gatewood, I've updated that classic tune. Here's my version. Maestro, hit it:

I saw Gatewood dissin' Santa Claus,
right outside Northgate Mall last night.
"You don't have to spent
every last red cent
Just because they say it's Christmastime."
Yeah, I saw Gatewood dissin' Santa Claus
outside South Square mall in Durham last night
He didn't see Bob Booth creep
in the middle of the street
With a gun that was big enough to stop Jaws.

December 04, 1995

A holiday wish in the hospital

It wasn't the dumbest question I've ever asked, but it was certainly within shouting distance of it.

I'm standing in Travis Monroe's hospital room at Duke University Medical Center two days ago, talking about the typical stuff 16-year-old boys talk about — basketball, girls, basketball — when I hear myself ask, "What do you want for Christmas?"

As soon as I asked it, I wanted to crawl under the bed on which he lay propped up with tubes running into his body.

He looked at me and, without a trace of sarcasm, said, "A heart would be nice."

For you see, for the past month and a half, Travis has been at Duke awaiting a heart transplant. The student at Fairmont High School in

Robeson County had open-heart surgery last year after collapsing at basketball practice and having 24 pounds of fluid back up on his heart. Right
now, he is third on the list of Duke patients needing a transplant.

But he might as well be 103rd, considering the shortage of available
hearts and the unwillingness of many people to part with their organs
even when they no longer need them.

Dr. Michael Higginbotham, Travis' doctor, spoke of the critical shortage of heart donors, especially among blacks. "Only about 2,500 transplants are done annually," he said. "Several times that many people need
them. ... African-Americans are a part of the community that seems
reluctant to become donors, but they really need to contribute more."

Higginbotham seemed fascinated, and initially disbelieving, when I
explained that one reason some of my black friends aren't organ donors
is because they fear going into the hospital for a tooth extraction and
coming out minus, say, a lung.

"That's remarkable," he said. It is also understandable. But it is small
consolation to a boy who'd rather be spending the holidays at home with
his family instead of hooked up to tubes and machines in a hospital
room.

Not that his room is the drab, foreboding place hospital rooms
appear on television. Far from it. Considering the tubes sticking in him
and the computer in the corner monitoring his heartbeat, Travis' room is
as close to home as one could expect. It is decorated in what can best
be described as NBA-chic, with posters of Grant Hill, Shaquille O'Neal and
of course, his hero, Michael Jordan. He has an autographed picture of
Jordan along with a Chicago Bulls' jersey. "A friend of Michael's visited me
and told him about me," Travis said, brightening noticeably.

Tutors work with him daily on his school assignments, and he spends
much of his day reading or watching action movies and basketball on
television. When I entered his room, his brother, Trayfer — a sophomore
at Methodist College — was visiting. Both seemed relaxed and happy.

But late at night when Travis is alone, he confesses, he sometimes
wonders why such a fate befell him. "Yeah, sometimes I ask 'Why me?'
But I never blame anybody. I know the Lord is working with me. ...The
worst part, especially right here at Christmas, is missing my church and
my family. If it wasn't for the teachings I got at church, I don't know if I
could take this."

But faith can sustain Travis for just so long. The kid needs a heart.

December 18, 1995

Toss coins in kettle — or else

No soldier in Bosnia could receive harsher looks than the ones I received when I enlisted in the Army this week.

The army I joined, by the way, was the Salvation Army, and for a couple of hours I assumed my post outside a Wal-Mart store, ringing a bell to raise money so some poor kids might have a merrier Christmas.

The N&O ran a story about a severe shortage of bell-ringing volunteers and about how the Salvation Army was being forced to pay people to do it. So, since ringing a bell seemed like something even I couldn't screw up, I volunteered to help.

I didn't mess up, but let me tell you, if looks could kill, then I'd be taking the dirt nap for sure this holiday. It's not that the people I saw and who saw me weren't concerned: More of them gave than I expected. Across the Triangle, giving at Salvation Army kettles is up, but a lot of money goes uncollected because they can't find enough volunteers to man — or woman — the kettles.

Despite the generosity of some customers, others scurrying to get in out of the cold and rain shot me gazes that would have chilled the Grinch who stole Christmas.

To be honest, I don't know whether they gave me the evil eye simply because my presence reminded them of their own Scrooge-like behavior — when it came to others, that is — or because they were irritated by the bell and my heartbreaking vocal renditions of Christmas classics such as "Please Come Home for Christmas," "White Christmas" and "Grandma Got Run Over by a Reindeer."

Indeed, one old woman stopped and agitatedly searched her purse for money.

"Here, honey," she said, thrusting a couple of bucks into the red kettle. "Don't sing."

She then disappeared into the store, but not before shooting me a glance that suggested I perform a physically impossible, not to mention unnatural, act with my bell.

After the first hour, long after the cold weather had numbed my feet and hands, I tried to anticipate who would and who wouldn't feed the kettle based on how they were dressed and the kind of car they drove into the parking lot. I reached no definitive conclusion, but I recognized early on that a woman driving a BMW was no more likely to give than one driving a car that was BMI ("Barely Making It").

I asked my commanding officer, Capt. Charles Powell of the Durham Salvation Army, whether the relative affluence of people or the status of the store had any impact on the amount of money donated.

"We haven't studied that, but usually, the end result is determined by the traffic flow rather than by the type of store," he said. "It doesn't matter if it's Roses or Belk's."

Go ahead, you can call it extortion — the fact that during my hours-long tour of duty I often used my voice to get people to contribute.

"Y'all better put some money in this kettle before I start singing again," I told two well-dressed young ladies laden with gifts.

But even if it was extortion, it was for a good cause, so I'm figuring the Lord will cut me some slack.

December 21, 1995

Sick and tired of 'Waiting'

When publisher William Randolph Hearst was having trouble selling newspapers at the turn of the century, he received a cable from the reporter he'd sent to cover colonial unrest in Cuba. The cable informed Hearst that nothing was shaking.

Hearst's reply: "You provide the stories; I'll provide the war."

He then proceeded to publish inflammatory, made-up stories of Spanish atrocities that forced the United States to enter the conflict — thus sparking the Spanish-American War. More important, he sold oodles of newspapers.

Ol' man Hearst would be proud of Terry McMillan, author of "Waiting to Exhale" and co-writer of that hit movie. McMillan has obviously adopted Hearst's philosophy in order to foment war between black men and women. Her objective: to sell books and movie tickets and munch caviar with Oprah.

The movie purports to be a celebration of black women. It is not: It's a two-hour denigration of black men with a hip soundtrack.

Every female character on the screen was portrayed as a long-suffering saint being bamboozled by a jive-talking, loutish Lothario. While watching the movie, I could've sworn I heard Waylon Jennings in the background wailing, "She's a good-hearted woman in love with a good-timin' man."

Even when Bernadette (her name should've been "Burn every damn thing") calmly poured gasoline on her husband's clothes and car and torched them, women in the theater cheered as though she'd struck a blow for their freedom. (Hey kids, don't try this at home: Arson carries five to 10.)

Other than the fact that there were no legal repercussions for her arson — or when she publicly slugged her husband's white secretary/girlfriend — I am most perplexed by the response of some men who saw the movie. And not all of them are your typical henpecked pantywaists, either. They say, "Y'know, I found the movie refreshing. I know dudes just like that."

Well, gollllly. Surprise, surprise. I imagine if Ray Charles threw enough mud, even he'd hit somebody everyone recognizes, too.

I can't really blame McMillan, though. She merely mined a rich literary vein: Books dogging black men. That phenomenon dates back to at least the 1970s, when:

• Michelle Wallace wrote "Black Macho & the Myth of the Super Black Woman." The book's premise: that black men are holding sisters back and they should let us sink or swim on our own merits.

• Ntozake Shange wrote "For Colored Girls Who Have Considered Suicide ..." in which the evilest dude in literary history, Bo Willie Johnson, spitefully dropped his two kids out of a window.

• Alice Walker, the queen of that tradition, wrote "The Color Purple," which portrayed us as either incestuous beasts or timid milquetoasts. All of those books were heralded as "events."

A few years ago when I was bedridden with the flu, I watched 18 straight hours of television. During the entire day of channel-surfing I saw only two black women in movies: both played prostitutes. That's the year the NAACP was unable to give out its Image Award to a black woman because none had a decent movie role.

So you see, I really long to see a good "sister" movie. But one that's not also a bad "brother" movie.

As a film critic, I'm giving "Waiting" two gasoline cans down.

January 11, 1996

The rap on O.J.'s big interview

With all due modesty, I have to say that I'm so smart that I scare my own self sometimes.

How so? Check this out: Who is the man who predicted that pop star Michael Jackson would suddenly "discover" he was black soon after his legal problems forced millions of parents to rip his posters from their children's bedrooms?

Me.

And who is the man who said O.J. Simpson would likewise own up — albeit involuntarily — to his ethnicity after realizing his halo was irreparably tarnished and Paula Barbieri was kicking him to the curb?

Me, again.

Think back. Right after Jackson paid that kid $20 million not to tell what he claims never happened anyway, he showed up at an NAACP awards program — an unprecedented act for a Jackson. Listening to him standing there with mock contrition all over his bleached and surgically altered face, I halfway expected him to do like Dorothy when she returned from Oz: "Oh, Auntie Em, Uncle Henry. I'll never leave you again. There's no place like home."

Of course, Michael said no such thing: as soon as his CDs started selling again, he immediately put as much distance between himself and other black people as he could.

O.J. is doing the same thing. He appeared on Black Entertainment Television last night to discuss his life since the trial ended and to hype his new video. It's no coincidence that he granted that network an interview only after every other network in the world told him to go suck exhaust fumes from his Bronco. But BET — whose call letters increasingly seem to stand for Bad Entertainment Television — leaped at the chance.

It sickens me that the nation's only black network would suck up to O.J. like this and allow itself to be used by him. Why, if it weren't for my need to see the half-naked video babes they feature 22 hours a day, I'd never watch it again.

If the BET network brass were smart, they'd have gotten "Video Soul" host Donnie Simpson — no relation — to conduct the interview. Donnie is an honor graduate of the Arsenio Hall School of Celebrity Butt-kissing Interviews. Also, he is so used to interviewing vapid, foulmouthed rappers that I'll bet he missed the entire O.J. media spectacle. But Donnie's a trouper, so he'd slosh on even if O.J. had shown up trying to be black by holding a 40-ounce Bull, wearing a dashiki and dreadlocks and reading Jet magazine.

Donnie Simpson: Good evening. We're joined here on the couch by a hot new rapper, D.J. O.J. Welcome to "Video Soul," brother.

O.J. Simpson: Uh, thank you Donnie, but I'm not a rapper. I'm a famous defendant.

Donnie: Of course you are. Sort of like Snoop Doggy Dogg and Tupac, eh? What did The Man get you for, brother?

O.J.: Supposedly for killing my ex-wife and another dude. But I didn't do it.

Donnie: Shhh. Don't say that, fool. You'll sell more CDs if people think you're a notorious rapper.

O.J.: Listen dammit. I'm no rapper. I'm an ex-jock, Grade-B actor who just got off on charges of killing my ex-wife.

Donnie: Oh. So you're not a rapper with a CD to sell? Well, what are you selling?

O.J.: Videos. Learn the whole truth. Just call 1-800-I'M BROKE.

January 25, 1996

Where there's a will...

You know how there are certain events that serve as guideposts to let you know when you've moved into another phase of life?

Well, for me, the first occurred one morning last year, when "Sesame Street" didn't seem as witty as it used to and I actually watched the "Today" show with Bryant and Katie instead.

The second occurred the first time I said, "Not tonight, dear. I have a headache." And actually had one.

But what happened a couple of days ago really made me understand that I am entering another phase — the phase where you are frighteningly close to qualifying for the senior citizens meal deal discount at Denny's: I drew up my will.

My attorney, Little Seymour Pettigrew — hereafter referred to as "Cool Breeze" — praised me for having the foresight to draw up a will at such a young age. But foresight had nothing to do with it.

Y'see, I am fixing to take a trip to a foreign country, a country where terrorists set off bombs with about the same frequency as Magic Johnson retires and unretires from basketball. With my luck, I'll probably wander up moments before some terrorist targets the neighborhood for annihilation.

Because of that, and because I don't want anyone fighting over my estate when I join that great news staff in the sky, I figured a will was something I'd better take care of now.

I strolled happily into Cool Breeze's office, expecting a perfunctory little meeting in which I'd sign some papers, we'd exchange lies about our love lives, and then I'd split.

But when I got through reading all those "parties of the first part" and "parties of the second part" and what have you, I knew that I was facing up to my mortality for the first time. (Well, for the second time: The first time I faced up to it occurred when I changed my mind at the last minute and decided not to marry this mean, straight-razor-totin' woman with blue gums whom I loved.)

Let me tell you, folks, it's an eerie feeling when you realize you're not talking about if you die, but when you die. In order for this will to go into effect, I will have to die.

That was my first sobering thought. My second one was when

Breeze gave me a pad and told me to make a list of my assets and how I wanted them distributed.

Remember on "Sanford & Son" when Lamont accused Fred of being selfish? Fred, genuinely wounded, stood in the middle of his junkyard and spread his arms wide.

Fred: You don't know me, do you, son? Look at this empire. Who do you think I did all this for?

Lamont: Yourself.

Fred: Yep, you know me.

As I, like Fred, stood in the middle of my empire with my son, cata-loguing all the neat stuff I plan to bequeath to him, I quickly and sadly realized one thing: Outside of the dudemobile and the little pup tent that we call home — (referred to in the will as "Barryland") — I have precious few assets.

I'm leaving one of my most prized possessions, my membership card to the 14 Karat Dinner Theater, to my buddy Peacock. But I'm taking my box of eight-track tapes with me. I just couldn't bear the thought of strangers picking over my collection of Al Green tapes.

February 26, 1996

Societal breakdown? Not hardly

Normally, I'd think anybody who said what I'm about to say was a couple of gallons short of a full tank, but I'm now convinced that there is nothing like a little automotive misfortune to make one feel blessed.

"How so, Saunders?" you ask.

Y'see, the adversity I ran into last weekend brought out the best in everybody I met and even had me rethinking my position that the world is heading to Charlotte in a handbasket. It also had me wondering if I would have done the same thing for a stranger that strangers did for me.

Y'all know that I'm a positive, upbeat guy, right? That's how I got my nickname: Mr. Sunshine. (Well, at least that's what I call me.) But my out-look on life was pretty bleak when my car broke down and left me stranded on Interstate 77 in South Carolina.

This is what happened: I was tooling along, minding my own busi-ness, when I heard a strange, ominous sound under the hood. I instinc-tively did what I always do in such a situation: I turned up the volume on the oldies radio station and tried to ignore the rattle.

I pulled to the shoulder just before the car cut off and, for some unknown reason, lifted the hood. Now, I don't know a CV joint from a marijuana joint, but I stood there gazing at the engine for about an hour. I finally started hoofing it down the road, singing "Me and You and a Dog Named Boo."

The sun was hot and it was early, so I wasn't worried — not until I'd walked a couple of miles and noticed some buzzards circling optimistically overhead.

After about three miles, a beautiful little sports car — driven by a young woman — pulled over. Now, I know I'm a mean-looking dude, and I've been known to send little kids screaming for their mommies just by smiling at them. So I was not expecting anyone — least of all a pretty woman traveling alone — to stop and give me a ride. I thought it was a mirage and the car, when I reached it, would turn out to be a discarded soda can or something.

"I don't usually stop and pick up strangers on the highway," she explained, "but I saw your car back there and figured you looked safe."

We finally saw an exit with a little country store and gas station, and she pumped gas while I tried to find a mechanic in the telephone book. As I said, my benefactor was a pretty little thing, and while she pumped the gas, a truckload of grease-covered guys in overalls drove up. They crudely expressed their admiration for her while I prayed they would go on into the store before she was ready to go.

"Oh, Lord," I thought to myself, "the last thing I need is for these white dudes to see me getting into a little sports car in Ridgeway, S.C., with a white woman."

A couple of them did give me looks that were none too friendly, but no one said a thing. The woman, an ex-cop turned country music singer, took me to Jerry's Garage, then followed Jerry and me back to my car.

Jerry, a big-bellied stock car racing fan whose car bore the license plate "Go Dale," looked under the hood, saw the problem and fixed it. He didn't charge me a dime. "Looks like you've already had a rough day, Hoss," he said.

I thanked him and the woman and drove off, feeling much better about the world I live in.

The only thing I regret, though, is that I didn't ask Jerry if he meant "Dale" Jarrett or Earnhardt.

February 29, 1996

Hardly a public service

If you hear a big "KABOOM" and see something big and black circling the moon the next time it gets really cold outside, don't worry.

That'll just be me after trying to ignite the pilot light on my furnace.

Anybody who knows me will tell you that you don't want to let me around gas — or anything else — with matches. And until last week, you wouldn't have.

But then Public Service of North Carolina, my gas company, recently ended a service it had provided to customers: relighting pilot lights.

The whole "operation" takes about 90 seconds for anybody with a modicum of technical know-how. But because I don't know a pilot light from an airplane pilot, I always called Public Service for help.

Twice this miserable winter my pilot light flickered out, leaving the kid and me shivering in the cold. Each time, though, I met a couple of extremely friendly, professional PSNC servicemen who didn't even laugh when I showed them how I'd been trying to light my water heater because I thought it was the furnace.

According to the card PSNC sent me in the mail one day — ONE DAY! A coincidence? I think not — before my pilot light went out, the company is changing the policy "to serve you better .... Next time you need your pilot turned on or off, you can contact one of the licensed heating contractors in your area."

I did that, grumbling all the while about what an impersonal world this is becoming and how I could do a lot of other stuff with the $20 or so it was going to cost for someone to come out and light my pilot.

Almost as soon as I started talking on the phone, the woman at the heating contractor's answering service said, "Let me guess: You need your pilot light lit." No, she hadn't been talking to Dionne and the Psychic Connection: She had been deluged with similar calls. She explained that they were fielding scores of frantic calls and that it could be the next day before someone could come out and light my fire.

She was wrong. My fire was lit as soon as one service guy called and informed me that it'd cost $89 for him to come and light the furnace.

I didn't need any heat after that, because I was hotter than any furnace.

So I called Public Service's local office. A service supervisor patiently explained: "We've decided to get out of that part of the business. We'll just concentrate more on the systems in our line and just service the ones we sell."

Despite my lack of technical knowledge, even I can interpret what he meant: "We don't make any money off of it, so we'll let someone else handle it."

The most galling thing about the card I received in the mail is that it was titled "Changing to serve you better." I wish someone would tell me how being charged $89 for a service that until a few days ago was free would serve me better.

The gentleman I talked to at PSNC assured me the company received no complaints, and he sounded sincere.

But even if no one else called to complain — I reckon most people are resigned to the futility of complaining — I can assure him that no one is pleased with the new policy. Except for heating contractors who charge $89 for 90 seconds' work.

April 11, 1996

"Sweet thang" put to the test

Honestly, folks, if it were just me, I'd let it slide — that nasty little letter syndicated columnist Paul O'Connor wrote about me in the N&O.

I can take it. But when Mr. O'Connor impugns the integrity of Sweet Thang her ownself — the embodiment of all that is pure and chaste — well, he has gone too far.

O'Connor, responding to my well-thought-out criticism of his buddy, Associated Press reporter Dennis Patterson, responded with an emotional attack on this newspaper and me, accusing us of ruining his pal's impeccable reputation.

Our sin? Reporting that the House speaker's former press secretary, Don Follmer, and Patterson frequently engaged in politically incorrect banter and that Patterson didn't consider it newsworthy when Follmer referred to protesting UNC housekeepers and their supporters at the General Assembly as "niggers and wormy kids."

Lo and behold, it turns out that Patterson's bosses considered it newsworthy and said he should've reported it. I wonder if O'Connor fired off an angry missive to them and called them, as he did me, hypocrites, racists and sexists?

I don't know how he could fix his mouth to call me a hypocrite. Of the myriad sins to which I confess, that is not one.

But he called me sexist and racist for using the endearing term "sweet thang" for Sweet Thang.

By calling me racist, is O'Connor saying that white men don't call their women "sweet thang"? Well, they do, because it was a white dude whom I first heard call his woman that. He said it so soft and sweet that I vowed, "If I ever get me a woman who's sweet, I'm going to call her that, too."

I used to call her "my li'l caramel-covered kumquat," but that took too long to say. So I stick with Sweet Thang, and she calls me B.S. That stands for Big Sugar. Sometimes.

But I realize that in these — uh-oh, Paul, here's that term that you deplore — politically correct times, it is not kosher to use terms of familiarity or endearment to women with whom one is neither familiar or endeared. Being on the back side of 30, it's tough for me to stop. But I'm trying.

It was no threat from a jealous boyfriend — or even fear of a sexual harassment suit from my secretary, the lovely and talented Miss Blue — that made me think twice.

What made me see the error of my words was my 7-year-old son. A few months ago, we had just pulled away from the drive-through window at McDonald's after ordering two sausage biscuits, when he looked at me earnestly and said he wanted to be like me when he grew up.

Swelling with pride, I asked, "Oh, so you can be a newspaper columnist with your finger on the pulse of the community?"

"No," he said. "So I can call everybody 'darlin' ' and 'sweet thang,' too."

Ouch. There is a possibility — a slight one, as you know — that I could be wrong. Perhaps St. Paul is right and I am sexist and racist and a blight on humanity.

Naaaah. But I'll leave it up to you women: Should "sweet thang" and other such terms be banished forever from our language — and more important, from my columns? Your letters and calls will determine whether I ever refer to her again on this page. It's up to you. I'll let you know the verdict.

May 02, 1996

The sweet sound of vindication

The Triangle was shaken recently by a controversy that threatened to split the region and set brother against brother. Or at least cousin against cousin.

No, the dispute wasn't over whether Superior Court Judge Henry Barnette should replace the Mercedes-Benz he wrecked with a green one or a blue one. It wasn't even over whether Judge Susan Renfer should wear something pink and discreet to her complaint hearing or go for titillation.

The biggest controversy to hit these parts lately was whether I should continue calling Sweet Thang "Sweet Thang."

Syndicated columnist Paul O'Connor fired the first volley when he wrote a letter to The N&O calling me a racist and sexist for using that term. St. Paul was upset at me for criticizing his pal, Associated Press reporter Dennis Patterson, after Patterson failed to report disparaging

and racist comments made by Don Follmer. Follmer, a former state
employee, had called protesters at the Legislative Building a bunch of
"niggers and wormy kids."

I was hurt by O'Connor's criticism, especially since I've read his stuff
since I was a kid. Why, I was unable to eat or sleep for what must have
been minutes.

But what if O'Connor was right and I was wrong? What if Sweet
Thang secretly hated it when I called her that — and what if she, in turn,
didn't really mean "Big Sugar" when she called me "B.S."?

I decided to let you readers determine whether "Sweet Thang" was
an appropriate term of endearment or whether I was a latter-day Robert
"Pinch" Packwood or state Rep. Ken "Sweet 16" Miller, with as little
respect for women. I vowed to abide by whatever y'all said.

After tallying the results, I concluded that few women are offended
by "Sweet Thang." I stopped counting after 300 responses, but by then
the results were so overwhelming — easily 80 percent in favor — that it
was obvious where public sentiment lay. With "Sweet Thang."

Here are some of the responses:

• "I'm a lesbian, but I'm not offended .... If Sweet Thang isn't offended, no one should be."

• "I have been calling ladies Sweet Thang ever since I was 14 or 15,
and I'm not about to stop because some educated @#$%$#% thinks I
should. I've never yet had a lady tell me she didn't like it."

• "I'm a 75-year-old white female — that shouldn't matter — and I
love your column and 'Sweet Thang.' "

• "Two votes for Sweet Thang from our house."

• "I've never seen one indication that you are a hypocrite, but you are
the biggest racist I've ever seen."

• "I'm a 32-year-old white female, and I think 'Sweet Thang' is so
adorable. I call everybody 'darlin' ' and 'honey.' "

• "I think you are the most racist columnist I've ever read, but I enjoy
your column."

• "I've been trying to get my husband of 45 years to call me 'Sweet
Thang.' I love it."

• "You stink, and so does Sweet Thang if she can't do better than
you. Get a life."

• "My name is Carol, and every time I see 'Sweet Thang' it makes my
blood boil. Please stop."

• "I think 'Sweet Thang' is redneck terminology, and I think being
called 'redneck' is comparable to being called 'nigger.' What I want to
know is, who's going to take up for wormy kids?"

May 23, 1996

Writing under the influence

A couple of weeks ago, radio commentator and liberal-basher Tom Joyner got drunk on the air to demonstrate the deleterious effects of alcohol and to persuade people not to drink and drive.

He did such a good job that I vowed never to take another drink unless I was by myself or with someone else. (Some of y'all probably think I was drunk when I called Alexander Killens, ex-director of the Division of Motor Vehicles, "Alexander Kitchens" in a column this week: I wasn't, and I apologize, although Killens might be glad I goofed up his name.)

I'm breaking my vow of abstinence only after deciding that, hey, if a juiced Joyner can do a radio show, then a soused Saunders can write a column.

Joyner imbibed a concoction of cranberry juice, vodka and orange juice in the presence of a uniformed State Highway Patrol officer who administered breath tests.

I couldn't get a uniformed trooper, but I got my cousin Tommy, who still had his uniform from his days as a security guard at Kmart.

So here we go.

11:25 p.m. I break the top off my first 40-ounce bottle of Olde English 800 malt liquor and take a sip. My mind is clear and filled with such weighty issues as, "Will there be any money left in Medicare when I'm 65?"

12:40 a.m. I can't get the words to "Me & You & a Dog Named Boo" out of my head. Also, I'm getting a headache from trying to figure out how to get in touch with the man who called me last year and said he has copies of every "Sanford & Son" episode ever made. Hey, Homey, if you're out there, call me.

1:45 a.m. Who was the mysterious woman who picked up Durham Police Capt. Reginald Taylor after his car accident last month and sped away? HEY, SWEET THANG! Where were you the night of May 16?

2 a.m. I send Officer Tommy out to get another 40-ounce, some pot-ted meat and some white bread.

2:15 a.m. Burrrp. I'm feeling no pain — and no sympathy for M.C. Hammer, who filed for bankruptcy the other day. If he has a yard sale, I want some of those baggy britches he wore. I could use 'em as curtains.

2:30 a.m. After two 40-ounces, I'm higher than the cost of a house in Cary. Am I dreaming, or did I just see the hair of one of those TV news dudes really move?

2:45 a.m. I'm so lit up that I'm actually beginning to believe the right-wing kook on the radio. He is ranting that Bill Clinton killed Vince

Foster and about two dozen other people. (No kidding, folks. That's what he claims in some new book.)

3 a.m. The way my head is feeling, I'm about ready to confess to something my ownself. I'm being flooded with guilt over a crime I committed 25 years ago. Anybody know the statute of limitations for stealing sugar cookies from the kitchen at Providence Baptist Church, from which I was chased by the Rev. Sawyer, who shouted, "If I catch you, you're going to Morrison Training School"?

2 a.m. Hey, wait a minute. It was just 3 a.m. Whatever time it is, I'm watching Donnie Simpson interview some rap star on BET, and I am thoroughly convinced I can be a rap star, too. All I need is a scowl, some oversized clothes, a toboggan and the ability to answer every question with a sentence beginning with "Yo" or "Word up, Donnie."

And if you needed any evidence of the dangers of alcohol, that's it.

June 13, 1996

This idea isn't hot — it's bunk

You don't need Philip Michael Thomas' private psychic hotline numbe to know an election is coming up. (If I had his number, though — and if it wouldn't cost me $3.99 a minute — the only thing I'd ask him is why, in 1996, he's still wearing a combination afro and Jheri curl.)

Actually, all I have to do to tell election season — also known as the silly season — is upon us is listen to the absurd rhetoric emanating from the statehouse.

We've still got a few months to go, but I'm betting the most absurd crime measure you're going to hear is the proposal to reduce overcrowding by forcing inmates at Lincoln County prison to share beds.

No, not at the same time, silly. Although, come to think of it, that might actually help the state raise money: I know I'd be willing to spend a couple of simoleons for pay-per-view to see two inmates fighting over the lone blanket in their cell on some freezing January night.

But hotbunking, the name given to the concept about to be instituted in Lincoln County, won't work. Even in Alabama, a state not noted for its sensitivity toward convicts, hotbunking was deemed cruel, inhuman and just downright unworkable. Charles Jones, warden of the prison in Elmore, Ala., called hotbunking the worst episode of his 27-year career in prisons. "It was a nightmare," he said, noting an increase in violence and, when convicts of different races had to share a bed, racial tension.

Y'all might think it is ludicrous that two incarcerated men who can't even go to the bathroom without getting permission would still find time to hold onto racial animosity.

But it's possible. Believe me. Having been an involuntary guest of a couple or four states myself, I know the slightest thing can set inmates off:

Inmate No. 1: Hey, warden. Tell him to quit leaving Afro Sheen stains on the pillow case.

Inmate No. 2: Oh, yeah: How can you tell, with all that Brylcreem that was already on it?

But that's greasy kid stuff. Here is how World War III will erupt in prison if hotbunking is instituted:

After a hard day of busting rocks or picking up trash along the interstate, some white dude is going to return to his cell, anxious to tell his cheesecake poster of Pamela Anderson Lee of "Baywatch" all about his day — "Here, Pam baby, I brought you this half a bag of potato chips I found on Highway 70; I even picked out the ants for you." Afterward, he'll brush the crumbs off his cot and rock himself to sleep while gazing longingly at her.

No problem, right? Wrong. Because the fireworks will ignite when the black inmate who slept in that bed during the first shift doesn't share his bunkmate's taste in poster women and replaces the Pamela poster with one of, say, Whitney Houston. He sings to her image each night and plots how to wipe out her hubby, Bobby Brown, without ending up back in the slammer.

"Hey, Whitney, I've got 'the greatest love of all' for you right here, baby," he tells her each night before he drifts off to sleep.

The ensuing fight will make the Attica prison riots look like a pillow fight at a frat house. Indeed, the only way the violence could be worse is if somebody replaced either Pamela's or Whitney's posters with one of Pamela's co-star, David Hasselhoff. Or, worse, Fabio.

June 17, 1996

Former jerk finds true path

What do you do when you discover that the person you love most in the world is a jerk?

More specifically, what do you do when that jerk turns out to be you?

I had to face that unpleasant reality this week when it became obvious that I was — if not a certified jerk — then at least engaging in jerk-like behavior.

It has even forced me to change the type of person I am. I hope.

Three days ago I was driving down Chapel Hill Street in Durham, singing along with the radio — which was playing "I Need a Good Woman Bad" by Latimore — when I had to slam on my brakes.

The reason? A big, black BMW had stopped in the middle of the lane, getting ready to make a right turn into a service station.

"Pardon me, kind sir, but what the heck are you doing?" I shouted at the driver (or words to that effect) as I swerved around him and honked my horn.

As I passed him, he shouted back, "What you want me to do — hit them?" That's when I saw the young woman with a baby in her arms walking in front of his car.

How low did I feel? Well, do you remember the price of chitlins in 1929? That low.

I tried to put the incident out of my mind, but a couple of blocks down the road I felt my car make a U-turn and head back toward the gas station.

The BMW driver, who was pumping gas when I drove up, eyed me suspiciously and angrily.

"Uh, excuse me," I stammered before he had a chance to say anything. Or start shooting. "Hey, Homes. That was my fault. I'm sorry I acted like that. Honest, that's not the kind of person I am."

After a couple of minutes of conversing, during which time I tried to convince him that I really am a member of the human race, he said, "That's all right, my brother. I know how it is when you're in a rush to get somewhere."

I didn't have the heart to tell him that the only place I was in a rush to get to was the corner grill to get me a pickled pig's foot. That's what made my behavior so bad.

And that's also what made me realize I was a jerk.

There are only two things in life I'm sure of. One is that the supremely untalented Jim Belushi and Whoopi Goldberg must have made a deal with the devil. The second is that there is already enough ugliness in the world without my adding to it.

Like George Bailey in the movie "It's a Wonderful Life," I feel now as though I am getting a second chance on life. A chance to do and be better. A chance to add joy and beauty to the world.

Or at least a chance to stop honking angrily at drivers who creep along 20 mph below the speed limit — and then run a red light. I promise also to stop shooting death rays at people in restaurants who take their same dirty plates to the buffet bar despite signs all over the place telling them to get a clean one for each visit, and to stop sighing audibly when people in bank lines wait until they get all the way to the teller before fill-ing out their deposit slips.

But mainly, I vowed to stop fussing at my son when he forgets to clean his ears, especially when we are going to the barber shop.

Little things, yes. But I'll bet the world will be a much better place with one less jerk.

June 20, 1996

The man who made a reporter

Bear with me here for a minute, will you, while I try something a little unusual. Instead of hurling bricks at somebody, I'd like to toss a bouquet.

My former editor, Glenn Sumpter of the Richmond County Daily Journal down in Rockingham, retired last week. Not because he wanted to. But because he's going blind. Had a stroke that affected his optic nerve, or something like that.

Whatever it was, for a journalist — especially one like Glenn, who was never without a book or a fat newspaper — it is a fate pretty much akin to death.

I have a tender spot for him because he is the one to blame for giving me my first newspaper job.

I had quit college after being cut from the St. Augustine's College basketball team and was working laying asphalt on roads when I stormed into Glenn's office and asked, "Why don't y'all have some black people writing in this paper?"

Without even looking up, he said, "Who you got in mind?"

Of course, I replied, "Me." He let me write a few columns — for free; I never said he was generous — before I eventually found a college in need of a shooting guard and went back to school.

Technically, Glenn wasn't my first editor. My first newspaper job was at the Atlanta Constitution, where I fetched the dry cleaning or coffee for reporters and editors too busy to be bothered by such mundane chores. But he was the first for whom I was a real reporter.

I knew before I applied that the Daily Journal had never had a black reporter. But Glenn and the publisher, Neal Cadieu, simply said, "It's time." And it was.

(Dr. Alan Mask of WRAL—TV wrote for it while in high school, but then he decided to make some real moolah and become a doctor.)

I often meet young reporters who yearn to work at the biggest newspaper in the biggest city, as though that will automatically legitimize their work. It won't. You can learn more at a small paper in a small town, where an editor like Glenn will go over every word you write and where you actually see and know the people you're writing about.

For instance, in Atlanta, I wrote the obituary of a man whose name was Ray. Somehow, the "y" turned into a "t" and Ray became Rat.

Embarrassing, yes, but it would've been worse in a small town like Rockingham, where I'd have been likely to run into Ray's family at the Piggly Wiggly, Dairy Queen or the Crooked Window, the name of Fun Wall's nightclub.

I made similar goofs in Rockingham, and Glenn never failed to let me hear about it, although seldom loudly. He'd been a drama major at West Virginia University, and he could convey cutting emotions merely by raising an eyebrow.

"Hey, Saunders, let's go eat," Glenn shouted at me my first day at the Daily Journal. I looked at the clock. It wasn't even 11 a.m.

Oh man, I'm going to like this guy, I thought. I liked him even more the next day when he suggested a meeting. The meeting room turned out to be his junky, mustard—colored Datsun, in which we drank a six-pack we picked up from the 7-Eleven and talked about what great jobs we had and his college years spent hanging out with West Virginia basketball star Hot Rod Hundley. Oh, and how much he loved reading The Sunday New York Times.

He'll no longer be able to read newspapers, but every time I write in one, I'll think of him.

June 27, 1996

Denzel? Denzel who?

Y'all will have to excuse me if I am not my usual ebullient, "Mr. Sunshine" self today.

I'm feeling kind of low because, contrary to what I predicted back in January, this has not been the "Year of the Barry."

First, Bob Dole snubbed me a few months ago to chase after Colin Powell as his vice presidential running mate.

Then yesterday I was in line at the Piggly Wiggly — fixing to stock up on some fish sticks they had on sale — when I saw this week's People magazine on the rack.

For the 11th year, the magazine named its "sexiest man alive." And for the 11th year, it wasn't me.

People bestowed this year's honor on actor Denzel Washington. Ain't that a hoot — that someone could find Denzel sexier than I?

Nothing against Washington, you understand. I am all man and then some, but even I can acknowledge that he's a handsome guy — if you want someone who's tall and dark with a perfectly symmetrical face. Oh, and did I mention he gets $10 million a movie, too?

But what about me? I'm not exactly chopped chitlins, you know. Why, there are certain streets in Durham and Raleigh where women actually try to flag me down or get into the car with me when I stop at a traffic light.

True, their interest in me is of a commercial nature and not exclusive enough to be flattering, but why quibble?

But after the Dole debacle, I was really steamed by this People snub. So I called Susan Ollinick of the magazine's public affairs office.

"What," I asked, "are the criteria y'all use to select the sexiest man alive?"

"It's really subjective," she said. "If a name elicits more sighs than groans, we know we're onto something .... There's a sexuality that some-one emits or doesn't.

"We've been rooting for Denzel for a couple of years, and with his lat-est movie, we sense there's a lot of heat around him right now — just like it was with Brad Pitt last year."

I didn't tell her that I knew Denzel was hot two years ago. That's when all these little boys named "Denzel" started showing up at my son's school.

Ollinick was underwhelmed when I told her I've been known to emit some heat of my own. She also acted as though she had never heard of me — which made me wonder if Sweet Thang really sent in my "sexiest man" application along with those autographed 8-by-10 glossies of me in a purple Speedo.

So sure was I of victory this time around that I'd spent a year prac-ticing the "come hither, li'l girls" look with which I'd planned to grace the magazine's cover.

"Is there a chance for me next year?" I asked Ollinick.

"Maybe if you become internationally famous and hot," she said.

She didn't notice, but I'm already hot. I'm also predicting a backlash. I think the American public will tire of its fascination with wealth and beau-ty, making magazine covers more receptive to the not-so-obvious charms of average-looking — ok, not-quite-average-looking — Joes like me.

Yes, I foresee a day when, instead of working out at a gym for three hours a day to sculpt their physiques, dudes like Washington will be eat-ing five Moon Pies a day and washing them down with a six-pack of Yoo Hoos to get that rounded, Pillsbury doughboy look popularized by me.

July 25, 1996

A pathetic take on Southerners

I know it's unfair to stereotype a whole region of people, but what the hell, I'm going to do it anyway: There appears to be an attack of lunacy striking some Noo Yawkers.

I feel justified in engaging in such an unfair generalization only because that's what Wall Street Journal editorial writer Hugh Pearson did last week. In case you missed it, he portrayed native Southerners as snuff-dipping, Coke-drankin' hayseeds who don't know their butts from apple butter. Oh, and they also walk around "with a hint of shiftlessness in their gait."

And that's just what he said about whites!

Black Southerners fared even worse. We were portrayed as hapless "oppressed subordinates ... predominantly conditioned to be antagonistic to intellectual curiosity." In other words, we don't know nothing and don't want to know nothing.

Pearson summed up the relationship between white and black Southerners this way: "The willfully ignorant have done their best to maintain a populace even more willfully ignorant than themselves." In other words, Southern whites and blacks are dumb and dumber.

Travel five minutes to the north or south of the state's metroplex — its big cities — where rural folks have not been graced with the edifying urbanity of Northerners, and it gets even worse, he says.

In Pearson's tome, Northerners are suave Cary Grants or Jackie O's, while every Southerner comes off like Gomer or Minnie Pearl.

"Many of them," Pearson notes, "sit on porches in suspenders, felt hats and rocking chairs, shelling peas." And, no doubt, wistfully whistling "Dixie," eh, Hugh?

Every Southerner should be offended by Pearson's anti-South broadside, but what stuck in my craw — I know we don't talk that way, but Northerners like Pearson love to hear us use such quaint colloquialisms — was Pearson's contention that the only hope anyone has of beating Sen. Jesse Helms is for sophisticated Northerners to move here and vote him out.

And that's unlikely to happen, he says, because most of them came here "precisely because they wanted to escape what too many Northern cities now represent" — uppity black politicians, I reckon.

My anger at Pearson has abated to the point that I'm now willing to help him look for a job. I'm betting he'll need one — as soon as his editors realize what he has done.

Seems like they sent him down here to write about the South, but he apparently spent his expense check on opera tickets or some other cultural extravagance. Still needing a story, though, he went to the video store, checked out "Driving Miss Daisy," "Hee Haw" and "Deliverance," and — voila! — concluded that he had captured the true Southern experience.

Of course, his bias against Southerners and the South is nothing new. As a boy visiting Washington, D.C., each summer, I stood a whole lot of kidding from my sophisticated Northern peers who cruelly dismissed me as an irredeemable hick.

Yet, while many of them slept on top of each other in tenements and choked on bus fumes, my li'l ol' country self was able to swim in a real creek, snatch a pear or a plum off a tree whenever I got hungry and actually breathe fresh air.

Still, I envied them because I didn't recognize how well off I was.

Nor, apparently, does Pearson.

August 01, 1996

Food stamp cheats merit the abuse

I won't go so far as to say I hope everyone who got food stamps they weren't entitled to last week chokes on a neckbone sandwich, but I will wish upon them a severe case of Montezuma's Revenge while stuck in a dirty public bathroom listening to Michael Bolton. In stereo.

I know Hurricane Fran caused thousands of people to lose whatever food they had in their refrigerators and freezers. And because the state was declared a disaster area, Uncle Sammy came to the rescue and offered emergency relief in the form of food stamps.

But it's like my Aunt Jennie taught me years ago: Just because somebody offers you something doesn't mean you have to take it.

Yet, some of the same middle-class folks — blacks as well as whites — who begrudge the truly needy any government assistance conveniently placed their consciences in mothballs for the several hours it took them to stand in line and clamor for a handout they truly didn't deserve.

All of them ought to be ashamed. One friend who lost a considerable amount of food to Fran told me she never even considered trying to take advantage of the food stamp offer — not even when one of her friends called to tell her how she'd gotten one over on the government: $427 worth of food stamps, and all she'd had to do was stand in line for three hours.

"She and her husband have great jobs in RTP," my friend told me. "That just wasn't right."

I agreed and, like her, rejected the government's largesse — and not just because I'm a wonderful, caring person. (Although I am.) Even though I must've lost $500 worth of fish sticks to Fran, I rejected the offer primarily because of an unpleasant encounter I once had with the food stamp bureaucracy.

It was while I was in college in Atlanta and somebody in school discovered that as struggling college students, we might qualify for food stamps.

So one day, when I didn't have a class, I snatched my cleanest dirty shirt from the floor, dabbed a little Brylcreem on my Afro, grabbed a handful of Cap'n Crunch — with crunch berries; I was on a health food kick then — and hit the road.

The people at the food stamp office regarded all the people there — including me — with a level of contempt usually reserved for a rat that dashes across the living room when company's present. They asked all kinds of personal questions and were just this side of hostile. I left with my head spinning and face burning with shame over the treatment I received.

It was, all in all, the most embarrassing experience I've ever had with the lights on.

So imagine my shock when, a week or so later, I received a letter informing me that I qualified for $80—something a month in stamps.

Now, I don't know if it was part of an official government strategy, but they so thoroughly humiliated me that to this day I'd rather drink muddy water and sleep in a hollow log than eat anything I got with food stamps.

But I do remember feeling sorry for people who, unlike me, had no choice but to accept the stamps — along with a heaping helping of bureaucratic abuse.

Of course, maybe I wouldn't have felt so bad if I — like some of you — had waited for a hurricane.

September 19, 1996

No tears to shed for Tupac

At first, I thought it was me. I really thought the reason I felt no great sympathy or sense of loss when I heard that rapper Tupac Shakur had died from gunshot wounds was because I'd grown old, cold and jaded from having viewed the murdered bodies of too many black boys and men over the years.

I've thought about it, turned it over in my mind, considered it from every angle. And I have reached one inescapable conclusion: There ain't nothing wrong with me. I just don't give a damn about Tupac.

The reason I know it's not me — but him — is because I still hurt and sigh all day when I read about other senseless deaths, such as the 8-year-old boy from Harnett County who was strangled to death last week — allegedly by his mama.

But when I think of Tupac? Nothing. Nada. Zilch.

Call me heartless, but I'm all out of tears for foulmouthed, misogynistic rappers who revel in their violent proclivities and their "thug life." As it says in the Bible — He who liveth by the Uzi shall die by the Uzi.

I know I shouldn't feel that way. I remember a line in some poem I read in high school that says, "The death of any man diminishes me" — and the senseless, violent death of yet another black man certainly does that — but I can't even muster up a crocodile tear for Tupac, who not only gloried in his violence, but profited from it, as well: Last year, when he was in prison for sexually assaulting a young woman with members of his posse, he earned the dubious but profitable distinction of being the first musician to reach No. 1 on the charts while in the pokey. Coincidence? I think not.

Of course, I realize I could be wrong and my inability to see the social relevance of Tupac's life and death could just be one of those generational things. Because Tupac wasn't making his music for old farts like me, perhaps he was connecting — the way James Dean did decades ago — with alienated, rebellious young people on a level we old coots can't dig.

No doubt, his death resonates with a lot of young people. One young lady, a student at the N.C. School of Science & Math, said students at that prestigious institution were devastated by news of Tupac's death. Even my 7-year-old son offered me his theory — which he got from his older, wiser 9-year-old cousin — on who killed Tupac. (Psst. Just between us, they think it was a rival rapper from New York.)

Was Tupac's death tragic? Yes. The dude was talented and more insightful than the average garbage-mouthed rapper — even I bought one of his tapes.

But those rich record company executives would not have been interested in releasing any CDs he might have made about being tardy with a term paper, unrequited love or other such mundane "middle-class" problems.

Even so, Tupac had said recently he was tired of the "thug life" and wanted to drop that baton. But we'll never know whether he was for real or merely repositioning himself to sell more music. Either way, I'm not about to join the chorus of voices who would have us believe Tupac died for our sins or was more than what he was — a rapper.

His death could have some positive meaning if it shows young, impressionable boys the ultimate futility of the "gangsta" lifestyle.

What I'm afraid it will do, though, is make some people view a violent outcome for themselves as inevitable.

As inevitable as it was for Tupac.

September 23, 1996

The state of tapping bumpers

I knew there was a good reason why I like Richard Petty.

A couple of months ago, I wrote about how I've been a Petty fan since fifth grade. That's when my buddy Lorenzo McDonald chose Fred Lorenzen as his race car idol — because their names were similar — and I attached my stock car star to Petty's bumper because he was the only driver at Rockingham's N.C. Motor Speedway in a Plymouth.

But I now have another good reason for liking him: He drives the way I'd drive if I were rich and famous Petty, a candidate for secretary of state, is catching grief — from "the liberal media," no doubt —and for what?

For gently tapping a car that was diddling along in the passing lane. Now I ask, who among you hasn't felt like doing the same thing upon encountering some slow-driving, moronic motorist who defiantly blocks the passing lane?

Far from hurting The King, this incident will only enhance his stature among true believers. A caller on a certain right-wing kook's radio show excused Petty's transgression thusly: "Ain't nothin' wrong with tradin' a li'l paint on I-85."

Truth be told, I'd love to trade a little paint with those bozos who, when they see two lanes merging into one, try to drive to the very front of the lane before sliding over.

I'll bet you a case of Moon Pies that, by year's end, Petty's name will be a verb in honor of his recent highway histrionics.

Lem: "Clem, I was running late for a meeting with my probation officer the other day when I come up on some city slicker hogging the passing lane while he gabbed on one of them celery phones."

Clem: "What'd you do, Lem?"

Lem: "Why, I pettied his [expletive deleted] right into a ditch, tee hee."

Not only will Petty's road-warrior act not hurt him politically, but it shouldn't hurt the state, either — not if we play our cards right. Indeed, it might even turn out to be a boon to tourism.

Before you go accusing me of sniffing exhaust fumes, let me

explain: You know how some people spend their vacations seeking excitement through such mundane acts as whitewater rafting, mountain climbing or driving 200 mph on the autobahn in Germany?

Well, if the state's tourism board is wise, it'll market the thrills to be found on our very own highways. I can just envision some orthodontist from New Jersey returning home and boasting of his exciting vacation on North Carolina's roads.

Throckmorton: "Hey Vito. What happened to your car? Looks like you were in a demolition derby or something."

Vito: (Beaming proudly.) "No, better than that. Went to North Carolina. See that dent in the back? Got that from Richard Petty on I-85."

Throckmorton: "Wow. Well, what happened to the driver's door?"

Vito: "Congressman David Funderburk. Ran me right off the road."

Throckmorton: "A congressman did that?"

Vito: "Scout's honor."

Throckmorton: "And isn't Petty running for secretary of state?"

Vito: "Yup."

Throckmorton: "I don't know what kind of politicians they got down there, but that's where we're going.

"Hey Ethel. Cancel those reservations for Disney World. We're going where we can really have some excitement."

September 26, 1996

Duke can't bank on 'Dollar' Bill

I've got a severe case of the blues. No, this is not Post-Fran Depression, a condition that afflicts Triangle residents who realize their insurance company is paying only enough to fix half of their caved-in roof. (Come to think of it, I have those blues, too.)

But the main affliction I have could be called the Post-Melinda Blues, and it descended upon me when I opened my newspaper and learned that I was passed over for the board of trustees at Duke University in favor of Melinda Gates.

John Burness, Duke's vice president for public affairs, called Mrs. Melinda French Gates "an extremely strong candidate."

He didn't say anything about me.

I really thought I had a chance this year. The only real difference between Melinda and me, as far as I can see, is that she was a dean's list student at Duke and hails from the Northwest, another reason Burness said she was chosen. Other than that — and the fact that her husband is worth $18.5 billion — we could be the same person.

Some cynics among you might think that Melinda Gates was named to the board of directors solely because she is married to Bill Gates, Microsoft's fabulously rich founder, and the school sees her appointment as a way of lassoing a hefty endowment.

Balderdash. If they wanted moolah, they wouldn't have gone for Gates' wife. Or even for the old — er, young — boy himself. Because even though Gates has more money than Robin Hayes has bad things to say about Jim Hunt, he has been known to squeeze a dollar bill until the eagle cries "Uncle."

That's right. The "g" in Gates definitely does not stand for "generous." Why, I'll bet if some homeless bloke asked him for 50 cents for a glass of Chablis, Gates would probably tell him, "Go invent something: I did." He has promised, though, that he will give away 95 percent of his vast fortune to charity and science when he reaches his 50s.

Promises, schmomises. Dollar Bill is only 39, so by the time he's 50, he can say, "Just kidding."

I want to be around in a decade or so when Duke officials go to his mansion to collect what they think they have coming to them.

Duke prez: "But Mr. Gates, remember when you said you'd ..."

Gates: "Sic 'em, Rover."

I'm no billionaire, but I have extensive holdings that could be worth a lot some day. And just between us, I'd be willing to turn them over — when I reach 50 (wink, wink) — to whichever local university sees fit to bestow a suitable honor upon me.

Among my assets is a membership card to the 14 Karat Dinner Theater in Durham. That alone is good for $5 off at the door, or five table dances before 1 a.m. (Oops. Did I say "table dances?" I meant "interpretive dances." This is a high-class joint.)

And even though I am not rich, we almost had a millionaire in our family. Or so we thought: When my Aunt Pearl from Washington called home to tell us that her boyfriend Eugene was coming to Rockingham with her, my other aunt thought she called him a millionaire.

So, we broke out the good china and silverware, killed a fatted calf and even invited the Rev. Mr. Sawyer for Sunday dinner.

Unfortunately for us, Aunt Pearl had said Eugene was a "milliner" — a hatmaker — not a millionaire.

Well, at least we all got hats from Eugene. Which is more than Duke will get from Bill Gates.

October 13, 1996

Not as easy as black and white

Comedian Godfrey Cambridge told a story once about a black guy having a conversation with God.

Bro: Lord, why did you make my skin so dark?

Lord: My son, the reason I made your skin so dark is to protect you from the scorching African sun's ultraviolet rays and to prevent you from getting sun stroke.

Bro: Well, Lord, why did you make my hair so coarse?

Lord: My son, I made your hair that way so that when you run through the jungle chasing the wildebeest and the antelope and the swift gazelles, your hair won't get tangled in the branches. ... Now, do you have any more questions?

Bro: Yeah, Lord, one.

Lord: Yes, my son?

Bro: What the hell am I doing in Cleveland?

I remembered that joke after reading a story last week about how some scientists now reject the entire notion of race as a valid way to divide human beings into separate groups. They've concluded that the only differences between people are physical ones that result from environmental pressures and genetic mutations.

"Race," said Jonathan Marks, a Yale University biologist, "has no basic biological reality."

When I read the story, my first thought was, "Oh hell, what's Jesse — Helms and Jackson — gonna do if it turns out we're all the same?"

Those ideological foes could form an unlikely alliance, joining forces to keep their names before the public and their butts out of the unemployment line.

Helms: Hey, Jesse, d'you read what these egghead scientists said in the paper today?

Jackson: I'm reading it now, my brother. We must move assiduously to ensure that this cockamamie crap never sees the light of day.

Helms: Right on, my brother. I need black people. Without y'all, who would I use to scare white people into voting for me Nov. 5?

Jackson: That's nothing. Without y'all, I might have to get a real job.

Helms: Amen, bro. Keep hope alive.

And what would people in these hoity-toity, prefab communities do? Well, because they could no longer fight to keep people of a different hue from building next door, they'd have to steal a page from the folks in Cary and just fight to keep folks from building homes of a different hue next door.

To me, this story on race — or, more accurately, the lack of race

— is far more significant than what O.J. Simpson had for breakfast or whether Madonna is going to breast-feed, both of which are things I have seen reported on the news.

But if you blinked, you would have missed it. We ran it on our front page, but I saw nothing in any other paper or on any television station's news. Why? Because the notion that we are all alike under our skin is not controversial enough, not at all like the premise put forth by William Shockley, the Nobel Prize winner who contended blacks are genetically inferior to whites.

Anyone with any sense — and any sense of history — will dismiss such "science" as nothing but racist quackery. After all, it was accepted "scientific" knowledge during slavery that — this is the truth — we blacks had a gene that caused us to break shovels and hoes with astonishing regularity.

Hmmph. I don't know about you, but to me, breaking a shovel when you're being forced to use it for free makes perfect sense.

October 14, 1996

Seamless love in a soiled world

I fell in love Monday morning. That's when I looked at the front page of my N&O and saw Mrs. Argin Laney of Durham.

No, I'm not fixing to ask another woman to take my name and, invariably after I mess up, everything else.

Laney, if you must know, is 62 years old and — in the picture in the newspaper — accompanied by six adorable grandchildren.

That is what I love about her. She was featured in a story on the rising number of grandmothers being forced by circumstances to raise their children's children. Being "forced" isn't quite right in Laney's case, since she seems to need the kids as much as they need her. "I couldn't manage without them," she said.

When I was growing up in Rockingham, there was a particularly strong wine known on the street as "Fight Your Mama," because after a couple of swigs your brain would be so messed up that you'd be ready to tangle with anybody — including the woman who brought you into this world.

Now, 20 years later, there's a drug out — crack — that could be called "Forget You're a Mama," since that, no doubt, explains why so many young mothers lack a maternal instinct and so readily turn the rearing of their children over to their own mothers.

But grandmothers raising grandchildren is no new phenomenon.

Many of my classmates in Rockingham were raised by grandparents while their own parents were off somewhere — usually up North — trying to make it the best they could in a cold, cruel or, at best, indifferent world.

My mother sent me to North Carolina — where the sweetest old woman in the world took me to her bosom like I belonged there — because our neighborhood in Washington was changing for the worse. Being young, I thought she sent me there because she didn't love me. I later realized she sent me there because she did.

That same grandmother who took me in and lavished me with love had already taken in four other grandsons whose mother had died young. I heard the story once of how several of my aunts were sitting around the kitchen table discussing how best to split the brothers so no one would have too great a burden.

My grandma listened awhile, pushed back her chair, stood and squelched all talk about splitting anybody up. "Bring me them young 'uns," she said. And that was that. She and my granddaddy raised us all until their health gave out. And then the greatest aunt in the world took over.

Many of the grandmothers in N&O reporter Michele Kurtz's story attend a grandma support group at C.C. Spaulding Elementary School in Durham in which they commiserate as well as share the joys of being mothers again. Principal Eunice Sanders, bless her heart, started the group after seeing an overwhelmed grandmother in her office break down in tears.

In a perfect world, grandmothers would never cry, mothers and fathers would be real parents, and grandmothers would be the people we visited on holidays bearing gifts, figgy pudding and glad tidings.

This isn't a perfect world, though, and much more than glad tidings are being dropped off on grandmothers' steps these days.

But for children lucky enough to land on those steps and in the bosoms of loving grandmothers, that is about as perfect as it gets.

October 31, 1996

He'll be home for Christmas

If you heard some crying in Cary last month, it was probably angels weeping over what happened to Antonio Vindel.

Vindel works seven days a week at three different fast-food restaurants so he can visit his family in La Ceiba, Honduras. He was giddy with glee when he finally saved enough money to see them for the first time in years.

Then Kelly Kirk decided she'd had enough of being a respectable businesswoman, packed up her family and skipped town, taking with her thousands of dollars belonging to clients of her Garner Travel Inc., according to police. Some of the missing money — $685 of it — was Vindel's, and now Kirk, charged with several counts of obtaining property by false pretenses, has gone from booking exotic trips for clients to being booked into the not-so-exotic Wake County Jail.

And while many of Kirk's customers are hurt and wondering why she ruined their vacations and her own life — and why she'd run away to West Virginia, of all places — none of their stories can be as heartbreaking as Vindel's.

You see, this wasn't the first time the Honduran native has been robbed. A few years ago, some guy jumped on him as he walked along a Tampa, Fla., street, pummeled him and took his money.

Then, while he struggled to recover from an emotionally and financially devastating divorce, he lost the travel money. Which, I asked, hurt worse?

He answered quickly. "It hurts worse when you trust someone and they take advantage of you than if someone comes out of the blue and beats you up," he said.

It took him months to earn the money to visit his family, and he thought nothing of it when Kirk asked for a down payment. "I should've known something was wrong when she threatened to cancel my reservation if I didn't pay up quickly," he says now.

He got a little worried, but not much, when he delivered the rest of his money to her office and noticed nothing but packed boxes — no computers, no typewriters, nothing. "I thought something was weird, but I trusted her."

Things really got weird for Vindel when he kept calling for his ticket and got no answer. Finally, he went to her office. What he saw made his heart drop and almost stop. "I saw a bunch of papers piled up outside the door. I was angry, upset."

So Vindel, who has been in Cary nine years, resigned himself to spending the Christmas holidays as he does every other day — slaving away over a hot oven or grill.

But Aaron Spaulding and his employees at Prestige Travel Agency in Raleigh saw a news story of Vindel's plight and were moved to tears. And action.

"We were touched because he was affected by a situation which he had no control over. He was out of that money and wasn't going home for the holidays," Prestige manager Kimberly Armstrong told me. So they decided to pay for the trip themselves. "This," she said, "is our way of doing something for the holidays."

When pressed, Armstrong admits that she and her co-workers have a somewhat selfish motive for helping Vindel. "Antonio is a very genuine person, and we definitely feared that something like this [Kirk's very public arrest] could give all travel agencies a bad name. People might think, 'If I can't trust a travel agent, who can I trust?' "

So now, thanks to the kindness of strangers, any noise you hear in Cary is likely to be Vindel singing "I'll Be Home for Christmas."

December 15, 1996

Ebonics as lingua franca

Make no mistake about it. I come to bury Ebonics, not to praise it. But before tossing dirt on the lame-brained notion that black kids should be taught that their slang, broken English and slovenly speech are worthy of consideration as a legitimate language unto itself — and thus worthy of federal funds — let me confess that sometimes even I Ebonic, and sometimes I don't.

Say what you want, but there are times when the king's English just won't hack it, when appropriate speech is inappropriate — because it's just not expressive enough, it lacks rhythm or it just doesn't sound right. I still smile when I think of the erudite, intellectual pastor of a large

church in Washington who, after a learned sermon in which he quoted
Plato, Langston Hughes and Shakespeare, asked me, "Who yo' people?"

I knew what he meant, and he knew I knew. Ebonic-ing me was his
way of showing me he was letting his guard down and being himself, of
making me feel welcome. It did.

But teaching kids that there is something noble in not speaking with
good grammar is absurd, even criminal. I don't care what the Oakland
(California) School Board says as it struggles to revise its monumental
gaffe, or what the Rev. Jesse Jackson now says — he went from con-
demning Ebonics to saying it was justified because of racism. Letting
bad English slide in school is an insult and counterproductive to blacks.

It is also a cynical ploy by the Oakland school system to qualify for
federal funds through bilingual programs meant for people from other
countries. In Oakland, some kid who went to bed unable to master one
language could awake to find himself declared proficient at two.

"For real? Oh, that's def," he'd exult.

Teachers could also receive merit pay for studying Ebonics. Now,
that's really def, because if anything could make me want to teach, that
could be it. Just imagine, I could get paid for hanging out in the pool
room — one of the most fertile places for Ebonics I've ever found, a
place that truly has its own distinct language. For instance, everyone
knows there's no such word as combinate, but I've never heard anyone
ask for an explanation when John Wall tells Louis he's going to "combinate the four ball off the six ball."

Fluency in Ebonics won't help you get the job replacing Bryant
Gumbel on the "Today" show, but not being able to speak it at all could
be hazardous to one's health.

Say what, fool? Here's a true story that illustrates my point. Six
years ago, while a reporter in Gary, Ind., I came upon a dead body surrounded by police and onlookers. I gingerly approached one gentleman.
"Pardon me, sir. Did you happen to see who killed this fellow?" I asked, or
something to that effect.

The dude shot me a look — and a stream of profanity — that let me
know there could soon be two bodies lying on the pavement in the rain if
I didn't get out of his face.

Gary led the nation in per capita murders every year I was there, so
it wasn't long before I was on the scene of another homicide with yet
another young dude lying dead on the ground. This time and from then
on, I knew how to handle myself. "Hey, Homes, y'all see what went
down?" I asked.

I still got no answer, of course, but at least no one looked at me as
though I were crazy. Or a member of the Oakland School Board.

In any language, that's the same thing.

January 13, 1997

Parents let childhood die young

I thought it was cute at the time. A couple of years ago, my then 5-year-old son rushed into the room and told me about something he'd seen on the news. "Dad, I just saw where a 6-year-old man got hit by a car," he excitedly informed me. (Relax: The kid turned out to be OK.)

The thought of a 6-year-old "man" was amusing then. It's not now, not after seeing haunting pictures of what looks for all the world like a real 6-year-old "woman" on television news the past few weeks.

I'm talking, of course, about JonBenet Ramsey, the little girl who was found raped and murdered in her Boulder, Colo., home.

Like everyone else, I was sickened when I heard what had happened to her. Also like everyone else, my sympathy for her is tempered by a feeling I have toward her parents that is less than charitable.

Don't look at me like that. I'm sure some of y'all, if you're honest, will admit to harboring thoughts about the parents that are less than Christian, too.

No, I'm not implying they have any complicity in this horrible crime. I hope they don't. But even if they didn't take her life, I think they took something equally precious from her: her childhood.

I am haunted by the endless news clips of little JonBenet performing onstage, prancing on the catwalk, staring alternately soulfully or winsomely into the camera, her hair frosted and coiffed and her makeup professionally applied. She had such presence that it was easy to forget the kid was just 6. Apparently, somebody did.

Nor did the parents engender much sympathy, at least not from me, when they immediately went into a defensive crouch, hired not only "his" and "her" attorneys and refused to cooperate with the cops but hired a public relations agent as well!

I realize JonBenet's mother — a veteran of beauty pageants herself — is not the first parent to try to live her life vicariously through her children. We all know people who do that. I know a failed dancer who makes her 12-year-old daughter practice ballet until her feet bleed. I have a friend in Indiana — a former friend, probably, after I objected to the ruthless way he tried to raise his son (or, more accurately, tried to raise a basketball star) — who transferred his son to three different junior high and high schools to maximize his playing time.

Of course, I haven't met a parent yet who didn't think his or her children had star potential. Heck, after I heard my son rapping a song he wrote himself — "Riding down the street on my Big Wheel, trying to find a Happy Meal" — I started having visions, ever so briefly, of raising the next LL Cool J.

But unless you've got that rare star quality like a Paul Newman, Denzel Washington or Halle Berry, a winning smile won't get you 15 seconds on the evening news. Unless you are brutally murdered and your daddy is rich.

Yet, as we can see now that the JonBenet tragedy has pulled the cover off the often-sordid child beauty pageant industry, thousands of little girls are being taught to coo, purr and comport themselves like prepubescent sex kittens in hopes of catching the eye of a TV talent scout and, later, a rich hubby.

But even when they win a pageant as Little Miss This or That, they often end up losing something more important: their childhood.

January 19, 1997

Evasion — to save his loved ones

Anybody who knows me knows I never jump to conclusions. That's why I'm assuming there was a legitimate reason why Raleigh City Council member Kieran Shanahan trampled the spirit of the law — not to mention his wife's petunias — while fleeing a process server last week.

In case you missed the story, Shanahan was trying mightily to avoid being served with a copy of a lawsuit, which accuses him, Mayor Tom Fetzer and three other council members of violating the state's Open Meetings Law.

An affidavit says that the first time Carlton Gerald, who's a process server for Poindexter & Associates, arrived at Shanahan's house with the suit, Shanahan called him everything but a ham sandwich and ordered Gerald off the property.

When Gerald then called on the telephone, Shanahan slammed down the phone. When the dude went back to Shanahan's home the next night, the lights inside mysteriously went out and no one came to the door.

But the next morning, when Shanahan pulled out of the garage in his wife's red minivan, Gerald was there, blocking the driveway with his own car. "I reckon I've got you now," Gerald thought gleefully to himself.

But he didn't reckon on Shanahan's employing some of the evasive driving techniques he learned from watching all of those "Smokey and the Bandit" movies with Burt Reynolds.

The affidavit says that "Mr. Shanahan turned his wheel sharply and sped across his front lawn." He left the neighborhood "at a high rate of speed" and turned abruptly into the path of a school bus. That's when Gerald, fearing a crash or an O.J.-style white Bronco chase, wisely ended his pursuit.

The question I've heard over and over from Raleigh citizens is, "Is that any way for an elected official to act?" My answer is, "Darned tootin'."

Giving Shanahan the benefit of the doubt, I must ask: "How was he to know what the guy following him wanted?" Heck, he could've been a Jehovah's Witness peddling the latest issue of "The Watchtower," a rabid Amway salesman or someone from Fetzer's office begging him to vote "no" on more money for the proposed arena. Shanahan, to Fetzer's consternation, voted "yes" for additional funding, and it passed 5-3.

But, as Shanahan told a local TV station when news of his great escapes became public, "I have a right and duty to protect my family."

Scoff if you want, but I can see how running away and leaving your wife and kids at home — alone — could indeed be interpreted as a selfless, protective act.

K.S.: Honey, it's me that they want. I'm going to divert their attention in the minivan while you and the kids take the Benz and get away. I may not come back alive, but just remember I love you. And tell Mayor Fetzer I —

Mrs. K.S.: No, baby. You mustn't go. We can wait him out. I just got back from the Piggly Wiggly and bought a hundred dollars worth of potato chips and bean dip. That should last you through tomorrow.

K.S.: Is it the kind with the li'l bitty jalapenos in it?

Mrs. K.S.: Would I buy any other kind for you, Special K?

K.S.: But what are you and the kids going to eat?

Mrs. K.S.: Oh, we'll get by.

K.S. Baby, you're the greatest. But I still must go.

Mrs. K.S. OK, but watch out for my petunias.

February 06, 1997

Geraldo and O.J. Inc. will have to open another vault

If you've got a job, you'd better hold on to it, because this country is about to undergo an economic upheaval unrivaled since the Great Depression.

I don't care what those rosy economic indicators say: the jobless rate is going to soar and it will have nothing to do with fewer exports to

China, fewer homes being built or Roseanne's latest diet.

What it will have everything to do with is the end of the O.J. Simpson trial — and the fact that all of those people who've been making a living off Simpson are going to have to find real jobs.

Regardless of how you feel about Simpson's guilt or innocence, his liability or lack thereof in the deaths of Nicole Brown Simpson and Ron Goldman, you have to admit that this play has lasted one act too long.

Unless, of course, you're one of the scores of people for whom the aging jock-pitchman became a cottage industry.

I worry most about poor Geraldo Rivera, the premier Simpson pimp. Rivera's obsession with O.J. would have been funny if it — oh hell, who am I kidding? — it was funny.

I realize we're talking about the brutal deaths of two people. But admit it: for a long time, this case has been only peripherally about Nicole and Ron.

It became, if not comical, at least surreal, to watch night after night as Geraldo and an interchangeable group of second-rate sycophantic shysters whose only common trait was a disdain for Simpson postured in front of the TV camera and low-rated the prosecutors or the jury for letting Simpson go free.

They would then tell how they, in their jurisprudential genius, would have nailed his worthless hide to the wall with one hand tied behind their backs.

Now that Geraldo can no longer sup at the O.J. trough five nights a week, he may be forced to return to his former television profession: opening, with great fanfare, the empty vaults of long-dead mobsters or interviewing nubile 16-year-old girls who "can't say no to sex."

(That field will be a bit more crowded than when he left to embark on his Great Black O.J. Hunt. TV gabber Montel Williams now plays out his own lecherous fascination with young girls daily.)

Joining Geraldo in the unemployment line, I hope, will be his new bestest buddy, Christopher Darden.

During the first trial, Darden conducted himself with dignity, even in the face of withering criticism from some blacks who foolishly attacked him for prosecuting a "brother."

(This despite the fact that the blackest thing — indeed, some say the only black thing — about O.J. were his Bruno Maglis.)

You can trace the beginning of Darden's loss of dignity to the end of the murder trial, when he broke down and cried for the cameras, obviously distraught over failing to land "the big one." Considering how ineptly he and Marcia Clark conducted their prosecution, he's unlikely to find another job in a courtroom unless it's intoning "All rise."

Whatever job he gets, especially if it's in the food-service industry, let's hope it requires him to shave.

The lives of duh-namic duo Darden and Rivera aren't the only ones that will change profoundly. Others who have ridden the Juice Train to a measure of wealth and fame, such as Clark and Johnnie Cochran, will have to find work that doesn't include pontificating about O.J.

But those whose lives will undergo the greatest change are undoubtedly the Juice-man himself and his children. Sure, he won custody, but if these judgments hit him as hard as many people expect — and hope — he'll have to radically alter their lifestyles and his.

Dinnertimes that once consisted of such sumptuous fare as duck sausage enchiladas and filet mignon will be replaced by Hamburger Helper — which sometimes may even include hamburger.

Sydney: "Oh infamous father. What exactly are the ingredients that go into this dish called chitterlings?"

O.J. (Turning to manservant): "Uh, A.C. These things are rather aromatic. What are they made of?"

A.C.: "Hog guts, Juice."

O.J.: "What? Man, my children can't eat that. Isn't there some more of that foie gras in duck sauce left in the fridge?"

A.C.: "There was, but old man Goldman came and took it. Court order."

But the surest sign of Simpson's financial destitution will have nothing to do with what he and the kids eat. You'll know O.J. is truly broke when you see him on the cover of Jet magazine — with a black woman.

February 08, 1997

If it's cool to hide your smarts, there's a lot to learn

If you have trouble sleeping at night, you already know there is nothing on television worth watching at 2 a.m.

Despite having 44 channels at my disposal, my main choices a few days ago came down to watching an infomercial with George Foreman cooking hamburgers on some grill he was hawking, the smarmy Dennis Miller interviewing the unfunny, steatopygous Chevy Chase, or the charisma-challenged head of the National Urban League, Hugh Price, on a C-Span repeat.

Since nothing could have entertained me less than watching George cook — although I did eventually order one of those grills — or Dennis and Chevy congratulating each other on their wittiness and hipness, I decided to check out Price.

I'm glad I did. Although he spoke in a yawn-inducing monotone, much of what Price said was interesting and disturbing. The most interesting — and disturbing — thing he talked about was the current anti-intellectual climate among some young blacks.

Despite the proven ability of education to increase one's income and help shelter blacks from the most virulent forms of racism, some young blacks perversely view academic attainment as some kind of repudiation of their heritage.

In some communities, black students who can conjugate a verb or utter a sentence that doesn't begin with "Yo, Homey" are ostracized or hit with the most opprobrious term imaginable: "acting white."

Intellectual curiosity and achievement are held in such low regard, Price said, that at one school — Ballou in Washington — some honor students wouldn't even attend the awards ceremony for fear of being found out as "brains."

That is undoubtedly the culture that insightful comedian Chris Rock is talking about in his standup act when he refers to young blacks who revere their peers who've served time in prison — who are, in the current lingo, "keepin' it real" — while dismissing as chumps anyone who goes to college or otherwise eschews the street definition of "cool."

So pervasive is this disdain for learning that even young dudes with genuine intellectual curiosity feel compelled to hide it.

One of the most instructive — and saddest —eulogies of slain rapper Tupac Shakur was delivered by Andy Young, former Atlanta mayor and U.N. ambassador. Young recalled being at a bookstore promoting his autobiography when he noticed a limousine pass the store, make a U-turn — not an easy feat for a limo — and stop in front. Alighting from the limo was a clean-shaven young man who approached Young and conversed knowledgeably and thoughtfully about his civil rights work.

Of course, it isn't surprising that Tupac wouldn't speak, much less rap, about his incipient intellectual curiosity and certainly not about entering — egad! — a bookstore. Why, what would the homies think?

Perhaps if Tupac had broken off a rap or two about the coolness of being smart, then I wouldn't be experiencing my current problems keeping my 8-year-old son in his school's A.G. — Academically Gifted — program: He hates it because three times a week he is separated from his pals, who tease him for being smart.

Who would've thunk it: being placed in a class for advanced students would one day carry the same stigma that being placed in Special Education classes did 20 years ago? (I know, because I spent part of my junior year making clay ashtrays, reading Playboy and singing "Kum-ba-ya.")

Not that contempt for intellectual proficiency or shame about academic accomplishment is anything new. Back in the 1970s when I was in high school, kids were more admired for the height of their Afros, the width of their bellbottoms or their ability to score with the ladies than for their scores on the SAT. If, that is, they even dared take the college entrance exam and risk being derided as a "braniac," a "Poindexter" or a "white-acting" wannabe.

Heck, I still cringe at the memory of being ridiculed — in college, of all places — and losing the affections of some sweet young thang because I used a word that contained more than two syllables. (Although, in retrospect, I don't think "metamorphosis" was the best word I could've used to explain what her heavenly presence did to me.)

By the time she and her roommate picked themselves off the floor and stopped laughing, I had already slunk out of the door and out of her life. And I haven't said "metamorphosis" since then.

February 22, 1997

'Booty' rakes it in, while a fine 'Rosewood' wilts

Hush. Shut up. Talk to the hand — because I just don't want to hear it."

Oh, excuse me. I was just practicing up on my responses to black people I hear griping about the way Hollywood portrays us on the big screen.

What has curled my kente cloth is the fact that "Rosewood," a sad, disturbing, but ultimately uplifting movie on a shamefully ignored chapter of America's history, is being virtually ignored by moviegoers while "Booty Call" is a piece of irrelevant, stereotype-enhancing tripe turning a tidy profit.

Two weeks after its debut "Rosewood" was barely in the top 10 among highest grossing movies — it was hanging on at No. 10 — while "Booty Call" was a robust No. 4.

For decades blacks have complained loudly about the way Hollywood ignored or distorted our history. We have brayed against the demeaning images of Mantan "Feets do yo' stuff" Moreland, the head-scratching, foot-shuffling antics of Steppin' Fetchit and the gangsta idolizing of flicks like "Superfly" and "New Jack City."

So what do we do when director John Singleton makes a gem of a movie about our history from blacks' point of view — a first in itself, as far as I can tell?

Why, we greet it with a resounding indifference and hustle down to

the multiplex to plunk down $6.50 to see "Booty Call," a movie whose
very title reinforces the stereotype of sex-crazed black men.

Or else we queue up to see the re-releases of "The Empire Strikes
Back" or "Star Wars," old flicks in which Carrie Fisher wears two honey-
buns on her head and blacks are represented by Billy Dee Williams (sans
Colt .45 malt liquor) and James Earl Jones' voice.

Blacks buy more movie tickets in proportion to our percentage of the
population than any other group. We are disproportionately responsible
for inexplicably making stars of Steven Seagal, Bruce Willis and Arnold
Schwarzenegger. That makes "Rosewood's" imminent quick disappear-
ance from movie screens all the more infuriating.

Of course, whites need to see "Rosewood," too. If nothing else, it will
show boomers that racism did not end when Lincoln signed the
Emancipation Proclamation.

But white moviegoers are not responsible for the movie's ultimate
success or failure. That responsibility lies with blacks, because the ultimate success or failure of "Rosewood" will determine, in large measure,
whether such intelligent movies get made or whether Hollywood continues its assault on our image with the likes of Martin Lawrence's profane
alleged comedy, "Thin Line Between Love & Hate."

That 1996 movie not only defiled the Persuasions' great 1970s song
of that title, but it also may have set some record for the most uses of a
particularly vile 12-letter word in a five-minute span. (That's all I could
take of it.)

I am no cultural elitist who thinks every black-oriented film should be
a sober-minded polemic on the evils of racism or one that extols the
beauty of all things black. I appreciate mindless entertainment as much
as anyone, and as proof I am anxiously awaiting a feature-length version
of "Sanford & Son: the Movie."

There is a place for inane mind candy such as "Booty Call." But that
place is not ahead of movies such as "Rosewood" or Spike Lee's excellent
"Get on the Bus," which also disappeared from theaters without a trace.

Of course, the problem is not just with black moviegoers seeking
escapist, silly fare at the expense of socially redeeming movies. Some of
the blame can be placed with theater owners who refuse to show films
with black themes or aimed at black audiences. The re-releases of "Star
Wars" and "Empire" were both on more than 2,000 screens nationwide.
"Rosewood" appeared on 994.

But "Rosewood" is an excellent movie worth searching for, and if it
doesn't make enough money to encourage other black directors to make
stories of our history, then the fault lies not with the stars — be they
Bruce, Steven or Arnold — but with us.

A reviewer for The Wall Street Journal skewered the movie — surprise! — but it wasn't made for him, anyway. Indeed, the fact that he hated means it worked, if you ask me.

For a while, I thought a suitable punishment for black moviegoers who fail to see "Rosewood" would be to make them sit in a theater eating stale popcorn and watching any movie — with extended, explicit love scenes — starring Jim Belushi and Whoopi Goldberg. Alas, the Constitution outlaws cruel and unusual punishment.

In that case, I think a fitting punishment would be to make 'em watch every movie Woody Allen ever made.

Then they won't have to worry about negative portrayals of blacks. Because there won't be any portrayals of blacks, negative or otherwise.

March 08, 1997

Street's lessons hard at 68

Gertrude Young needs a friend.

She is 68, and all her belongings, as far as I can see, are a shapeless sweater and a jacket on two hangers in this tiny room in a rundown motel.

Oh, and dozens of tattered newspaper clippings spread over the bed. All of the clippings — some dating back 15 years — are in some way about homeless people: the unfortunate circumstances that forced them onto the street, the wrongs done them by an unfeeling bureaucracy, how they were helped by having their plight publicized.

That's why she called me three days ago. "Mr. Barry, can you help me?" the small voice on my answering machine inquired.

By the time I called back at the number she'd left, she was gone. I learned later that the weather had warmed up enough for her to resume her lonely vigil walking the streets all night, lugging the plastic bags containing her possessions. She said her other stuff — furniture and "fine clothes that still have the tags on them" — is in storage.

Miss Young ended up on the street when the city condemned the ramshackle apartment building in which she lived. The place was full of rats, she tells me, the four-legged kind and their human counterparts.

She makes the sacrifice and spends the money for a motel room when the weather gets too bad or she feels too sick to walk the streets. But even a spartan room like this one — bare walls, soiled carpet and torn sheets — is an extravagance.

I've never been good at math, but even I can tell that a $32.95-a-day room takes a healthy chunk out of a monthly income of $328 from Social

Security.

The frail voice I'd heard on the telephone matched the spindly arms and legs of the suspicious woman who finally opened the door to Room 109. Her stomach was bothering her. "There was a time I could eat nails at midnight and sleep like a baby," she says. "Now, my stomach stays tore up. ... That's what living out here like this will do to you."

Living "like this" — out on the streets — also makes one knowledge-able about certain things, like the schedule of the kind hotel security guard who will let her stay in the bathroom all night. And of the one who yells angrily at her on sight, "Get outta here!"

Remarkably, Miss Young still has a sense of humor, expressed wryly. "Seems like all I eat is soup," she says. "I've eaten so much soup I feel like a noodle." Then, holding up her skinny arm for inspection — "I look like a noodle."

She says she used to be a nursing assistant in Washington, D.C., taking care of elderly people. She was paid by the city's social services department, but the job was phased out when the city went broke.

She says she plans to resume her career — or take any job that pays — when she finds a place to stay. "I'm looking for someone to stay with," she says. "I can pay $250 a month. It doesn't take much for me to live off, and I can work two or three days a week."

I suggested she try the Durham Housing Authority. "I've tried them three times. How many more times should I try?" she asked.

I ask about her family. "Don't mention them," she snaps. So I don't.

But she still needs a friend. If you've got a suggestion — or, better yet, a room to let— call me. I know where to find her. At least when the weather gets bad, and she's feeling poorly and she has some extra money, I do.

April 03, 1997

A selfish pursuit of sound sleep

I'm used to people calling me dirty names, everything from a "racist" to a "ham sandwich."

I accept that as part of the job.

But my detractors have really outdone themselves this time, what with the vile, insulting epithets that have filled my answering machine the past several days.

Dozens of people called me "generous." "Almost human." And worst of all, "nice."

And what did I do to deserve such opprobrium?

Why, I merely wrote a column about a homeless woman I encountered last week who needed help.

I told how Gertrude Young spent her nights walking Durham's
streets, lugging plastic bags filled with her belongings. How when the
weather was bad — and she had some money to spare from her $328
monthly Social Security check — she'd get a cheap motel room.

That's when a friend looked at me all mushy—eyed and said, "You've
got a heart after all, don't you?"

I assured her and everyone else who misconstrued my interest in
Miss Young that I don't. I am the same old me, and my motto, taken
from my hero, Fred G. Sanford, is the same as it's always been: Do unto
others — and then run.

Oh, I can't deny that the scores of people who called seeking ways to
help Miss Young renewed my sagging faith in humankind, especially
when some offered to open their homes and pocketbooks to this
stranger they knew only from what I'd written. In the next few days, she
will meet with people who read of her plight and want to meet her to see
if their situations fit. One gentle, beautiful woman — who said she was
diagnosed with cancer five years ago — is offering a room in her home.
"People have been so wonderful to me," this woman told me. "This seems
like a way I can possibly show kindness to someone else."

I received many other calls from people of all races and religious
beliefs who seemed genuinely interested in sharing the bounty with
which they've been blessed.

Those are the "nice" people, and I'll keep you posted on how Miss
Young makes out.

But even as I do that, honesty compels me to confess that my own
interest in helping her was primarily selfish. No, not so I'd have a subject
for a column. Indeed, I agonized over whether to even write about her
and then about the heartwarming responses.

So what was in it for me, you ask? Let me tell you a little story I
once read about Abe Lincoln. It seems pre-presidential Abe and his law
partner were riding in a horse-drawn buggy arguing over man's basic
nature. Lincoln was saying that everything human beings do is motivated
by self-interest, while his partner argued that people are basically good
and truly concerned about others.

As they rode along in a snowstorm, they came upon a small lamb
whose leg was trapped in a wire fence. Lincoln got down from the
wagon and struggled mightily to free the animal, and after several minutes he did. The pair then rode on in silence for a while until the partner
said smugly, "See there? I told you man is good. What you just did was
totally unselfish."

To the contrary, said Lincoln, equally smug: "If I had ridden on without freeing that lamb, I would have wondered at its fate all day.

I would not have been able to eat, and it would have haunted my sleep. I freed it because I like to sleep."

So do I.

April 10, 1997

When they were kings: Courage in and out of the ring

I've got this bet with my best friend, Seymour Pettigrew, but it's going to take awhile to collect. At least 30 years.

Seymour is betting that basketball star Michael Jordan will still be as popular — and still be hawking everything from hamburgers to drawers — 30 years from now as he is today.

Me? I'm betting that, within five years of hitting his last jump shot, Jordan will be a mere historical footnote — albeit a rich one — remembered by none but the most avid sports fans.

What prompted this unusual wager was a movie Seymour and I saw together this week — "When We Were Kings," a fabulous documentary on Muhammad Ali. We picked 30 years to judge Jordan's lingering impact (or lack thereof) because it was 30 years ago this year that Ali was stripped of his heavyweight boxing title for refusing to compromise his beliefs and be inducted into the U.S. Army during the Vietnam War.

Regardless of how you feel about Ali's stand, you must admit that his importance transcends his sport. He risked his livelihood, even his freedom, rather than go into the Army, where he would've gotten as close to actual fighting as I did — and I was 10 years old at the time.

No, Uncle Sam would've given him some cushy position traveling from base to base putting on boxing exhibitions. As the government did for Joe Louis. But even that was an unsuitable compromise for Ali, who declared himself a conscientious objector and urged the government to "clean out my cell, 'cos I'm going to jail" rather than compromise.

It was during that period that Ali uttered what became his signature statement, one that should be in any book of historical quotations — despite its "ungrammaticism." When asked why he refused induction, Ali replied, "I ain't got no quarrel with the Viet Cong."

Compare that to the statement by which Michael Jordan will be remembered. His pithy response, when explaining his refusal in 1990 to campaign for Democratic U.S. Senate candidate Harvey Gantt against Sen. Jesse Helms, was, "Republicans buy basketball shoes, too."

Don't get me wrong, now. Jordan seems to be a likable, courteous chap, and when I interviewed him years ago while representing a small Indiana newspaper he was just as courteous and patient as if I had been with The New York Times. Nor is he the only present-day athlete whose interest in or knowledge of social issues is non-existent.

But as the one with the highest profile — and about the highest pay — he epitomizes the current crop of self-enraptured, unsocially-conscious athletes. One gets the impression from watching the tightly wrapped, unspontaneous Jordan that he confers with image consultants — or his agent, David Falk — before going to the bathroom.

Michael: But David, I've got to go reallllly bad.

Falk: Well, OK.

I just hope he asks Falk if he can go see "When We Were Kings."

There is a powerful, silent scene in that movie in which a dozen or so top black professional athletes of the era — including Bill Russell, Lew Alcindor (before he became Kareem Abdul-Jabbar) and Jim Brown — gather around Ali to speak out on the conditions confronting blacks in America.

It is inconceivable that today's athletes — direct beneficiaries of the courage shown by Ali et al. — would speak out on anything that might adversely affect their shoe contracts.

Sure, it could be argued that the problems confronting blacks today are more complicated, less easily identified, than they were in the 1960s. After all, there is no Sheriff Bull Connor with his high-pressure water hoses and vicious, snarling dogs. Indeed, many of the problems confronting blacks today are self-imposed — or at least exacerbated by ourselves.

But that's all the more reason for athletes who have the nation's ears, eyes and hearts to speak out. As the Rev. Jesse Jackson said recently of today's black celebrities, "The people who were direct beneficiaries of the civil rights movement can no longer have a free ride."

Yet, even when some brave athlete does speak out on something, he is ignored by the media. Craig Hodges, a former teammate of Jordan's on the Chicago Bulls, used the team's meeting with President George Bush in 1991 to present to the president a list of black America's grievances.

Didn't know that, did you? But I'm sure you knew all about Dennis Rodman dating Madonna, kissing transvestite RuPaul and generally behaving like an idiot, right?

If someone deigns to make a documentary on Jordan and today's pro athletes, a fitting title might be "When We Were Chumps."

April 12, 1997

(Former) Rev. Chavis finds you can't take it on faith

It was a hard choice, but in the end, the United Church of Christ had to take away the Rev. Ben Chavis' clerical collar after he joined the Nation of Islam and changed his name to Chavis Muhammad.

Allowing him to remain in both groups simultaneously would have knocked the whole religious applecart topsy-turvy. For one thing, as a member of the United Church of Christ, Chavis Muhammad would have been able to eat pork chops; as a member of the Nation, pork is strictly forbidden.

Perhaps fearing such gastronomical transgressions, a key commission of the United Church of Christ voted last week in Durham to revoke Chavis Muhammad's status as a minister. Commission members said it was not easy ousting the man who formerly served as executive director of its Commission for Racial Justice.

Chavis became a player in the civil rights movement in 1971, when he was sentenced to prison for taking part in a riot in Wilmington, and blacks today owe him and thousands of people like him for the sacrifices they made in the civil rights struggle.

Chavis, or Chavis Muhammad, is the kind of indispensable foot soldier without whom no army could succeed. But it is painfully obvious each time he tries to rhetorically arouse a crowd that he lacks the charisma or eloquence to galvanize people around him or a cause.

A perfect example occurred when I saw him at a national conference of black journalists in Atlanta three years ago. There, Chavis, then head of the NAACP, was able to stroll the hotel lobby or sit undisturbed by either well-wishers or journalists.

The next day, however, when the story broke of his profligate spending and his effort to pay off a former lover with NAACP funds, he was page one news across the country and sought after by every journalist who ever pulled on a trench coat.

No doubt about it, those embarrassing revelations led the NAACP to give him the boot. But what really greased the skids for his departure was his then-unofficial alliance with Minister Louis Farrakhan and his Nation of Islam.

When Chavis tried to appeal to younger blacks by reaching out to Farrakhan, the staid NAACP showed him the exit and snatched away his credit cards, cars and title quicker than you could sing the opening stanza of "We Shall Overcome."

More than anything else, Chavis Muhammad's flirtation with — and now marriage to — the Nation is an indictment of Christianity. His leadership style, what there is of it, has always been unorthodox. And Chavis undoubtedly recognized that Protestant religions have failed miserably in attracting disaffected young people — the people most receptive to Farrakhan's message.

But the theological implications of allowing Chavis Muhammad or anyone else to serve simultaneously in two faiths — whether it was Farrakhan's controversial Nation or any other — are surely what the UCC found most troubling.

For one thing, it would have necessitated an amendment to the Ten Commandments, making one of them read, "Thou shalt have no other God before me — OK, maybe one."

For another, well. . . Let me say it in a song, sung to the tune of — what else? — "Ben" by Michael Jackson. Maestro, hit it:

Ben, you'd found what you were looking for
Then, the NAACP showed you the door
They claim you spent up all their money
On your outside honey.
But they didn't comprehend
that you were just being Ben.
Ben, most churches would turn you away.
You don't listen to a word they say.
All you want to do is preach
but they don't like what you teach.
I'm sure they'd say "amen"
if they had a friend like Ben.
Ben, you've traded in your collar
(That made them want to holler.)
You now sport a bowtie
And try to sell bean pies
You used to say "Glory hallelujah."
But now it's "All whites'll screw ya."'
Some people say you're just a pawn
Of the Minister Farrakhan.
But you insist you're still the same
except "Chavis" is now your first name.

May 03, 1997

An assist by Eddie Murphy

I don't know why y'all are looking at Eddie Murphy like that, as though you don't believe his story of how and why police caught him in the company of a male transvestite prostitute at 4:45 one morning last week.

Doesn't everyone pick up grieving, seductively clad, uh ... women at that time of morning to offer words of encouragement?

Yet when Murphy the good Samaritan tries to put his Christian beliefs into action, he finds himself lampooned by Letterman, Leno and a skeptical public.

I don't know about yours, but my Bible advises to "judge not, that ye be not judged." And in the Book of Fred it says, "Let he who is without sin — pick up some."

For shame, for shame. Why, the ridicule to which Murphy is being subjected is almost enough to make one stop trying to help one's fellow man. Or woman. Or whatever.

Honestly now, how was Eddie to know that this beguiling damsel in distress was actually a fugitive, street-walkin' dude in drag?

Just goes to show, you never know.

Of course, some people contend that Murphy knew exactly what he was getting into — and what was getting into his wife's Land Cruiser in an area L.A. police have identified as a "prostitution abatement zone." The evidence for such conjecture, if one knows where to look, is compelling.

Cynics point to Murphy's concert videos from the late 1980s. The vitriol and hatred with which he attacked gays made one thing obvious to them: either Murphy had been traumatized by a homosexual as a child or he had some unresolved inner issues to work out.

There isn't a gay bone in my body, but the intensity of Murphy's gay-bashing in his movie "Delirious" was so offensive that it forced me to turn off my VCR. His homophobia was so pronounced that a gay organization even named a disease after him.

And now he's been caught — but not charged for — picking up a gay streetwalker. Murphy says he thought his passenger was a Hawaiian woman, but gay people with whom I've spoken said they wouldn't be surprised if he knew it was a Hawaiian-looking dude. According to two with whom I spoke, the most virulent — and violent — homophobes have ambivalent feelings toward gays and are uncertain about their own sexuality.

For proof, just look at lawyer Roy Cohn and former FBI Director J. Edgar Hoover, two moralists whose public personas were unrelentingly anti-gay, but whose own gay skeletons tumbled out of the closet after their deaths.

But even if Murphy does cover the waterfront, gays with whom I spoke sounded forgiving. Mark Johnson, spokesman for the National Gay and Lesbian Task Force in Washington, told me, "If Mr. Murphy is a gay person, I hope he'll find the strength to acknowledge that. He'll find that the personal pride and happiness and the weight lifted off his shoulders will far outweigh any negative publicity."

Me? I believe it's possible that Murphy really was just being a good guy and offering assistance to someone he thought needed it. As he said in his defense, "I've seen hookers on corners, and I'll pull over and they'll go, 'You're Eddie Murphy.' And I'll empty my wallet out to help."

You can smirk if you want to, but if I ever need a ride at 4:45 a.m. I hope Eddie'll stop and give me a lift.

But you can bet I won't be wearing high heels.

May 08, 1997

Children need help to dream

That was a real Hallmark greeting cards moment I had in the woods surrounding Raleigh's Shelley Lake last week. If I had seen it on television, I would have dismissed it as too corny to be believed.

But this was real life, and because of that it was a moment of such transcendent beauty that I didn't want it to end. There I was, huffing and puffing around Shelley Lake, trying to keep up with Jennifer Davis, director of programs for Loaves and Fishes Ministry, and about 20 pre-adolescent children. Davis and a handful of volunteers were leading them around the lake and to a picnic as part of the group's annual fund-raising walkathon.

Their immediate concern was making sure none of the kids, in grades K through 5, followed the ducks or geese into the lake. My main concern was wondering whether the corns on my feet would hold up for one more trip around the lake.

About 10 of the kids, succumbing to the youthful inclination to climb atop anything taller than they, took a break from petting every passing dog and clambered onto an observation deck overlooking the lake.

There, intoxicated either by the view or the height, a 9-year-old girl burst gleefully and unselfconsciously into song: "I believe I can fly." As if on cue, several others joined in. "I believe I can fly. I believe I can touch the sky."

Now, it's OK if that song by R. Kelly strikes you as vapid and hokey. That's how it struck me, too. But that was before I heard it sung by a bunch of poor kids freed momentarily from earthly constraints and their bleak neighborhoods. I felt giddy and sad at the same time, because the thought that popped into my head was, "Oh, if only they could fly — or if only they could continue believing that they could."

Dreams, you see, die young for cute, inquisitive kids like these, and too soon become merely what they do when they sleep at night. If they're lucky enough to dream.

For many of them, dreams of flight — literal or figurative flight — will soon give way to more mundane concerns, like how to play on their front porches without getting hit by a stray bullet.

But thanks to Loaves and Fishes, a nonprofit Raleigh organization that helps low-income kids develop school and social skills, those worries were miles away on this day.

But even as I basked in the glow of the sun and their laughter, I felt vaguely disturbed. Sure, I felt bad that these kids would soon be going back to neighborhoods that I wouldn't want to live in. And yes, I regretted that my back gave out when two tiny little girls jumped on it, pleading for a ride.

But it wasn't until I drove away that I realized why I was most distressed. It was the fact that all the children were black. And Davis and all her volunteers were white.

Where, I wondered, were the black volunteers interested in tutoring, mentoring or just lending a hand to these kids?

Sure, this is a stressful world and people feel they hardly have time for their own kids, much less some little urchins from the poor side of town.

But believe me, if you don't reach out to these kids today, some of them may be reaching out to — or at — you someday.

May 12, 1997

Fashion cops crack down on poor

Hey guys, I've got a great idea. Let's all go over to the projects and kick the #@#$ out of some poor people.

Naw, naw. Y'all sit back down. I'm just kidding. But a lot of you aren't. Indeed, you be ready at a minute's notice to go to Few Gardens or Chavis Heights and other public housing developments to beat the crap out of people whose only crime is being poor.

Don't deny it. I've heard from you new Minute Men and Women, and so has The N&O. Last week, we ran a story about the difficulty of reducing the welfare rolls in Durham County. The story revealed that a lot of poor people don't have access — educational, vocational or physical — to available jobs.

But despite the vivid, balanced portrait painted in the story, the only picture that callers wanted to talk about was the front-page one that accompanied the story.

One black caller objected, predictably, to the picture of the black woman on the front page because, she contended, it perpetuated racist stereotypes about welfare.

I understand the caller's sensitivity, since welfare and anything else considered "bad" are usually, unfairly painted black. But in Durham County, on which the story focused, 86 percent of welfare recipients are black and the odds are great that even a randomly selected welfare recipient would be, also.

But most of the calls dealt not with the 41-year-old woman's race, but with her accessories.

"My question is," said one caller, asking not a question but making an indictment, "what is she doing with such expensive jewelry? I counted at least six rings and two gold bracelets. I can tell it is very expensive jewelry."

She could tell no such thing. A jeweler at Reeds Jewelers in Durham said it is impossible to tell the value of a piece of jewelry — or whether it is real — merely by looking at a picture. For all we know, the woman could have gotten the bracelets and rings from a Cracker Jack box or from some dude named Slick standing on the corner going, "Psst, wanna buy a genuine imitation diamond for $2?"

But even if that were the case, some people will demand that she refund the government that $2. Because they think poor people shouldn't get help. Or if they do, they should pay a high psychic price for it.

Believe me, they do. As a broke, busted and often disgusted college student who for a long time couldn't buy a job, I once applied for food stamps. The questions asked were so personal, the experience so humiliating, that by the time I was approved I said, "To hell with this."

But many people don't have that luxury and therefore must open up their lives to some bureaucrat who, for all we know, might obtain vicarious sexual pleasure by asking applicants, "Does your boyfriend ever spend the night at your crib?"

But most respondents to the story displayed no regard for such niceties as privacy rights for welfare recipients. If anything, the tone of their calls indicated they'd be inclined to say, "Why stop at jewelry? The woman also had on a dress, and in her kitchen was a blender, a microwave and a washing machine. Take that away, too."

Ronald Reagan became president by politically attacking so-called "welfare queens." The incivility he bred may lead some to attack them physically. If they do, the rallying cry of these new Minute Men would be, "Don't fire until you see the whites of their appliances."

June 02, 1997

Growth binge has price tag

Right now, the Triangle is the greatest place in America to live. So go ahead and congratulate yourself for having the good sense to settle here. But do it quickly.

Because it won't stay that way for long. A conversation I had with a Durham City Council member a couple of years ago illustrates why.

We were talking about undeveloped land along U.S. 15-501 between Durham and Chapel Hill, parcels that were coveted by national firms wanting a piece of our good thing.

Despite the high-tech, high-paying corporations vying for the land — and despite the objections of its own planning department, Chapel Hill officials and The N&O — the Durham City Council approved a bid by Home Depot and, eventually, Wal-Mart.

"Why Wal-Mart?" I incredulously asked my council pal.

"Got an election coming up, and that's about 300 jobs," he said, as if that explained everything.

Sadly, it did. It explains what happens when you have leaders who place short-term political gain over long-term civic progress.

Never mind that most of the jobs at Wal-Mart and the other stores at New Hope Commons are part-time service jobs and don't pay enough to raise a family on. And never mind, also, that the Triangle needs another discount mega-store shopping center like Dennis Rodman needs another tattoo.

I've got nothing personal against Wal-Mart. Heck, where do you think I get these trend-setting polyester jumpsuits? And I'm no tree-hugging, granola-munching, Birkenstock-wearing environmentalist who goes ga-ga at the sight of a duck-billed, yellow-bellied sapsucker.

But you don't have to be an environmental fanatic to object to what's happening to the Triangle.

This criticism is not aimed exclusively at Durham's leaders; Raleigh officials also have fallen prey to the "if you've got the money, honey, we've got the land" approach to development. I mean, just how badly does Raleigh need another grocery store or video store?

But the mess that motorists battle daily on 15-501 epitomizes the shortsightedness that will doom the Triangle to mediocrity or, worse, a Charlotte-like unlivability.

Just as I predicted in this space four years ago, rush hour on 15-501 between Durham and Chapel Hill now lasts from 7 a.m. to 7 p.m., and many motorists I talked with say they are filled with a sense of dread whenever they have to travel on it.

Instead of commercial edifices housing highly paid and high-paying captains of industry and commerce, the area is populated by nondescript chain stores in which the most common refrain is, "You want to try that in a size 7?"

We all laugh, and we should, at the neurotically snobbish way Cary officials try to restrict the types of businesses and buildings they allow in the town. But you have to respect the fact that they actually want to control growth instead of having the growth control them.

It's like the first time I met a bottle of wine. "Hmmm," I thought, "if a little bit makes me feel this good, a whole lot will make me blissful."

Raleigh and Durham officials are laboring under the same misapprehension regarding development. And just as my overindulgence did me, theirs will leave them — indeed the whole Triangle — with a helluva hangover.

June 05, 1997

Even when they're singing Dad's song, they're not

Hey guys, let's try an experiment. Tomorrow is Father's Day, right?

So about 8 a.m., I want everyone with a daddy to pick up the telephone and call him.

You know what's going to happen? You'll get through, that's what.

And that is the clearest example I can cite of the inequity of the two parental holidays.

Father's Day gets nowhere near the publicity and reverence that Mother's Day does. In the pantheon of major holidays, Father's Day is a baldheaded, snaggle-toothed stepchild. Just try calling mom at 8 a.m. on her special day.

"We're sorry. All circuits are busy. Please try your call later." That's the recorded message you'll hear before you finally make a connection.

But the fact that you'll actually be able to call your father on Father's Day with little trouble is not the only evidence of the day's — indeed fathers' — relative importance. Or lack thereof.

Political, religious and social leaders held a press conference earlier this week in Washington to proclaim fatherlessness "one of the greatest social evils of our generation," according to Wade Horn, president of the National Fatherhood Initiative.

The absence of positive father images in many children's lives is an indisputable tragedy. But so, too, is the absence of positive father images on television and radio. Since Heathcliff Huxtable and "The Cosby Show" bombed in syndication, that leaves Andy Taylor on "The Andy Griffith Show" as one of the very few fathers on TV who isn't a nincompoop.

Radio is even worse. Have you ever listened to the pop songs about mothers and compared them to the songs about dear ol' dad?

On Mother's Day, we are deluged with saccharine songs about how loving and caring mom is. Remember "I Want a Gal Just Like the Gal Who Married Dear Old Dad"? Fortunately for me, I don't, either.

My favorite of that "gee-ain't mom-wonderful" genre is "I'll Always Love My Mama," by The Intruders. I defy you to listen to your radio on Mother's Day without hearing 10 requests for it. And if the radio station plays the long version, you'll hear this dialogue:

"What about Pop?"

"We ain't talking about Pop. He was hanging out, drinking more wine than we used, coming home at 3 in the morning with lint balls all over him."

As if that patricidal musical tribute isn't bad enough in a song supposedly extolling mom's virtues, the most requested song on Father's Day is most likely the Temptations' "Papa Was a Rolling Stone." It talks about an absentee dad with "three outside children and another wife." Not exactly a Hallmark greeting card sentiment, eh?

"Daddy Could Swear, I Declare" by Gladys Knight & the Pips praised dad for, of all things, his ability to curse a blue streak. Wayne Newton's — yes, that Wayne Newton's — "Daddy Don't You Walk So Fast" was about a little girl chasing her fleeing daddy who was walking out on the family.

The overwhelming majority of dad songs are like that, about philandering, shiftless men. The number of songs about bad mamas is infinitesimal. Actually, I can't think of a single one.

Lest I give the impression that no dad songs extol patriarchal virtues, there are some — most notably The Winstons' "Color Him Father." It's a great dad song but, I confess, not a great song. That's probably why it usually makes everybody's "10 worst songs ever written" list. Indeed, it contains some excruciatingly trite lyrics:

"Never a frown, always a smile
When he says to me 'How is my child?'
I say 'I've been studying hard all day in school
Trying hard to understand the 'Golden Rule.'"

Most critics of the song, and they are legion, make two main observations: anyone who smiles all the time probably has a serious mental disorder, and how hard can it be to comprehend a rule that says "Treat others as you want them to treat you?"

Alas, even the song's hero, who marries a widow with seven young 'uns, is a stepdad.

Oh well. When you're a dad in late 20th century America, I guess you take whatever acknowledgment you can get.

June 14, 1997

The name of the game for arena

All kinds of suggestions are being put forth as a name for the sports arena that N.C. State's basketball team and the Carolina Hurricanes hockey team will share.

The Pork Palace and the Swine Shrine are two that come to mind. Those names, while probably offered humorously, would adequately acknowledge the source of the wealth of Wendell Murphy, the man most responsible for making the arena a reality.

But such names would do nothing for the dignity of the university.

Nor would another suggested name, one not offered humorously.

Jim Valvano.

Hey, wait a minute, now. You don't have to talk like that. I actually liked Valvano and was inspired by both his coaching style and his courageous fight with the cancer that eventually killed him. Indeed, I would have played for him at N.C. State — if I'd been younger and quicker and had a better jump shot.

Valvano was an original, and his players loved him — probably because he didn't make them go to class. But the reason his fans want to affix his name to the arena is because, dammit, he won.

Never mind that he didn't always follow the rules or keep winning in its proper perspective. He took the team, the university and the state on a magic carpet ride in 1983 and won a national championship against great odds.

But, in the process, he oversaw — only nominally, at that — a renegade program peopled by kids who were astoundingly unqualified to wear the title of "student-athletes." Of his 54 players at State, 26 had grade point averages of less than 1.5.

Yet, when the NCAA lowered the boom, placed the school on probation and fined it $400,000, Valvano parachuted to safety — with a $613,000 buyout from the university — and took a job at ABC Sports.

You know how they say the making of laws and sausages are two things you don't want to look at too closely? Well, at N.C. State during V's reign, you didn't want to look too closely at the making of a winning basketball program, either.

Unless your constitution is stronger than mine, it could've turned your stomach to see him exploit all those young black boys, many of whom got about as close to receiving a degree from State as I did — and I didn't even go there.

But any blame Valvano deserves must be shared by the parents of those kids, parents who each year turn what should be their most prized possessions — their kids — over to facile-tongued coaches promising stardom and riches. I doubt that any of them asked V about his graduation rate or about N.C. State's world-renowned engineering program.

Mainly, it appears, they wanted to know how many minutes per game Junior would get and what his pro prospects were.

Now, if we want to end the hypocrisy and admit that winning is everything, then the arena should bear Valvano's name. Jim's Gym. Etched in granite. But if winning with principles means anything — and really, are we ready to tell our kids it doesn't? — then it should be named after Les Robinson.

Robinson won no titles, but he is a sweetheart of a guy who restored some integrity to N.C. State's hoops program and required students to hit the books with an intensity approximating that with which they hit the backboards.

And how was he rewarded? He got kicked off the bench.

Come to think of it, maybe we have already told our kids that winning is everything.

June 23, 1997

$587 tribute to our consuming interest in celebrity

CHICAGO — I was strolling down Michigan Avenue's Magnificent Mile here last week, while the nation — well, actually just the news media — was still in a frenzy over fashion designer Gianni Versace's death.

Versace was probably a nice guy who may indeed have revolutionized and energized the fashion industry, as he is credited with doing. But does that make his enviable life and tragic death worth 16 pages in Time magazine?

No.

I strolled into Neiman Marcus, an upscale monument to conspicuous consumption, and approached a shoe-laden table with my favorite word on it: Clearance.

"Is it just me," I asked the fabulously turned out but snooty sales clerk, "or are these shoes the ugliest things you've ever seen?"

"It must be you," she replied haughtily, looking me up and down as though I were the ugliest thing she'd ever seen, "since people are buying them as soon as we put them out."

Hmmmm.

"Well, if they're selling so well, how come they're on the 'clearance' table?" I asked.

For a response, I had to content myself with her withering look, a look generally reserved for a cockroach crawling around in your last bowl of grits.

She turned from me to another customer so abruptly I feared the poor thing might get whiplash.

But it wasn't the ugly shoes or the uglier-acting sales clerk that had me reeling when I stumbled out of that store and others along the pricey downtown shopping strip.

No, what had me fearing that I really am unhip was the price of some of the designer clothes, and the eagerness of so many to pay it. Specifically, the price of the Versace clothes.

I had been fascinated — and repulsed at the same time — by news reports after Versace's death about how items bearing his name were "flying" out of stores, as consumers wanted to . . . well, hell . . . I don't know what they wanted to do. Some said they were buying anything with the Versace label as a tribute.

Bull. What sparked the rush had nothing to do with tributes. It was the same thing that fuels much of what the public does: celebrity and a desire, a need even, to touch celebrity and feel — if only for the time we have on a $2,500 Versace suit — as though we, too, are connected to celebrity, however tenuously.

I guarantee you that some of the same people who insisted that their post-mortem purchases were somehow a tribute to Versace would be bestowing the same dubious "tribute" upon Andrew Cunanan if that murderer had come out with a clothing line bearing his name.

But I really wanted to be hip, so I counted up the discretionary income in my pockets — 40 bucks — and figured I'd pick up something by Versace, merely as a conversation piece, you understand.

I figured wrong. Veteran shoppers know how much — actually, how little — Versace you can get with $40.

By my reckoning, for $40 I could afford a button on one of the Versace shirts on sale at Saks Fifth Avenue.

It was a nice-enough shirt, but the only way I could envision it costing as much as it did — $587 — was if Elvis his ownself had worn it while performing "All Shook Up."

But more outlandish than the price of that shirt — or of a $200 Donna Karan T-shirt I saw — was the statement by Miami Beach Police Chief Richard Barreto moments after Cunanan's suicide had been confirmed.

"The nation can stand down," he said, as though the whole country had been walking around tensed up for its inevitable encounter with Cunanan.

As hard as it may be for Chief Barreto and the media to believe, most Americans were not walking around fearing Cunanan.

Clem: Lem, would you go see who that is at the do'?

Lem: No sirree. Could be that Cunanan fella.

Of course, a media-inflamed fever overtook some people who claimed they saw Cunanan in a South Dakota Wal-Mart or a Greensboro Burger King, but most people I know viewed the whole episode as a tragedy, yes — but also as a soap opera with about as much relationship to real life as, well . . . a $200 T-shirt.

July 26, 1997

Creaking toward the big Four-Oh

This is definitely not how I envisioned turning 40.

Relax. I'm not having a midlife crisis in which I want to go out and buy a red 'Vette, get a toupee and play "house" with a 22-year-old aerobics instructor named Vicki.

Lord knows, I didn't expect to find any fountain of youth at 40, but I did expect to be able to get out of bed without going "OHHHH!" and hearing my joints creak like a rusty door hinge.

But that is precisely what I have found as I stand here knocking on the door to 40, a door that'll open in about two weeks.

By 40, every man should have learned a thing or two. (And really, I wouldn't put the number above that.) What I've learned is that charm and a winning smile — qualities that can carry you a long way in your 20s — are no longer negotiable currency.

It's not as though old age snuck up on me. A couple of years ago, I was frightened by the reflection in a store window of a hobbling old man on a cane: The old man, to my horror, turned out to be me.

But the injury that hobbled me then was incurred honorably — on a basketball court. The one that has me limping and groaning now was incurred by, I swear, simply getting out of bed.

Like most men, I can heroically bear injuries sustained playing ball, rescuing children from burning buildings or being thrown off the stage by a bouncer at the 14 Karat Dinner Theater. Certain bragging rights accompany injuries incurred thusly. But how do you boast about pulling a hamstring when all you were doing was going to the fridge to get your son some ice cream? Especially when, by the time you got to the kitchen, you'd forgotten what you went there for anyway?

One writer described 40 as the age when you wake up and realize that the people you went to school with are running the country. Or, to quote one of those whining dudes on the dreadful television show "thirtysomething," it's the age where you realize you're invisible to teenage girls.

(I don't care about that, because it's their mamas I was always more interested in anyway.)

A deteriorating memory and body aren't the only things those of us approaching 40 have to look forward to. Here are some other things we can now kiss goodbye: Being called upon to pinch-hit for Ken Griffey in the World Series, playing bass for Van Halen or hearing Tyra Banks purr, "Baby, is this bikini too small?" Except when we dream, which is something we'll do a lot of because we're always tired and sleepy.

The thing that makes me want to stay in bed — even when I am physically able to get out of it — is realizing that I am now older than Dr. Martin Luther King Jr. was when he was killed, and knowing that no one will ever give me a Nobel Peace Prize or name a holiday after me.

It's not comforting to reach 40 and admit, even to yourself, that you peaked at age 12, when you won Mrs. Robinson's sixth-grade spelling bee at Leak Street School in Rockingham. And they don't put your face on a stamp for that, hoss.

You know that fabulous Willie Nelson song called "My Heroes Have Always Been Cowboys"? Well, at 40, you don't just hear it — you feel it, too — when ol' Willie laments a wasted lifetime spent "pickin' up hookers/ instead of my pen, I let the words to my youth fade away."

Aw, what the heck. Maybe I will buy me a red 'Vette.

July 28, 1997

Revenge is a dish best eaten cold

How insensitive of me. Remember last year when I said I hoped everybody who got food stamps they didn't deserve after Hurricane Fran choked on a neckbone sandwich?

Well, I take it all back. Fact is, I hope y'all enjoyed those T-bone steaks, expensive cheeses and yuppie cereals you bought with those purloined stamps.

Because that's not what they serve in the county jail, which is where some of you could soon be taking your meals.

Proving once again that there is no such thing as a free lunch — or breakfast or dinner, for that matter — the state Division of Social

Services is making noises about nailing people who took food stamps to which they were not entitled.

I couldn't reach Kevin FitzGerald, director of the Division of Social Services, on the telephone Wednesday, but in recent N&O stories, he addressed the possibility of food stamp fraud. "We take this very seriously," he said. "We won't tolerate people taking advantage of our taxpayers in the wake of a natural disaster. ... If we find that fraud has occurred, it will be dealt with very seriously."

If I may, I'd like to express my jubilation at that prospect in song. Maestro, hit it:

You're going to jail
They're cleaning out your cell
Don't ask me to go your bail
'cos you're going to jail.
If you were truly hungry and
Wanted something to eat
You could've just called me —
I'd have gave you some pig's feet.
But you had to go and be greedy
You took all that you could get
So now it looks like that could be
The most expensive meal you've et.
Na na na na na.

Now I understand why people got so angry at me and accorded me all the respect you'd give ... well ... a wet food stamp when I wrote disapprovingly last fall of those who gouged the gubmint. They knew their actions were indefensible, and my insightful comments — unlike their ill-gotten groceries — were hard to digest.

I wrote in September of an RTP—employed couple that together earns more than $100,000, yet the wife stood in line for three hours to get $427 in food stamps. And actually boasted about her big score!

But the state isn't relying on anecdotal evidence. Just a small sample of the 95,000 people who received emergency aid shows that 47 percent of them understated their income.

Many of the people with their hands out, I'm sure, were loyal Republicans who begrudge the poor any thin dime of assistance. Yet, they apparently put their consciences in the freezer — right next to their purloined groceries — when it was time to receive a handout they knew they didn't deserve.

That's shameful. If anybody had a right to feel wronged by Fran's wrath, it was me. Why, I'll bet I lost $500 — well, maybe not $500 — worth of fish sticks and barnyard pimp wings when my electricity stayed off for six days. But did you see me standing in line, trying to take advantage of my government, taking food from the mouths of people who truly needed assistance?

No.

Being the open-minded dude I am, I'll acknowledge the possibility that some people who understated their income may not have known just how much they earn. I just hope those people get a judge who's as open-minded as I am.

On second thought, I hope not.

July 31, 1997

Readers find whine not so fine

OK, maybe you're right. Perhaps I did overstate matters a bit when I wrote that "woe-is-me-I'm-'bout-to-turn-40" diatribe last week.

But really, was that any reason for y'all to come down so hard on me? Here are a few of the unkind responses to that column:

"Why don't you stop whining?" one woman e-mailed from Raleigh. "At least you're still alive. ... Try being a single, black woman over 30 looking for a husband. That's like being dead while you're still alive."

Or this telephone call: "Wait until you're 80, like I am, and then tell me about creaking, aching bones."

Or how about this one: "What? You're 40 and you don't want a 22-year-old aerobics instructor? You really are over the hill."

I also heard from a dude — I have forgotten his age — who said he dealt with his midlife crisis precisely the way I said I didn't want to. He went out and found a much younger woman and bought a red Porsche. "Neither," he concluded, "was worth the trouble."

My favorite response, though, came from a man in Raleigh who saw me on television: "I don't believe you're only 40. How did you get that ugly in just 40 years?"

That might be the second-greatest line on aging I've ever heard. The first was muttered by comedian Milton Berle, who lamented that, "It now takes me all night to do what I used to could do all night." Ba-dum.

True, there are certain obvious things you lose as you get older: the ability to party till sunup; the stamina to play three full-court games of basketball in an unventilated gym without fearing you're going to drop dead; and the ability to watch reruns of "The Three Stooges." This will strike some men as heresy, but I don't find the dudes as amusing now as I did when I was 9 and stopped by Jeffrey Robinson's house each morning before school for my daily fix.

Without getting too melodramatic here, I knew middle age was imminent the first time I channel-surfed past Larry, Curly and Moe (and the
underappreciated Shemp) without stopping.

But to me, the greatest loss I've incurred as an adult is the loss of
trust. Hate to sound misanthropic, folks, but it seems that the more you
know about people, the less you want to know. I could be wrong, of
course, and maybe it's just the quality of some of the people I know. But
in the past year and a half, I've loaned I don't know how much money to
distressed "friends" to prevent them from losing their homes or worse.
I've also loaned countless tools — and even two lawn mowers. Little of
the money has been repaid, and few of the tools — and neither of the
mowers — have been returned, despite requests and threats. I guess
that ancient philosopher was right: A fool and his tools are soon parted.

I'm not telling you this to show what a great guy I am: I'm not a
great guy, and I can provide signed, unsolicited testimonials to back me
up on that. I'm telling you only to show what has caused my faith in
humankind to plummet.

Lest I give the impression that there is nothing good about turning
40, let me assure you there is. The best benefit was cited by a reader
named Dean who turned 40 last week. He wrote, "At least we'll no
longer be associated with those narcissistic whiners on that TV show
"thirtysomething."

Amen.

August 04, 1997

Why should anyone help Don King promote himself?

I'm not going to lie to you. At first, I thought it was just me. But
then, I talked to Flora Garrett and realized, no, I am not losing my mind
just because I can't figure out why the NAACP and various other civil
rights organizations are treating boxing promoter Don King like he was
the Rev. Martin Luther King Jr.

Someone must have confused the two Kings, because in the past
month Don King has received the NAACP's highest award, as well as
honors from the Southern Christian Leadership Conference, Operation
PUSH and the National Council of Negro Women.

What Flora Garrett wants to know — and I do, too — is what the hell
has Don King done to merit a humanitarian award? Indeed, Garrett
would take it even further: She would question what King has done to
merit being called "human."

Because, she said, he certainly wasn't human that April night in 1966 when he stomped and kicked her husband to death.

"The man is a monster," Garrett told me in a telephone interview from her Cleveland apartment. "He is vicious . . . and doesn't care about anything but money and himself."

King has successfully reinvented himself as a grandiloquent, fun-loving jokemeister, but Flora Garrett said neither the old King or the new one has ever even called her to apologize for depriving her of her husband and her daughters of their daddy.

Don King killed Sam Garrett over a gambling debt. Some people say it was $500, some say it was more, others less.

Flora Garrett neither knows nor cares how much it was.

"My husband owed him some money, yes. If it was a dime or millions, you don't take a person's life for it," she said.

King served his own debt — just over four years in prison — and proceeded to climb to the top of the slag heap that is professional boxing.

Far from hindering him in that nefarious world, I'm betting his manslaughter conviction has actually proven to be an asset: King has left in his wake many broken and broke boxers who, aware of his violent past, probably figured they'd split with at least their health.

Certainly his conviction for killing Garrett, who, his widow said, was sickly and suffered from tuberculosis, has added to King's legacy and figures to be a prominent feature in a rumored movie on King's life. Actually, Garrett was the second man killed by King: 12 years earlier, he had shot and killed a man trying to rob one of his gambling houses. Police ruled that one justifiable homicide.

Some people, sadly, seem willing to justify anything King does — as long as he loosens his purse strings enough. I mean, how else can you explain this rush by the nation's premier black organizations to defend a predator like King? How else to explain what the hell NAACP President Kweisi Mfume was talking about when he likened Don King to Jackie Robinson?

I am not questioning King's right to make a living. The dude served his time, piddling though it was, and deserves the opportunity to ply whatever legal trade he wishes. Indeed, if you want to admire King's chutzpah in becoming the most successful promoter in boxing history, fine. If, even, you want to honor him as an entrepreneur, that too is deserved.

But there is no rational explanation for the NAACP to bestow its President's Award on Don King, or for the National Council of Negro Women to name him its Humanitarian of the Year or the SCLC to give him its Drum Major for Justice Award. (I wonder what Martin Luther King Jr. would say about that one?)

Anyone who thinks Don King is receiving these awards mere months before he stands trial again for an insurance fraud case probably also thinks it was mere coincidence that the National Baptist Convention gave King its highest spiritual honor — the Cross and Crown Humanitarian Award — soon after Mike Tyson offered the group $5 million to build its new headquarters.

I tell you what: I hope Mfume, Jesse Jackson and the leaders of the other organizations received a lot of moolah from King, because it will take a lot to clean this stain from their reputations.

The best thing one can say about these organizations is that they have been had. The worst thing you can say is that they have been bought.

August 09, 1997

Next time, they'll know better

When it came out in court testimony last week that Joseph and Dorothy Hutelmyer had not had sex since 1992, my first question was, "Hey, you mean I'm not the only one?"

But when Dorothy Hutelmyer's attorney nonetheless described their union as "a storybook marriage," the next question I asked was, "What kind of books has this dude been reading — science fiction?"

What attorney James Walker meant, though, was that although the Hutelmyers hadn't known each other in a biblical sense since the Bush presidency, Joseph had been knowing his secretary, Margie Cox, since 1994. And that knowledge is what persuaded an Alamance County jury to order Margie Cox — now Margie Cox Hutelmyer — to pay Dorothy $1 million for stealing Joseph's affections and thus changing the storyline in the Hutelmyers' book of love.

I tell you what: At those prices, I hope they knew each other well.

I don't know how y'all feel, but this absurd law has me so angry I can hardly see straight. Not because it portrays the man as some spineless twit who was overpowered by the feminine wiles of a shameless hussy. No, I'm upset because I didn't know about the law when some slick-talking joker made off with my first fiancé several years ago.

If I had, I might've sued, too. I was already broke — that's why she left me — and a million bucks would've come in really handy. If nothing else, it would've allowed me to drown my sorrows with a higher quality of booze.

Instead, I used to sit around pickling my innards with the cheapest firewater I could afford and listening to every sad country song I could find, plotting a suitable revenge for the low-down, egg-sucking snake who stole my beloved Cynthia from me.

But three things prevented me from acting on any of my dastardly plans: I couldn't think of anything bad enough to do to him, the Bible says vengeance belongeth to the Lord and, most important, she gained about 50 pounds and got real ugly.

After that, I wanted to give the soldier boy $1 million for stepping up and taking that bullet for me. But alas, he'll have to be satisfied with my eternal gratitude. And deepest sympathy.

I also have some sympathy for Joseph Hutelmyer. Although the jury's ruling makes it seem that he has no culpability in this menage-a-mess, he now finds himself in an impossible situation: No matter what he does, he's going to have a hard time living up to the price Margie must pay for him.

After a year or two of waking up to "Look man, I paid a million bucks for you. The least you can do is (take out the trash, pick up behind yourself, fix those shutters)," he may yearn for the relative serenity of a marriage in which he and his wife don't know each other.

Speaking of Dorothy Hutelmyer, she denies vengeance motivated her to sue the woman who alienated her husband's affections. Asked why she sued "the other woman" and not her two-timing husband, Dorothy cited her religious beliefs.

"Because that woman sinned."

Oh, well. I guess John and Paul were wrong. Not John and Paul the apostles — the Beatles. When they wrote "All you need is love," they hadn't read the Book of Dorothy, which says, "Yeah, but cash helps."

August 11, 1997

'Education' really isn't a dirty word

You know those Durham parents who don't want sex education taught to their children in school? Well, I'm with them.

No, really, I am. Let's take sex ed out of the classroom and keep it in the poolroom — which is where I mislearned everything I don't know from a couple of brothers named Money and Joe Willie. Why should today's teens and prepubescent playground-dwellers be better informed than I was? Let 'em walk around as ignorant as my pals and I were.

I applaud the state for requiring that any school sex ed program stress abstinence. That's what we should be stressing. But despite our best efforts — and our worst, such as telling them premarital sex will make you go blind — not all of them will resist temptation. And as much as we might want our little tax deductions to abstain until they're old enough — or even too old, in some cases — they still need to be armed with knowledge about contraception, abortion and other things some of you can't say even to yourselves.

Not only that, but sexuality for today's children is far more complicated than it was for us. Think about it: Just as there were only four food groups, there were only two sexes — male and female. Today's kids could burn up tons of brain cells just trying to figure out what the hell Dennis Rodman is.

As a parent my ownself, I can understand the parental reticence about having one's adolescent offspring exposed to too much too fast. I mean, I don't want my boy at 8 years old coming home telling me about the joys of S&M or of sky-diving nude into a vat of low-fat tapioca pudding — not that there's anything wrong with that, if that's your thing and you're old enough to afford your own parachute.

But I see nothing wrong with teachers talking responsibly to kids about pregnancy, contraception and abortion. Indeed, I see everything right with it, especially when many of the most vociferous opponents of comprehensive sex ed probably answer their kids' normal curiosity with a backhand, or with, "Go ask your mama."

Still, let the parents have a say. Under the current system in Durham's public schools, students are given consent (lack of consent?) slips that parents must sign to prevent their kids from being taught about such things as contraceptive use. Students who don't return the forms are permitted to learn everything possible about the birds and bees.

Problems arise, predictably, because many parents say they never see the forms and thus can't make a decision for or against their children's participation.

I could be wrong — which we all know is quite unlikely — but why don't the geniuses at Durham Public Schools dictate that students not be allowed to participate if they don't return the slips?

True story: Several years ago, when I was a teen counselor for 4-H camp in Rockingham, I overheard some 9- and 10-year-old campers discussing — as 9- and 10-year-old campers are wont to do — where babies come from. Not one of them, I'm proud to report, mentioned a stork. But one did boldly hypothesize that a Barry White cassette and a six-pack were essential to the process. His "knowledge," I'm guessing, came from overhearing his dad.

Or Joe Willie.

August 14, 1997

The spell of Sweet Baby James

Usually, I'd rather pick the jam from between Mickey Rourke's toes than listen to a remake of a classic song.

But when James Taylor did his version of the Drifters' "Up On The Roof" at Walnut Creek the other night, all I wanted to do was find me a roof to climb up on. Not so I could jump off and kill myself — as I'd want to do if, say, Michael Bolton did that same song — but so I could experience the tranquility that Taylor makes sound so darned accessible in his songs.

Taylor's music epitomizes what life in North Carolina should be — soothing, guileless and, to use a word from the '70s, "mellow."

Am I the only one who has experienced this? While in some other part of the country, you mention you're from North Carolina and are greeted by a look of scorn or pity, followed by, "That's where Jesse Helms is from, isn't it?"

My response — or the only one that can be printed here — is often, "Yeah, but it's also where James Taylor is from." So there.

Stop me before I get all mystical here, but when I was standing beneath the glittering stars listening to Taylor, with a bucket of chicken in one hand and a good pal standing beside me, I actually felt a chill run through me. And it had nothing to do with the weather.

Indeed, I wanted to turn to the people standing around me at that moment and say, "Y'know, it doesn't get any better than this." I resisted the temptation to do so, though — not just because some beer company already has spoiled that line, but because one look at everyone's face told me they felt as I did.

That was especially true when this brother named Arnold McCuller — remember that name — joined Taylor on "Shower the People" with a voice so beautiful it had everyone wishing the song had lasted 10 minutes more.

I don't know about the other 20,000 people who were at the concert, but the whole next day I drove around singing, "Shower the people you love with love." Let me tell you, that is a wonderful sentiment even when expressed by a voice as bad as mine.

When Taylor sang "Carolina in My Mind," it became possible to forget for three minutes all the superfluous megastores and prefabricated apartment complexes that threaten to turn the Triangle into Charlotte.

Several years ago, when I was serving a 6 1/2-year sentence at a newspaper in Indiana, it was that song that helped me survive the Midwest's brutal winters. Just about every morning, before I'd go out to shovel snow off my car — often in June — I'd crank up the old

Victrola and play "Carolina in My Mind." Call me crazy, but I'd swear it had a therapeutic effect on me then, and on people at The Creek the other night.

On the highway and exit ramp leading to the amphitheater, my buddy Tony and I watched sadly as angry, inconsiderate drivers tailgated or drove straight to the front of a long line and cut in, giving one-finger salutes to anyone who impeded their date with J.T.

After the show, though, the karma in the cars changed. While leaving, we marveled at how patiently people waited — if they waited at all, because other motorists smilingly waved them into the driving lanes.

They seemed — and here's that word again — mellow. Why, I halfway expected the guy who waved us in to say, "Have a nice day." Have a nice day.

August 28, 1997

Public to blame for Diana, too

You know how some people are blaming the news media for Princess Diana's death? And how even some journalists are engaging in self-flagellation in seeking to ascribe blame?

Well, include me out. I'm not buying it.

I do agree with Diana's grief-stricken brother, who said, "Every proprietor and editor [who paid millions for intrusive pictures of the woman] has blood on his hands today."

The swinish picture-takers — paparazzi seems too dignified a word for them — contributed mightily to the accident that killed her by shoving cameras in her face every place she went and turning her whole life into a "photo op." Her chauffeur reportedly was fleeing rowdy photographers — I prefer to call them stalkers with cameras — when he lost control of the car.

But if you really want to know who contributed to her death, I'll tell you: Y'all did.

Yup, if you ever bought one of those ridiculous tabloid newspapers you see at the grocery store checkout line featuring salacious stories on every aspect of Diana's — or any other famous person's — life, you bear some responsibility.

I have, a time or two, picked up one of those pseudo-newspapers while waiting to pay for my Cap'n Crunch, but only to read about a two-headed pig or about some woman who was impregnated by Elvis' ghost.

I couldn't have cared less about Diana and Dodi Fayed or their private life, and I made it a point to skip over stories about their love life — as I hope they would have done with stories about mine. But someone was buying those papers, thus feeding the beast that led photographers to chase Diana's car and then to jump out and snap pictures of it and her after the fatal crash.

Some of my friends are photographers, but I admit that when I heard that bystanders in Paris had attacked the ghoulish ones who snapped pictures of the mortally wounded Diana without trying to help her, my first response was "Good!"

My second response was "Great!"

But if you think attacks — physical or otherwise — on a few photographers are going to cause them to be more respectful of the living or the dead or to become more circumspect about the havoc they're wreaking in people's lives, you must be dreaming.

If anything, it could lead to a whole new genre of checkbook journalism.

Photographer: Hey boss, how much will you pay for a photo of Madonna locked in a fiery embrace with her new lover?

Editor: Ah, that's old news. But I'll pay you a million squid if you get me a picture of her locked in a fiery car.

I'm not going to overstate the global implications of Diana's death. Truth be told, there were none. Like so many people, she was essentially famous for being famous.

But to her credit, she used her fame — she was probably the second-most-recognizable person on Earth — to focus attention on serious, overlooked issues: AIDS before it became a "sexy" issue, battered women and, most recently, land mines in Bosnia and Angola.

That's far more admirable, don't you think, than the way the single most recognizable person on Earth uses his — to play golf with Bugs Bunny and to sell everything from underwear to overpriced sneakers?

September 01, 1997

Hizzoner's painful chore

When it comes to spankings, my philosophy is taken straight from the Bible: "'Tis way more blessed to give than to receive."

I think I'm a hip, swinging dude — although the fact that I still say "hip" and "swinging" probably means that I am neither — but I just can't understand the thrill some folks derive from sadism, masochism and humiliation.

Oh, hundreds of women have hit me and called me out of my name, but not one did so with the intention of giving me pleasure. And those whippings I received from my Aunt Jennie in Rockingham and the almost daily schoolyard humiliations? They are still vivid, and neither memory conjures pleasurable images.

But that's me. If just the thought of a knotted cat-o'-nine-tails whistling through the air sends you into paroxysms of delight — or if you get all tingly inside from crawling on all fours while a woman in leather and studs refers to you as "loathsome goat vomit unworthy of death" — boy, have I got a place for you. If, that is, our moralizing mayor would just sit down and shut up.

Two women, known professionally as Delilah and Diana, want to open an establishment in Raleigh for people who wish to be dominated and humiliated. The club, the name of which I don't know — I'm partial to "The Whipping Post" or "The Beaten Path: Where Your Pain Is Our Pleasure" — will let people experience the joy of corporal punishment in the discomfort of their parlor.

The proposed pain palace, no matter what you personally think of it, is perfectly legal. I missed that particular civics class, but I'm sure the U.S. Constitution guarantees "life, liberty and the right to wear a dog collar."

But that won't deter Mayor Tom Fetzer of Raleigh. Sensing votes from people as closed-minded as he is, Fetzer plans to use the whipping business as a whipping boy, Constitution be damned. "No chance. ... Dead on arrival," he said of the proposal, trying to sound forceful but sounding like a petulant schoolboy instead.

If Delilah and Diana — known in Sunday school and elsewhere as J.B. Popplewell and Patty King — were planning to go out on Triangle streets and snatch people at random — "C'mere. You look like you've been bad" — then Fetzer would make sense.

But as I understand it — and slap me if I'm wrong — people desiring a hand from Diana and Delilah would have to ask for it.

Actually, they'd have to beg for it. At least that's what the voice mail of the woman I called two days ago said. Mistress Alexis, a dominatrix whose phone number I got from the back of a local weekly newspaper, said she is "once again accepting pleas from sincere submissives."

I left several messages, at $2 a minute, but she hadn't called back when I began writing this. Guess I didn't sound submissive enough.

Since Fetzer has obviously mastered this mayor thing to the point where he can do it with one hand (or maybe both) tied behind his back, perhaps he now wishes to enter the advice-column business. Good, because if he's going to tell adults how they can't get their kicks, he'd darn well better be prepared to tell them how they can.

Indeed, Triangle residents concerned that their pleasures are violating the Mayor of Love's moral code should just write and ask. (Dear Mayor of Love: My wife only gets amorous while munching red M&Ms and humming the theme to "The Rocky & Bullwinkle Show." Is that immoral?)

September 04, 1997

The offense was real, so why not real punishment?

Poet Maya Angelou is a bad lady. For those of you who didn't come of age in the 1960s, "bad" means good.

But when I saw Angelou recently at the N.C. Black Press Association awards banquet in Chapel Hill, I wanted to tell her how dangerous, misguided — how downright wrong — she was in that beautiful eulogy she gave for Betty Shabazz, Malcolm X's widow.

Shabazz died June 23 of injuries she suffered when her angry 12-year-old grandson set fire to the apartment he reluctantly shared with her. Turns out the kid wanted to stay in Texas where he could hang out with his homies and indifferent mother, not in New York with his strict grandmother.

But in eulogizing Shabazz, Angelou, who is usually right about so many things, sought to portray young Malcolm Shabazz as the victim, not the perpetrator. Don't be angry with him, she urged: He needs protection and nurturing.

Maybe so, Maya, but he also needs an ass-whipping.

Oops. That thought reflexively and instinctively popped into my head, where it had remained until now: I figured mine was a decidedly and dangerously minority viewpoint which would be better kept to myself.

But I recently read an interview with college professor Michael Eric Dyson — and before that, a column by writer Bill Maxwell — in which they said pretty much the same thing. Albeit, I confess, more eloquently than I.

What Maxwell, Dyson and I are all saying in different ways is that some black men have gotten off too easy too long and have not been held accountable for their actions.

Of Angelou's funeral speech, Maxwell wrote, "Instead of so easily forgiving them, black people — especially black women — must start forcing our males to grow up . . . to accept responsibility for their actions."

Let me ask you something: How is someone like Malcolm Shabazz going to learn to accept responsibility for his actions if he's hearing people portray him as a victim even as his grandmother's charred body lies smoldering in the church? Indeed, why should he?

Dyson, in the Independent weekly in Durham, called Betty Shabazz's death at the hands of her grandson a "powerful metaphor and symbol of the lack of memory among black folk(.) . . . Had he an appreciation for this woman's grandeur and merit, could he have struck the match?"

The answer, of course, is hell no.

Don't get me wrong, now. I understand how some of us feel so protective of brothers who are, unfortunately, national scapegoats for just about every social ill. But denying that some black dudes are just plain sorry and not worth defending is, ultimately, self-defeating. (And admitting it doesn't make me an Uncle Tom, so don't call me with that jive.)

There are less-tragic instances each day of blacks overlooking the foibles of black men because of the very real hardships we endure. But that willingness to suspend blame and make excuses for anti-social behavior can be taken to extremes, as is being done by a female friend of mine who told me she stays with her abusive boyfriend because he catches hell "from those white folks on his job . . . He needs me."

Wrong. He needs the same thing Malcolm Shabazz needs. And she needs a bus ticket to anywhere that creep isn't.

An incident I experienced recently provides another example of black men's misbehavin' being rewarded or excused.

My car window was broken out. All signs and eyewitnesses pointed to the retromingent, vile-smelling boyfriend of a young lady in whom I had expressed the most casual — and to my way of thinking brotherly — interest. No, really. (Don't look at me like that).

But did she rebuke him or distance herself from this vandalizing punk? Fuhgeddaboutit. His act, she said, was just his way of showing his love. Say what?

I am in no way equating my broken car window to the death of the woman Dyson called "one of the mothers of the black liberation struggle." But when we can, with a straight face, portray either of those acts as "love" or the actions of a "victim," we are in trouble. And that's really bad.

September 06, 1997

Justice must be a gymnast

I'll admit that I am not a lawyer, although in my younger years I logged enough time in courtrooms to qualify for the bar in some states.

Of course, I was usually standing humbly before a black-robed dude and saying something like, "I swear, Your Honor, I thought she was 18."

But I didn't have to be a lawyer to be aware even then of something criminal defendants call "po' time." That's the time — usually heavy —

behind bars that judges give to guys who aren't rich or white-collar.

Now, don't confuse po' time with "Poe time," which is what Superior Court Judge "Let 'em Go" Orlando Hudson gave to W. Alex Poe last week in Raleigh.

Judge Hudson, fooled by Poe's calculatedly manipulative attempt to pay back some of the $342,000 he stole from the Greater Raleigh Chamber of Commerce, levied an infuriatingly light sentence: Six to eight months. On work release. Unbelievable. Disgusting.

In addition, Poe has to continue paying the Chamber back only as long as he is on work release. Thus, if he gets a minimum-wage job at his wife's high-class steak house and tavern saying, "Would you prefer another olive in your extra-dry martini?" the $2 or so he contributes each week for six to eight months will legally satisfy the judge.

But it won't satisfy me, nor should it you.

I am not a heartless grinch, and if Poe had an ill relative and stole the money during a moment of stress-induced weakness so he could buy a hospital in the Bahamas, I might have some sympathy for him. But this was no one-time lapse in conscience.

No, Poe's thievery was systematic — over several years — and inspired by pure greed.

But don't blame Poe for accepting the puny sentence. Heck, what was he supposed to say — "No really, Judge, you're too kind"?

You should wonder, though, about the prosecutor in the case, Assistant District Attorney Howard Cummings. Chamber representatives met with Cummings and told him they wanted Poe to do some time, but when Cummings presented sentencing suggestions to Hudson, he said only that they wanted Poe punished. (Duh!)

Sounding for all the world like Hamilton Burger, Perry Mason's perpetually bested courtroom rival, Cummings said, "If they had asked for something specific, I would have asked for something specific."

Huh? So now prosecutors need to be told that violating the public confidence and stealing $342,000 merits severe punishment?

You know how they say "Justice is blind"? Well, she is also a gymnast. Because in this case, the old girl has bent over backward and sideways to ensure that Poe experiences minimal discomfiture.

Even after the theft was discovered, Poe never went to jail, because the prosecutor said at the time that he wanted to wait until an audit was completed so he would know exactly how much was stolen.

Crapola. They knew he stole something. Forget how much. Toss his butt in the slammer — he could've easily made bail — and then tally up the damage.

Remember that old song called "I Want a Gal (Just Like the Gal

Who Married Dear Old Dad)"?

Defendants appearing in Wake Superior Court will be crooning an updated version of that one, titled "I Want a Judge Just Like the Judge (Who Sentenced Dear Old Alex Poe)."

September 15, 1997

All's fair with love at the fair

Sandie Martin is a lot like me. We both can recall experiencing a warm, tingly feeling while at the N.C. State Fair.

Mine, unfortunately, came from eating too much cotton candy and barbecue. Hers came from meeting her dream man, the one with whom she intends to spend the rest of her life.

Martin met her husband, David, at the fair five years ago. They were standing in line at the Marlboro cigarette booth for a free pack of smokes when they got more than a cigarette: They got a match.

They got married three months later, on Jan. 1, but Sandie Martin still sounds positively giddy when she talks about meeting her husband.

"There was this gentleman standing there in blue jeans and a plaid shirt, and I thought he was cute. ... We started a conversation, and he asked if I was married. I told him I was divorced with three children. When he asked if he could call me, I asked him, 'How do I know you're not a serial killer?' He asked me, 'How do I know you're not one?'

"He said he would call me at 6 o'clock, and he called at exactly 6. I almost broke my neck trying to get to the phone before he hung up," she recalled.

He didn't hang up, and the spark that started in a cigarette line is still burning.

Now, anyone who knows me knows that I have been kicked in the butt by love — or something dressed up like love — many times. But hearing the sheer joy in Sandie Martin's voice as she talks about the man she met while surrounded by powdered elephant ears, stuffed animals and amusement park rides is enough to make even me think about going back to the fair. Almost.

In an age in which men are constantly derided as insensitive louts and advances in cloning technology threaten to make us obsolete, it is refreshing to hear a wife say this about her husband: "I just think he's wonderful, a gift from God. He is everything in a man I could ever want. There is absolutely nothing about him I would change. And I still think he's cute."

(I almost got a Valentine's Day card saying those exact same things about me. But I wasn't willing to spend that much for a card.)

I talked to Sandie Martin on Wednesday, an hour or so before she and David headed for the fairgrounds. Only this time, the Wendell couple wasn't looking for the Marlboro booth. They were looking for a chapel so they could take their vows again.

I realize there is nothing terribly novel about people getting married at the fair or in other unusual places. We've all seen on the evening news people being married while jumping out of airplanes, on motorcycles and even at the Church of Elvis in Las Vegas. Such vows are usually exchanged merely as publicity stunts precisely to get on the evening news, and I'll bet they're in trouble before the parachute opens.

But to the Martins, renewing their vows at the place where they met is no gimmick. Indeed, when Martin called me, she was merely trying to find out whether they could renew their vows there, not seeking a story.

"I'm not getting on any Ferris wheel or anything," Sandie said. "I want to stay on the ground. ... We want to renew our vows at the same place we met and see if we can do it another five years."

October 23, 1997

Air Jordan grounded by foot trouble? That's UnNikely

Come on now. Y'all didn't really expect Michael Jordan to miss that game at the Dean Dome in Chapel Hill on Friday night, did you?

I doubted, even before he said his hobbled feet were miraculously healed, that he would sit out the meaningless exhibition game.

How'd I know? Was it because of Jordan's legendary competitive-ness?

Or does he so love his alma mater and home state that he couldn't bear to disappoint fans who'd shelled out as much as $100 for a ticket? Could it have been his special way of paying homage to his college coach, the recently retired Dean Smith?

Get real. I can sum up in two words, four if pressed, why I think Jordan changed his mind and decided to limp onto the court: "Phil Knight." The other two are "Nike stock."

Those are, unfortunately, the same words that dictate Jordan's every action and inaction, why he has been afraid not only to speak out on any issue more complicated than a jump shot, but also why he won't even tacitly support any issue that might cause someone to dislike him or, Heaven forbid, leave one of the myriad items he hawks on the store shelf.

— When Jordan was approached in 1990 about supporting Democrat

Harvey Gantt's U.S. Senate campaign against Republican Sen. Jesse Helms, Jordan demurred, saying "Republicans buy gym shoes, too."

— Earlier this year, Jordan donated $1 million to UNC-Chapel Hill's School of Social Work after refusing to give a nickel to the campus' fledgling Black Cultural Center. "I want to give to something that will help everybody, not just one group," he said, betraying shameful ignorance about the BCC's mission. Which is to educate everyone, not just one group.

Jordan is undeniably the greatest basketball player to ever lace up a pair of overpriced sneakers, but I'm beginning to wonder if the dude can even say "Good morning" to his wife without Phil Knight's permission.

Mike: Uh Phil, I just woke up and was wondering if I could roll over and say "Good morning" to my wife.

Knight: Gee Mike, I don't know. Didn't you speak to her yesterday? You know we've got to save your voice to sell stuff.

OK, that might be a slight exaggeration. But with each passing day, it becomes more obvious why Arthur Ashe expressed extreme disappointment in his autobiography with Jordan's "demureness" on social issues. And when the Rev. Jesse Jackson railed against those who have been the direct beneficiaries of the civil rights movement yet shirk their responsibility to those less fortunate, he must've had fellow Chicagoan Jordan in mind.

I've got a question: Since Jordan makes more money than several countries, how much must he earn before he feels free to speak out on something other than his vertical leap? Or, even, to sit out a meaningless exhibition game if his feet hurt?

After initially saying he wasn't going to play on Friday, Jordan reconsidered, saying "The quicker I can get back to playing basketball, the better. . . It isn't as tender as I thought it was going to be."

Loosely translated, that means "Phil Knight called and told me Nike stock would drop lower than Dennis Rodman's free-throw shooting percentage if I sat out because of a foot injury."

Hey Mike. Must be the shoes, eh?

October 25, 1997

Light a candle for the au pair? Why not for the baby?

To tell you the truth, I thought the lady whose picture appeared in newspapers across the country was, euphemistically speaking, a little touched in the noggin.

Hours after that au pair in Massachusetts was convicted of killing

Matthew Eappen by slamming him against a wall or floor like you would a dirty rug, I saw a picture of a woman holding a sign. It read "OJ Simpson Innocent? Louise Woodward Guilty? I think not."

What kind of mental gymnastics were being performed inside her head for her to compare the au pair trial to Simpson's criminal trial that everyone — except, perhaps, Geraldo — would like to forget?

Lady must be dingey, I thought, tossing the paper aside and continuing what I felt was a far more important mission — polishing off my bowl of Cap'n Crunch.

But it turns out the sign-holder was not a refugee from the Hoo Hoo Hotel after all, but was merely expressing feelings I've since heard elsewhere.

I don't know about you, but to me the Simpson case and the Woodward case are connected the same way the music of Travis Tritt and George Jones is connected, or that of Ray Charles and Michael Bolton. That is to say, not at all.

But some people are citing the two cases and their different verdicts as irrefutable evidence of the inherent unfairness of the U.S. justice system.

Stop that laughing; I'm serious.

But if you think it's absurd that people are ready to scrap the entire judicial system merely because two high-profile trials had unpopular endings, wait until you hear how others are trying to connect them.

Some of the scores of "legal analysts" fouling the airwaves — a definite byproduct of the Simpson trial — think the presence of attorney Barry Scheck on Woodward's defense team may provide grounds for a mistrial.

What did Scheck do? Did the dude drop his pants and moon the jurors, or address them in his summation by doing "Elvis"? Did he call the judge a gaseous old windbag?

No, worse. He had been a member of O.J. Simpson's Dream Team.

I am not kidding. Some razor-sharp legal minds have actually surmised that the jury cared not one whit about justice for Matthew Eappen and his family. Oh no. Its members were really angry at Scheck for defending O.J., and by sending Scheck to inglorious defeat they were really expressing contempt for Simpson.

Nothing personal, Louise, but you just happened to get in the way, hon.

That's what psychiatrists might call "transference." That's what I call "a crock." But if Woodward gets a mistrial based on that, Simpson could soon replace "The dog ate my homework" as the most overworked excuse for every misstep since the McDLT or tuna-flavored toothpaste.

J.B.: "Throckmorton, where's that assignment I asked for yester-day?"

Throckmorton: "Uh, sorry, J.B. O.J. broke into my house last night and . . .

J.B.: Say no more, my son. Do it tomorrow.

I guess if you look hard enough, you can find at least one thing the two cases have in common: in both the real victims quickly became mere afterthoughts.

In the Simpson case, at least in the courtroom of public opinion, some people swept the memories of Ron Goldman and Nicole Brown under the rug in their eagerness to "get O.J."

Likewise, in the au pair case, the memory of tiny Matthew Eappen has been swept under the rug as people on both sides of the Atlantic anguish over the injustice they imagine is being done to poor little Louise.

I've been extremely impressed by the well-attended candlelight vigils, marches and petitions expressing support for her.

That's why I'd like to take a moment to offer all who participated in them these heartfelt but admittedly overused words of consolation: "Get a life, dammit!"

Just as the jury in the Simpson case had access to more evidence than did the people out contorting their faces and minds after that verdict, so, too, did the jurors in the Woodward case know more than you know.

If you're going to march for somebody, why not for an 8-month-old baby who was slammed against a wall or floor like a dirty rug.

November 08, 1997

UNC road for the rich gets bumpy

Last week I wrote a column praising college students for the new wave of activism washing over campuses as they raise a stink about — among other things — UNC's malodorous deal with Nike and the visit by China's main mean man, Jiang Zemin.

I was all for those protests and said so. But guys, enough's enough. Because now it appears that those crazy kids have gone one toke over the line, sweet Jesus: This time, they are picking not on ruthless mega-corporations or ruthless rulers, but on rich people. And that's something we cannot abide.

In case you missed it, a coalition of UNC students, faculty members and Chapel Hill town officials announced plans to block a road that leads to the Dean Dome on Friday night before the Tar Heels' basketball season opener. They are outraged that the state Department of Transportation ramrodded the $1.3 million Ram Road project down the town's throat without even consulting town officials.

OK, I'll concede they have some justification for being peeved. But geez, guys, we must all try to be a bit more sympathetic toward the overprivileged. We're talking, lest you forget, about rich people here. And they, as F. Scott Fitzgerald wrote, aren't like you and me.

The ostensible purpose for the "private" public road was to allow well-heeled Tar Heel contributors to avoid pre- and post-game traffic jams when they park in the exclusive parking lot close to the Dean Dome. Another reason that some people paid $40,000 to park at courtside is so they won't have to park their Bentleys, Rollses and Benzes next to the rusting '67 Dodges driven by unmonied minions like me.

Letting poor people park next to rich people is just the first step down a slippery slope toward socialism or even anarchy. Why, I'm betting that if poor people park next to rich people, the next thing you know, they will be wanting to speak to 'em. And that is the real reason people shelled out so much moolah — so they wouldn't be accosted by regular people in the parking lot after the game.

Poor dude: Say, Hoss. Some game, huh? Don't look like the Heels are gonna miss Coach Smith after all, huh?

Rich dude: Pardon me, but why in the hell are you speaking to me, especially driving an American-made car?

But it's not just snobbishness — one's parking proximity to the arena is definitely a status symbol on the golf course and at the country club — that's driving people to desire their own little road.

Have you seen how bad traffic can be after a game? The great unwashed middle class — at UNC games, they're the ones driving their own Mercedes Benzes or Saabs with "Harvey Gantt" bumper stickers — might be able to afford to spend 30 to 40 minutes getting onto the highway after a game, but rich people have more important things to do, things like ... well, I'm sure there's something.

Some of you will laud the protesters' courage in forming a human chain across the rich folks' road, and so do I. But I'd have even greater appreciation for their selflessness if they formed a human chain on Ram Road when the Heels play Duke in February, not Middle Tennessee State in mid-November.

If they did that, I'm sure I — or someone here at The N&O — would write about them. Only, I'm afraid it wouldn't be a column.

It'd be an obituary.

November 13, 1997

Teacher robs the cradle, gets glorified detention

C'mon guys, admit it. When you first heard that a sixth grade male student had had an affair — and a baby — with his teacher, you probably smirked and said (if there were no women around) "Lucky kid."

Even if you didn't take it that lightly, the law did — treating Mary Kay LeTourneau much less harshly than it would have treated a male teacher who'd impregnated a 13-year-old. Really, can you imagine a male teacher skipping away from such an abominable crime with a mere six-month sentence — the judicial equivalent of being forced to stay after school?

Why, a male similarly convicted of two counts of second-degree child rape would be lucky if he saw freedom before the offspring of his illicit union was drawing Social Security.

And that's the way it should be. Relationships in which lecherous old men sexually exploit young girls are justifiably scorned. But the contempt for older women who prey on young boys is considerably less.

For a while, every comedian who's ever pulled on a pair of multi-colored suspenders made LeTourneau's May-December "affair to forget" in Washington state a part of his act. I guarantee you that such levity would have never been permitted had the situation been reversed.

Society and the law have gone to great lengths to protect girls from predatory older men who, by exploiting physically developed but emotionally fragile teenagers, account for more than half of all teen pregnancies.

But women escape such wrath. Somehow it is considered a rite of passage when a selfish older woman sexually exploits an equally emotionally fragile adolescent boy: 20 percent of all boys who are sexually molested are victimized by women.

Smirk if you want, but LeTourneau is guilty of sexual assault just as surely as if she had yanked the boy into a dark alley and assaulted him.

As an experienced educator, she must have known that 13-year-old kids are not emotionally equipped for sex, especially not with an authority figure such as a teacher.

As senior deputy prosecutor Lisa Johnson said, "She abused the trust placed in her as a teacher. . . She exploited him for her own needs, her own selfishness and her own inadequacies."

Even if she didn't wear a mask or use a gun, LeTourneau is guilty of robbing that kid of something he can never recapture — his youth.

I know I sound like a square, railing against something society winks at and even encourages. The story of the older woman who teaches the young dude the ropes and "makes him a man" is proverbial, a literary and Hollywood staple. (Do you think it's a coincidence that "The Graduate" is on just about every man's list of top movies?)

After watching "The Summer of '42," a 1970s-era coming-of-age movie in which an older woman tenderly initiates an underaged boy into the ways of manhood — or at least Hollywood's "ways of manhood" — I'll bet most teenage boys left theaters across the country wishing they could be similarly initiated. I know I did.

But Hollywood never showed the boy dealing later in life with the psychological scars that no doubt resulted from his one-night affair.

Just as Hollywood tried to justify the woman's obviously irrational and exploitative behavior — in the film she was seeking solace in the kid's arms a day after receiving a telegram saying her beloved husband had been killed in the war — LeTourneau's attorney convolutedly attempted to place the blame for her contemptuous behavior on men.

Two of them to be precise. First, it turns out her husband was having affairs of his own and verbally abused LeTourneau. Then her dad, well, he was dying of cancer.

So that justifies her raping — and stripped of its niceties, that is what she did — a kid whom she first taught in second grade? A mere four years earlier?

Oh please. If anything, it means only that her attorney saw the same movie I saw when I was 15.

November 29, 1997

The season for insincerity

Want to know what I hate about the holidays?

Well, I'm going to tell you anyway. Then I'll tell you about a heart-warming incident that will make you feel better about the state of humankind.

What I hate about this time of the year is the way dead-eyed, cold-hearted misanthropes who don't even acknowledge your existence for 50 weeks of the year all of a sudden feel it necessary to bare their teeth in a phony grin and say "Merry Christmas!"

Count on this: That pimply-faced clerk at the Piggly Wiggly who usually doesn't even glance at you when ringing up your Cap'n Crunch all of a sudden feels compelled to give you your change with a hearty "Happy Holidays." Same with that dour-faced cashier at the bank who normally barks "Melp you?" ("May I help you?") — and thrusts your money at you with all the tenderness of a sword-wielding matador running a bull through.

Is there something subliminal in hearing Bing Crosby sing "White

Christmas" that makes people say "Merry Christmas" when they don't mean it?

My philosophy is: If you can't speak to me during the rest of the year, dadgummit, don't bother speaking to me now.

I wish there was a law so that anyone caught muttering "Merry Christmas" to strangers whom they would not ordinarily greet would be arrested.

I feel the same way about philanthropy and charity. People who need help during the holidays need it during the entire year.

I despise seasonal altruism by seasonal do-gooders. But I love hearing of and seeing acts of genuine kindness and charity, such as that shown to my son and me by a couple of strangers in a Durham restaurant a few weeks ago. I found their kindness touching, mainly because I suspect they would have done the same thing in July, August or May.

This is what happened: The kid and I had just polished off some macaroni pie at a Greek restaurant at Brightleaf Square when the waitress gingerly approached and told me — in a voice that could be clearly heard in Cary — of a "PROBLEM" with my credit card. I went to the telephone, called the credit card company and was placed on hold — all the while sweating bullets as diners nudged each other, snickered or looked embarrassed for me.

I was still on hold 20 minutes later when the waitress approached again. Discreetly this time, she said, "That couple over there asked if you'd mind if they paid for y'all's dinner."

I faked a laugh and said, "Thanks, but tell them I really do have money. I think."

Minutes later, the credit card company realized the error — I hadn't activated the danged card — and I paid the bill. I asked the waitress to point out the couple who offered to pay for our dinner, and I caught up with them as they left the restaurant. I thanked them profusely and introduced myself, whereupon I learned they often read my column, They even mentioned a few of their favorites.

But when they offered to pay for our meal, they had no idea who I was, how much the bill was or that their act of kindness would end up in the newspaper. To them, I was just some broke bloke who needed a hand. And that's what made their offer special.

The bill was only about $30, but to me, their offer to help was worth a million bucks. I'm sure I'll remember it forever. Since my encounter with them, I've felt a lot better about people and the world in which we live.

So, "Happy Holidays."

December 15, 1997

Good-taste police about to strike out

Elizabeth Best knew something was wrong last month when a man in an official-looking car stopped in front of her house, walked across the barren front yard and asked if he could ask her some questions.

But the man wasn't interested in getting Best's opinion; he wanted to give her one — from Wilson city officials. They have concluded that the stuffed chair on Best's front porch is a tasteless eyesore. As such, it is not in keeping with the desired image of Wilson and will have to go.

No, you're not suffering the delayed aftereffects of that last carafe of MD 20/20 wine you drank on New Year's Eve. Nor is this some kind of premature April Fools' Day gag: The City of Wilson really is banning indoor furniture such as Best's from porches and yards.

This proposal, I admit, doesn't have the same dramatic effect as General Sherman's burning of Atlanta, but it is an attack on the South just the same. The only difference is that when Sherman visited, his target was wealthy slave owners. The target this time is poor people.

Oh, city officials swear they aren't targeting poor people specifically, but how many rich people do you know who feel compelled to hold on to a tattered Naugahyde Barcalounger that isn't quite good enough for the living room but isn't quite raggedy enough for the trash heap?

When I was growing up in Rockingham, it was as predictable as the dew that each morning Miss Rosa, Miss Atlee and my grandma would sit on their porches and drink a cup of coffee and chat as they waited for their "rich folks" to come and take them to their homes to clean, cook and iron. It was just as predictable that at the end of each day, they'd plop down on the porch, bone tired, and talk about their day before trudging inside to clean, cook and iron for their own families.

I can't remember if they ever had stuffed, indoor chairs on their porches, because it didn't — and shouldn't — matter. The social interaction encouraged by porches, not the chairs on them, is what was and is important.

Best's stuffed porch chair gives her an excellent vantage point from which to watch her daughter at the park across the street or to chat with the neighbors whose house is a mere 5 feet from hers. And, she added, "I like to sit out ... and read me a book sometimes."

Best, 26 and a cook at Quincy's, said she and her friends — many of whom have indoor chairs outside — can't figure out why a city with myriad other problems is having a conniption over such a minor issue.

"A lot of people I know are wondering why they are passing a law about chairs and not doing something to protect these children or to get drugs out of our neighborhoods," she told me Saturday.

I suggested that maybe if dope dealers plied their trade from red vinyl recliners on the front porch, Wilson's good-taste police would run them out of town.

Sarah Rasino, a member of the good-taste police — also known as the Wilson Appearance Commission — was quoted in a New York Times story on the furniture ban as saying, "People who say 'I want to keep my couch' are looking at it from a very narrow perspective. Those become weather-beaten, and I don't think there's anything pretty about that."

Well, there's nothing pretty about what the city of Wilson is doing, either.

Dangerous, yes. Pretty, no.

January 05, 1998

Much ado about nothing

Hey, could somebody please pass me a hanky? I'm all choked up these days, what with Jerry Seinfeld deciding he no longer wants to do "Seinfeld."

I'm kidding, of course. But there are some people — mainly those with a financial stake in the multinational corporation that owns NBC — who want us to believe our lives will be somehow diminished without "Seinfeld" on Thursday nights.

The mundane reality is that a very rich comedian has decided to stop doing his television show. The only thing that will be diminished because of his decision is NBC's profits. "Boo freakin' hoo" is what I say.

Pure and simple, Seinfeld's fame derives from his ability to make money — which derives from his fame. The gnashing of teeth and mourning over his leavetaking illustrate clearly our reverence for anything that makes gobs of money.

When Tom Brokaw — who, not coincidentally, works at NBC, which airs "Seinfeld" — "reports" that the show's finale could be the most-watched show in television history, he is helping to make it so.

And when others in the media write breathlessly about the so-called funk descending upon a country facing a "Seinfeldless" future, they are helping to make that true, too.

Coverage the past couple of weeks of Seinfeld and his wacky pals eclipsed that accorded those wacky warriors Terry Nichols and Ted Kaczynski. It was, unbelievably, a cover story for "Time" magazine.

"Say It Ain't So," screamed People magazine from its cover while asking — without any discernible irony — how will we survive without Jerry, Elaine, Kramer, George and even Newman.

The answer: We'll survive quite nicely, thank you.

It appears that the present generation is suffering "big event envy" because it, unlike previous generations, has no defining event to rally around — no World War II, no political assassinations, no Vietnam.

Our parents had Presidents Eisenhower and Kennedy and King, among others. We have a moderately amusing comic. Devoid of any genuinely defining cultural icons, we seek to manufacture them — the death of a princess, the assassination of a fashion designer, the termination of a TV show.

Anyone who has watched "Seinfeld" throughout its nine-year run knows it has already begun to slip. The fact that it is, nonetheless, the wittiest show on TV merely points up how weak the others are.

Truth be told, even at its peak, the show was inconsistent and could range from inspired to insipid in a week. The episode this week in which George went berserk because his "Twix" bar got stuck in the vending machine was, quite simply, dreadful.

Of course, "Seinfeld" did have two of the funniest episodes of any sitcom in TV history: The ones about "mulva" and the "master of my domain" — if you have to ask, don't ask — rank right up there with "The Andy Griffith Show" in which Aunt Bee was fixing to leave Mayberry because Opie didn't cotton to her, and the "Sanford & Son" episode where Fred and Bubba conspired to reclaim some rare and valuable blues records. (Certainly you remember when Bubba, posing as the son of blues legend Blind Mellow Jelly, kept repeating "I want my daddy's records"?)

Those shows were just funny without pretending to define a generation or aspiring to some greater truths, truths which some people are bending over backward to find in "Seinfeld" even though the comic himself admits that the show is about "nothing."

Actually, I think its "nothingness" contributed mightily to its success. The show succeeded — sometimes — in making day-to-day banality entertaining and in making everyday blokes think "Hey, they're just like me." (Sure, pal, if you were wittier, richer and better-looking.)

January 10, 1998

Anchors aweigh from Havana — all for a sex scandal?

I have always thought of myself as a good American. Until now, that is. I mean, I always stand for the Pledge of Allegiance, take off my hat whenever the National Anthem is played and I get tingly (you'd have to be dead not to) whenever Ray Charles grabs ahold of "America the Beautiful."

But now, I'm not so sure. What has me doubting my patriotism is that, no matter how I try, I just can't seem to get outraged over the so-called sex scandal allegedly involving President Clinton and an adult intern.

(Now, if Monica Lewinsky was some starry—eyed, naive 16-year-old from Frogleg, Miss., who'd succumbed to a presidential come-on, I'd be just as outraged as Rush Limbaugh wants us to be.)

I, like most Americans, would prefer that our chief of state comport himself like some kind of national Ward Cleaver who goes to work and returns home to read the paper in a cardigan and a tie. But gee willikers, you'd have to go all the way back to . . . well. . . never to find a president like that.

Implicit in the media's hysterical coverage of the prez's possible sexual infidelity is the message that all "good" Americans should be storming the Bastille and demanding that Clinton be tossed out in the street.

I'm guessing the pope and Fidel got whiplash from watching every single news network immediately yank its big hitters from Cuba — "Hey, where'd everybody go?," the perplexed pope asked — and return them to Washington to cover a story they hope will match the hype.

Me, I believe our national Outrage-O-Meter should've jumped off the chart when it was revealed that President Reagan lied about financing Iran-contra and slept through much of his second administration, or that his wife helped influence national and international policy with the assistance of psychics.

Now those, more than with whom Clinton is sleeping, concern me and are issues that could legitimately knock Arafat, Netanyahu and the Holy Father to the bottom of page 6 of this country's newspapers.

Remember when the movie "Jaws" made such a big splash in the 1970s? The effective, chilling ad for the movie asked "Is it safe to go back into the water?" Since I'm a confirmed landlubber who never learned to swim, I never fretted about bumping into columnist-eating sharks.

But the question I'm asking is "Is it safe to turn on my AM radio?"

I am now terrified of turning it on and encountering rabid, right-wing sharks who are in a feeding frenzy over an issue most Americans find only salaciously interesting.

I don't know about you, but something seems slightly askew when morally reprehensible slugs like Oliver North and G. Gordon Liddy can get on radio stations and bust a gut in mock outrage because they contend the current scandal has made America an international laughingstock.

That's laughable, since according to my recollection there are countries in which both Liddy and North could have been convicted of treason and hanged for the offenses they committed against the flag they now claim to revere.

If G. Gordon and Ollie are examples of good Americans, that makes me doubt if I am — or even want to be — a good American.

If you have the same doubts, just take this simple "patriotism" test:

1. Which upsets you more?:

    A. That Clinton may have committed adultery.

    B. That Ollie North lied to Congress.

    C. That "Seinfeld" is ending.

2. When electing a president, do you:

    A. Study his moral fiber?

    B. Study his foreign and domestic policy?

    C. Check out his preference in women?

3. Do you think the next reporter who asks a politician "Have you ever committed adultery?" should be:

    A. Answered?

    B. Hung upside down by his toes?

    C. Asked the same question?

4. Would you rather have a president who, before setting policy:

    A. Fooled around?

    B. Lied to Congress?

    C. Consulted the Psychic Connection Hotline?

If you answered "D" to all four questions, you have what it takes to be a good citizen. Heck, you might even make a good president.

January 24, 1998

Are youngsters ready for cover-your-ears coverage?

Man, do I envy Ward Cleaver. Not only did he have a perpetually sweet-tempered wife who cooked and cleaned while wearing pearls and high heels, but he never had to explain to the Beav why everyone was so interested in the president's sex life.

That is the predicament I — as well as millions of other American parents — have faced these past two weeks.

Most of us already know to be forever ready to punch the car radio button as soon as we hear the opening strains of Marvin Gaye's "Sexual Healing." And of course, we know to keep the dial far away from stations playing profane, sexually suggestive rap music.

But I've discovered it's a lot easier to steer clear of Snoop Doggy Dogg than it is to avoid the frank descriptions of President Clinton's alleged sexual trysts with Monica Lewinsky.

Because coverage of the alleged affair has been inescapable, I shouldn't have been surprised when my inquisitive 9-year-old started asking questions about it. While lying in bed and watching Clinton's State of the Union address earlier this week, the kid turned to me after Hillary Clinton appeared on screen.

Him: She's mad at the president, isn't she?

Me: Uh, why would she be mad at the president, dude?

Him: Because of that Lewinsky woman.

Oy vey! I have never been one of those television sitcom dads who becomes mushmouthed and befuddled at the prospect of telling Junior about the birds and the bees. I actually relish the prospect, since I don't want my boy to learn about sex from the same source I did — namely, from a guy named Joe Willie hanging out in the poolroom.

But geez, I never thought I'd have to explain it this soon, or explain how the birds and bees relate to the leader of the Free World.

I mean, this is the same child who, I swear, a few short years ago was asking me "Where does Wile E. Coyote get the money to buy all that stuff" he uses to try to catch the Road Runner? Now, he's asking me "What did the president do" with Monica Lewinsky?

I explained, as elliptically as possible without actually lying, that "People say he went on a date with her."

That was actually a good response, says Mai Mai Ginsburg, a certi-fied clinical social worker who works with adolescents. "The simplest answer is the best way to go," she said in a telephone interview from her Chapel Hill office. "When children are exposed to a media frenzy like this, it can be disconcerting and they look to their parents for guidance and explanation."

At what age should children be told about what's going on? I asked.

"If the child is asking questions, no matter how young, you have to respond. You don't lie, but a one-sentence, simple answer is best," she said.

The presidency has always been viewed as the pinnacle of achievement in America, and parents have used the office as the carrot to motivate their kids. "Why, if you're smart, you can grow up to be president," we all heard growing up.

But now, that can have a different, unintended connotation. On an episode of the old television show "Cheers," a teenage boy approached the lascivious former baseball star Sam Malone.

Kid: Mr. Malone, I want to be just like you when I grow up.

Malone: Oh, you want to be a great relief pitcher?

Kid: No. A babehound.

But Clinton's alleged actions aren't the first to tarnish the mystique surrounding the office, and one can diminish the office's mystique even without being accused of sexual peccadilloes: Jimmy Carter, a born-again Christian who confessed to pangs of guilt when he merely lusted in his heart, diminished it some when he tried to be a "regular Joe" — wearing those cardigan sweaters and carrying his own luggage on and off planes.

History has shown us that other ex-presidents were not the paragons of sexual purity we'd been led to believe they were. Indeed, they have often been a bawdy lot. They just didn't have to contend with the present Washington press corps, which means parents didn't have to explain why the Father of Our Country always looked so happy when his wife wasn't around.

January 31, 1998

The Gloved One's hometown could use a helping hand

Aha, y'all almost had me this time. You almost made me think I was wrong. Of course, you know as well as I how unlikely that was.

But you had me going there for a minute, bless your hearts.

It seems that every time I mention how successful people — especially blacks — have an obligation to help those less fortunate, I am deluged with calls and letters from angry people calling me everything but a reuben sandwich. "Get a grip" is often the kindest, most printable thing they say. Many of my most vicious critics, surprisingly to me, are blacks.

This is especially true whenever I talk about richer-than-God jock Michael Jordan. So virulent are people's feelings on this issue of "giving something back" that I was beginning to waver, to entertain the possibility that "Hey, maybe they're right and I'm wrong. It's a dog-eat-dog world out there and perhaps it is indeed every man for himself."

But then reality sets in and I again know I am right.

Relax, Tar Heel fans. This column isn't about your beloved MJ. It is obvious that dude will never speak out on or contribute to anything that doesn't have a dollar sign attached to it or that won't polish his pollyan-naish image. So I shall just leave him alone to bask in the empty adulation of people who actually want heroes without backbones.

Did I say it's not about MJ? Well, it is in a way, but not the MJ you know and love. This is about the sexually and racially confused MJ — Michael Jackson.

I woke up yesterday mad enough to chew nails. That was unusual, since Sweet Thang wasn't there snoring in my ears or snatching the covers off of me.

No, I was angry because I had left my radio on all night and the first story I heard upon awakening was about how the almost terminally ill South Korean economy was showing new signs of life.

What happened? Why, Michael Jackson happened.

The King of Poop agreed to invest $100 million in an amusement park in that country, and investors responded with optimism that sent certain stocks soaring like Jordan on a slamdunk.

"Well, what's wrong with that, you #@$$%&?" you snort.

Nothing, except this: I used to live in Jackson's hometown, Gary, Ind. — a city that, rightly or wrongly, has come to exemplify urban blight and despair, and I remember the frustrations of city and civic leaders who tried to get Jackson to contribute anything. He contributed nothing to Gary, not even his presence.

So that leaves me wondering "How much could Jackson have done for his hometown, full of people who look like him — or at least who look like he looked when he was born — with just one-tenth of that $100 mill he invested in a country half a world away?

When the bottom fell out of the steel industry in the 1970s, Gary and the thousands of people who depended upon its belching steel mills for handsome livelihoods were devastated.

How badly? So badly that, in the late 1980s, the opening of a Wendy's restaurant was announced with great fanfare — even a ribbon cutting by city officials — and heralded as the beginning of the city's renaissance.

It wasn't. There have been fits and starts in recent years as the city tries to right itself, but that task would be so much easier if Jackson — and the other world-renowned natives, many of whom are (or were) black — tried to help.

I talked yesterday to Vernon Smith, an Indiana state representative, former Gary City Councilman and probably Gary's biggest booster. He was baffled by Jackson's attitude.

"He's more interested in helping everybody else but Gary, a city that was very supportive of him" when he was beginning in show business, Smith said during a legislative break. "I've got the pictures (of MJ as a kid) to prove it. . . We asked him to donate the family's old house, a very modest donation, and he refused. That could be a gold mine sitting right there as a museum."

The name of Jackson's proposed amusement park in South Korea — like the one he's proposed for California — is Neverland. Which seems to sum up his attitude toward Gary: Never-everland.

February 28, 1998

Here's one Jordan who'll go the extra mile for anybody

That's all, folks. Balloting is over. Thank you for your time and please, drive safely.

Voting for "humanitarian of the year" is over, and the winner in a landslide is none other than — Vernon Jordan.

Jordan, First Friend and Washington super lawyer, deserves the award for his tireless efforts on behalf of Monica Lewinsky. Not only did Jordan take time from his busy, $200-an-hour schedule to escort the former White House intern to a defense lawyer, but he also called a couple of his big CEO pals trying to secure her a job commensurate with her qualifications.

Vernon: "Hey Homes, I've got this great young lady who's looking for employment. She's a a real go-getter and Bill is extremely impressed with her office skills. Think you can hook her up with a nice entry-level job paying around . . . hmmm. . . $150,000 a year?"

But how is Jordan repaid for his diligent altruism? By being hauled before Independent Counsel Kenneth Starr and grilled like a tuna.

Sure, Jordan is perceived by some as having distanced himself from black people to the point where Randall Robinson, in his fabulous book "Defending the Spirit," named an affliction after him: Vernon Jordan Disease.

But I'm betting Jordan would have pulled a "Lewinsky" for any struggling single mother in Southeast Washington who wanted to better her lot in life. (All she'd have to do is look on her Rolodex and call him up.)

Now, I admire Randall Robinson greatly, but I think he is underestimating Jordan's proletarian influence. For instance, in some neighborhoods, dudes no longer even ask for a "hook-up" from their brother-in-law's cousin's friend who works down at Stereo World.

Oh, they still want that major discount off the regular price of that phat CD system, but now they ask for a Lewinsky, not a hook-up.

Instead of greeting Jordan's actions with skepticism and automatically assuming they were part of some kind of devious quid pro quo — "You don't tell what you and the president did, and I'll hook you up with a fat job for which you're astoundingly unqualified" — we should view Jordan's actions as representing America's highest ideals.

I think it is admirable that a man of his stature and importance would deign to help an obscure young woman he hardly knew. As for charges that Jordan was acting only at the behest of President Clinton, I say "So what?"

If anything, that makes what he did even more praiseworthy. I'm proud — proud, I tell you — to live in a country where two powerful men would take such a personal interest in a regular Joe. Or, in this case, Josephine.

Could you imagine Boris Yeltsin or some other country's leader — or even some of this country's previous leaders — taking a personal interest in a 24-year-old, unpedigreed ex-intern? Not likely.

One of the major criticisms of Ronald Reagan was the "imperialism" of his presidency. He was criticized for lacking the common touch because everyone he knew was as rich or richer than he.

But now that we have a really common president, we suspect him of having impure motives.

Frankly speaking, it is no longer possible for every kid to grow up legitimately dreaming he or she can become president. For one thing, you have to win too many primaries.

But thanks to Vernon Jordan, every kid can still grow up dreaming that — with the right Rolodex — the president's best friend can Lewinsky them up with a good job.

If a special prosecutor doesn't find out about it.

March 07, 1998

Talented teen a step ahead, and a size behind

You know how Mary McLeod Bethune once described singer, football star, scholar and social activist Paul Robeson as "the tallest tree in our forest"?

I'm predicting the same thing will be said about Tijan Jarra one day, too. Tijan is a mannerly, brilliant 16-year-old junior at the N.C. School of

Science and Mathematics, which accepts only the state's best and brightest high school students.

On the day I talked to him while strolling along the bucolic campus, he had just finished practicing a rap routine for a school talent show. He also has made a movie with classmates and wants to be a surgeon.

But right now, more than anything else, he needs shoes that fit.

Tijan wears — or more precisely, needs — a size 23 shoe, which means he can't just walk into Thom McAn, plunk down a few simoleons and strut out with a pair of Italian loafers. He is currently walking around with his feet crammed into a size 22 shoe.

I learned of the agony of his feet after receiving a call from a concerned friend in Congressman Bob Etheridge's office, who put me in touch with Tijan's father, Hassan.

I immediately set out on a hunt for shoes for Tijan.

My first call was to Duff, a friend in Rockingham who owns a sporting goods store. He promised to get back to me today, although he said the largest shoe he'd ever ordered was a 19.

Then, I called a place where the only thing larger than the shoe sizes are the egos and paychecks.

That's right, the NBA. Specifically, I called the Charlotte Hornets basketball team, where I talked to Susanne Conley, a team official.

Conley was the essence of sympathy and kindness, inviting Tijan and his family to a Hornets game where they could sit on the bench before tipoff and possibly meet some of the players. She also inquired around the league, but found that the player with the biggest feet, Shaquille O'Neal, wears only a size 21. What about Gheorghe Muresan, the 7-foot-7-inch center for Washington, you ask?

Not even close. He wears a relatively petite size 19.

Tijan's father, a janitor for the Rocky Mount Post Office, told me he has found one company that could make shoes for his son, but it wants $500. In advance. Not only that, but they take four to five months to make.

Clothing Tijan — he's 6-feet-9-inches tall, 325 pounds — is also expensive. As he and I walked along the campus on a chilly Saturday, he wore a lightweight cotton jacket that cost $73 — about 50 bucks too much.

But as hard as it may seem to believe, Tijan's size isn't the main thing you notice when you're talking to him. His smile is. The kid has a great smile that faded only once: when he talked about the hardship his size and — although he was far too modest to say it — his genius is causing his family.

He explained that he has usually worked to help with his expenses — one summer at McDonald's, the next in the neurobiology department at Duke University, which is what he says led to his desire to be a surgeon. But the School of Science and Math prohibits students from working. So, the responsibility for clothing him and his siblings falls solely to his parents.

It's an awesome responsibility for Brenda and Hassan Jarra, who met and married while she was working for the Peace Corps in Hassan's native Gambia. They now have four biological children and four they adopted from Hassan's relatives in Gambia and brought to America to continue their educations.

Eight would be enough under any circumstance. But when one of the eight is 6-foot-9, 325 pounds, then Hassan's salary as a post office janitor and Brenda's as a captain at Nash Correctional Center are stretched like, well, like a size 22 shoe trying to contain a size 23 foot.

Let's get one thing straight. The kid and his family aren't asking for anything: I am. It doesn't have to be Christmas to help someone, and people don't have to be destitute to need help.

The Jarras are hard-working people who know the importance of education: Tijan is the second of their children to qualify for and attend the prestigious school in Durham. Walking and talking with Tijan was a real pleasure, especially compared with some of the teenage miscreants I meet, and I got a feeling after just an hour with him that this kid is on a journey to make the world a better place someday.

But every great journey begins with a single step, and of course, every step must begin with shoes that fit.

March 30, 1998

His feet get helping hands

I agree with people who boast about what a great place the Triangle is to live, work and raise a family.

But I have little in common with those Chamber of Commerce types who tout such irrelevancies as the number of superfluous shopping centers per square foot, the high-tech jobs per person or Ph.D.s per university.

No sirree. The reason I think we're all blessed to live here is quite basic: It's the people.

Now don't get me wrong. Nobody complains about the boorishness of some area residents more than I do, a boorishness that has at times brought tears to my heart, if not my eyes.

Well, what y'all did last week brought tears to this old cowboy, too.

But they were good ones. I was overwhelmed by the outpouring of assistance Triangle residents offered to Tijan Jarra and his family after I wrote a column detailing their hardships in trying to clothe him and fit his unusually large feet.

Tijan, you recall, is the big man on campus at the N.C. School of Science and Mathematics, not necessarily because of his academic prowess — every kid at the Durham school is extremely bright — but because of his size. The dude is only 16 years old, but he is 6 feet 7, weighs 325 pounds and needs size 23 shoes. I wrote that even though both his parents work — his dad as a post office janitor, his mom at a prison — they were being overwhelmed by his special needs. I asked if some of y'all might could help.

Boy, could you ever. The first telephone calls came in before 6 a.m. the morning the column ran and continued for days.

"People have really been nice and helpful," Tijan's mom, Brenda, told me. "They have sent money and called with information on where we could find big clothes." Some local radio disc jockeys mentioned the column on the air, prompting their listeners to respond, and some readers themselves contacted shoe companies. As a result, Nike and Converse have requested outlines of Tijan's feet and promised to make shoes for him at a nominal fee.

I myself received hundreds of calls from people asking where to send money or telling me about a big man's clothing store in this city or a maker of big shoes in that one.

Tijan's parents have set up a fund to help their still-growing son. If you want to contribute, the family's address is 331 S. Grace St., Rocky Mount, N.C. 27804.

If pressed to explain this outpouring of concern, I'd guess it has something to do with the fact that Tijan is a bright, well-mannered kid who, as several callers said, "seems to have his head on straight." Often, the only young people we're exposed to in the newspaper are those who've shocked our sensibilities with one act of barbarism or another. Lord knows I get tired of writing about those creeps, and I'll bet y'all get tired of reading about them.

A steady diet of such youthful pathology makes Tijan's story even more refreshing. The most refreshing aspect of the story — well, next to your generosity — was Tijan's response when his mother told him that people were calling and offering to help him.

"For real, Ma?," he asked incredulously. "They're doing that?"

Yes, they are. But would you expect anything less in the greatest place in the world to live?

April 09, 1998

Sanford accentuated the positive

Over the next several days, you're going to read lots of stuff about
Terry Sanford as writers try to figure out his legacy and where he made
his greatest contributions.

Was it as governor? Senator? President of Duke University?

An argument could be made for any of those, because Sanford was
a political and intellectual giant.

But if you ask me, Sanford's most enduring contribution to America
was as an environmentalist.

I don't mean as one of those tree-hugging, granola-munching "save
the humpbacked whale" zealots who seem more concerned about the
plight of the yellow-bellied sapsucker than about their fellow human
beings. The species Sanford was interested in saving from extinction
was one that's very close to me: the black male.

In 1990, he was named a co-chairman of the 21st Century
Commission on African American Males, a bipartisan group of scholars,
business and political leaders seeking to stem the tide of destruction —
OK, sometimes self-destruction — that threatens to make brothers as
rare as spotted owls.

I can't say that Sanford and his colleagues succeeded — after all, the
leading cause of death for young, black men is still young, black men —
but the fact that our senator brought this issue to the Senate floor for a
series of hearings is remarkable and gratifying.

During a dry recitation of statistics showing how bad things are for
some black men, it was Sanford who broke that depressing litany during
the first day of hearings by noting that "the level of success [for black
males] exceeds the level of failure."

Whenever I mention I'm from North Carolina, which I do every time I
leave the state, there are three names that come to everyone's mind.
This trinity — although I dare not call it a holy one — is comprised of
Michael Jordan, Jesse Helms and Terry Sanford.

Jordan, of course, is an ultimately inconsequential jock whose influence begins and ends with his ability to shoot a ball through a hoop and
to hawk overpriced shoes.

Helms is known for meanness, obstinacy and for invariably being on
the wrong side of any issue.

Sanford, conversely, was known for being on the right side of most
issues. He was "the anti-Jesse."

It is no coincidence that Sen. Sanford was selected to be host of the
official Washington dinner for South Africa's current president, Nelson
Mandela, when he was freed from prison after 28 years: Sanford had

used his clout as a member of both the Senate Foreign Relations and Banking committees to cajole bankers into withdrawing their financial support from South Africa's apartheid regime.

Kathy Wellman, a former member of Sanford's Washington Senate staff, told me he did this "with no fanfare. He never instructed us to call the press and say 'Look at what I'm doing.' "

It wouldn't be accurate to call Sanford a prophet without honor in his own home state. Most of us know we were blessed to have him born a Tar Heel. But his stature around the world is equally great.

No matter how anyone else eulogizes Sanford, nothing will be as appropriate as what President Clinton said: "He was a wonderful man who fought for the right things in the right way."

What an epitaph. But then, what a man.

April 20, 1998

Last meal ought to be oh, so fine

What a dirty, rotten trick. If you want to talk about cruel and unusual punishment, let's talk about what the state of North Carolina did to Wendell Flowers a couple of weeks ago: It let him live.

Now, ordinarily, that might be reason to celebrate, but not this time. You see, not only did Flowers want to die for killing an inmate in prison — where he was doing life for killing an 81-year-old man — but he had already eaten his last meal: chitlins and cherry cheesecake and strawberry cheesecake washed down with a bottle of Cheerwine.

Burrrrp.

Flowers was all ready to walk — or, after that meal, perhaps trot — to the death gurney and a one—way ticket to the hereafter when his mom filed a petition on his behalf, against his wishes.

Patty McQuillan, a Department of Correction spokeswoman, said Flowers seemed dejected after learning he wouldn't be executed.

Heck, who wouldn't be dejected after eating chitlins and cheesecake together and then learning they were going to live? If Flowers was ready to take the dirt nap before eating that "last" meal, imagine how he must've felt about 4 a.m. when it started dancing the macarena inside his belly.

That he and those who went so ignobly before him could eat at all is remarkable in itself. I'll tell you one thing: If I were about to pay the piper, grace — not gravy — would be foremost in my mind.

McQuillan, the prison spokeswoman, ran down for me the "special meals" of some inmates who've dined, then died:

John Rook, class of '86, ordered a dozen hot dogs; he ate only two.
Velma Barfield, '84, munched Cheese Doodles, a Kit Kat and a Coke.
Ricky Lee Sanderson, '97, had a Dolly Madison honey bun.
David Lawson, '94, ate pizza with everything but anchovies.
Kermit Smith, '95, ordered four pieces of extra-crispy white-meat chicken from KFC and washed it down with a Mountain Dew and a Pepsi.

There is obviously nothing "haute" at all about these death-row chow choices, nothing that Wolfgang Puck will be whipping up for the beautiful people.

But at least the state has never encountered an order it couldn't fill, McQuillan told me, although, she added, "we were concerned about the chitlins."

Chitlins is an intimate dish, one that you should eat only if you trust the hygiene habits of the person cooking them — or are about to die anyway. I mean, I came out of the closet only a few years ago and acknowledged that I'll eat a chitlin, but only those that have been cooked by either my Aunt Betty or Aunt Jennie.

I recently switched my position on the death penalty. I now oppose it, not because I don't think people should pay the ultimate price for the evil they've done, but because it is meted out exclusively to poor people. Just look at these choices for "last meals." It's obvious that people, even those near death, eat what they're used to eating in life.

Call me crazy, but just once I'd like to see someone facing the hot squat order up some filet mignon, duck a l'orange or lobster tail.

Until then, the only thing I want to see get fried is chicken.

May 07, 1998

The public has a right to dough

Trying to crack the code at Krispy Kreme doughnuts' corporate headquarters is, I've concluded, only slightly less difficult than trying to figure out how 40-year-old Michael Jackson manages to look more like a prepubescent white girl with each passing year.

And I'm talking just about cracking Krispy Kreme's information code, not its zealously guarded glazed-doughnut formula.

I wasn't about to try to find that out, not after an N&O reporter told me about the hoops she had to jump through to tour the company's headquarters in Winston-Salem — which has a special floor where no visitors are allowed and where, presumably, the secret recipe is kept locked in a safe.

Indeed, the only reason I called the company was the telephone calls I received from a couple of irate Krispy Kreme customers.

Granted, two distraught women do not constitute a flood of calls, but their distress moved me.

The women called to express their dismay over what they regard, if true, as an act of Southern heresy: Krispy Kreme has changed its doughnut recipe.

"I've been eating Krispy Kreme doughnuts for 40 years," one caller said, close to hysteria, "and I've never had to throw one away. I just threw half a box away."

She couldn't tell what had changed. All she knew is that they don't taste the way they did when she was a young'un. That was the unscientific but strongly felt conclusion of the other caller, too.

Sensing a potentially trend-setting story with great social implications — and an excuse to eat some doughnuts — I got on the phone to the local Krispy Kreme. Yes, the lady who answered the telephone confirmed, "changes have been made" in the 61-year-old formula, but she wasn't about to tell me what they were.

A manager at that store said the only change he knew about was that the doughnuts were bigger, "but they don't really let us know what goes on with the mix."

Because I'm a journalist, I went out and bought a dozen doughnuts — which I planned to pass out to my co-workers and then quiz them to see if they detected any changes.

Unfortunately for them, traffic on the Beltline was slow, which caused my beltline to grow: I ate all 12 before I got to the office.

So I called Krispy Kreme's corporate offices, where — upon hearing that I wanted to talk to someone about the famous formula for glazed doughnuts — the woman slammed the phone down in my ear.

I eventually succeeded in contacting someone who contacted someone who contacted me. And of course, I had a mouthful of doughnut when Jack Mcaleer, an executive vice president, returned my call.

He admitted that changes in the "formulation" have been made over the years but said, "It's always based on the original formula."

Huh? He told me more than I ever wanted to know about doughnuts but not what I kept asking: "Did y'all change the recipe?"

I'll keep investigating that one. Of course, that could entail eating dozens of doughnuts. So, if I acquire a resemblance to the Pillsbury Doughboy, just remember: I did it all for you and your right to know.

May 28, 1998

What I really really want: fewer Spice Girl stories

As someone who attended college — several of them, actually, although to no great effect — I at times feel compelled to do certain things.

You know, stuff like watching "Jeopardy" and listening to National Public Radio for at least 20 minutes a day. So one day this week I turned the radio dial from the oldies station to the local NPR station, hoping to find out the latest on the burgeoning arms race between Pakistan and India, to hear if Ken Starr has finally subpoenaed Monica Lewinsky's third-grade teacher and to find out just how fast the rain forests of Brazil are disappearing.

So imagine my surprise when the top story on NPR turned out to be whether the Spice Girls can survive the departure of Ginger Spice. The Spice Girls, for those who don't know, are a media-created bevy of bare-bellied beauties whose musical talents are — quite frankly — inaudible to the naked ear.

Yet, according to the NPR reporter, millions of fans the world over are worried that the defection of Ginger from the quintet signals the end for the group that made "Girl Power" its mantra. This "power," ironically, was mainly manifested by telling millions of 12-year-old girls that hey, it's all right to dress like a hooker.

Don't look at me like that: I call 'em as I see 'em.

The reporter, with a mock solemnity befitting the death of a head of state, told of the personality clashes between the five group members that led to Miss Ginger Spice's decision to seek her fortune as a solo sea-soning condiment on the stage of life.

To the reporter's credit, she did not say that "creative differences" led to the breakup of the Fake Five, since "creative" and "Spice Girls" is as oxymoronic as "giant shrimp" or "ethical politician."

The report was brilliant in one regard — not because the reporter revealed intimate, heretofore unknown aspects of the group, but because I, even after listening to the whole thing, still couldn't tell if it was a joke or if the reporter was taking it as seriously as some of the group's crestfallen fans.

The departure of Geri Halliwell — that's Ginger to you, pal — and whether it invariably signals the demise of the group was even debated in Parliament in London. Since British humor is so naturally droll, I could-n't tell whether those dudes were serious or whether their comments were, as I suspect the reporter's were, meant to be taken tongue in cheek.

There was definitely nothing playful about the response of a young

British journalist who was interviewed for the piece. She sadly spoke of the group in the past tense, as though its demise is imminent now that its acknowledged leader is gone. "The Spice Girls were a classic," the young woman said. "There'll never be another Spice Girls."

Oh, fiddle faddle, girlfriend. I felt the same despondency when the Archies broke up soon after making "Sugar, Sugar." I was certain that no other group, real or animated, could touch my heart with such saccharine yet Dylanesque lines as "I just can't believe the loveliness of lovin' you."

Now, when the Spice Girls can drop some classic lyrics like that, I'll join in this international wailing and doff my bowler to their accomplishments. In the meantime, I'd like to quote a line from the Archies' seminal '60s anthem, "Sugar, Sugar:"

"Pour a little sugar on me, honey."

June 06, 1998

Home is where the hurt is

I could be wrong, but it just seems to me that a man should be able to walk out of his own front door without being insulted.

But twice this week that is exactly what happened to me.

On Monday, a woman jogging on the sidewalk mere steps from my house dashed into the street and nearly got creamed by a car rather than jog past me as I walked to pick up my son from school.

Then Tuesday, a carful of teenage girls pulled onto the sidewalk to turn around about 20 feet from my front door and 10 feet from where I was walking with two kids.

The girls saw us and, with military precision, locked their car doors in unison. The clicks were so loud that, if I hadn't been looking directly at them, I'd have sworn someone was firing at us.

I know some of you are already rolling your eyes and sighing in exasperation, thinking, "Here he goes again, whining."

Well, you can call what I'm doing whining if you want to. I call what was done to me demonizing and dehumanizing, and it's one of the most painful experiences a person can have. After 30 years of it — it's been happening since I was 10 — I still can't accept it.

Now, don't get me wrong. I definitely understand why some people are leery of some black men. Aimless, sometimes conscienceless young punks — I won't call them "brothers" — commit a disproportionate share of crimes, and others are disproportionately depicted as criminals on TV news and in newspapers.

But that's no reason to treat us all as malevolent ne'er-do-wells. In recent days, I've read stories of two white men who burned a black man and beheaded him with an ax and of three others who tied a black dude to their truck and dragged him for three miles — a crime that left parts of his body strewn on the road and veteran cops speechless.

Yet, you don't see me recoiling in terror and locking my doors every time a white guy walks past me. Well, damn it, I deserve — no, I demand — the same respect.

I'm all for women keeping their car doors locked, regardless of the neighborhood they find themselves in. But don't make me the impetus for locking your doors!

That's why I applaud what I consider a great technological innovation: cars with doors that lock automatically as soon as the ignition switch is turned. I call them "insult-proof" cars.

I am writing this column at 5:30 in the morning. No, I didn't get up early: I haven't been to sleep. I couldn't, not after what occurred right outside my door.

The fact that the female jogger was white and the carful of girls was black matters not at all. It just means that they have accepted the same stereotype that all black men — even when accompanied by two little boys — are violent criminals. If anything, I'm even more insulted that the black girls — whose daddies may be blacker than I — would be so insensitive. Had I been able to catch them, I'd have asked, "How would you feel if someone did that to your brother, father or boyfriend?"

Now, I realize there are neighborhoods where I will automatically be perceived as a sociopathic pariah. So, to spare my feelings, I try to stay away from those neighborhoods.

But damn it, I shouldn't have to contend with that crap in my own neighborhood. I just shouldn't.

June 11, 1998

Equal wrongs: Murder is murder, no matter the race

I got a telephone call the other day. It was my old pal Joe from down in Johnston County. Calling Joe my pal is probably stretching things a bit, since I only hear from him when he's angrily — often profanely — disagreeing with me.

But what I respect about him is the fact that, after he's angrily rebuked me for some "liberal, racist nonsense" I've written, he always leaves his full name and telephone number and invites — no, dares — me to call him back.

When I returned his call this week, he was talking about the racially motivated death-by-dragging of James Byrd Jr. in Jasper, Texas.

"I seen where ol' Jesse Jackson and all the rest of them were on television raising sand about them killing that black man down in Texas," Joe said in his thick drawl.

After assuring me that he thought Byrd's killers should be killed, he continued, "How come I don't hear 'em saying nothing when you blacks kill the whites? Or when you kill each other?. . . Is (Byrd) any deader than if he'd been shot by one of his 'brothers'?"

I've never been able to quiet Joe down once he gets on a roll, but this time I did: I agreed with him.

I have long contended that black leaders turn up the volume when a hate crime is perpetrated against blacks by whites, yet they seemingly push the "mute" button when it comes to fratricidal black thugs who run amok in our communities.

Part of the blame for this lies with the media, which are far less enthusiastic about reporting reaction to a run-of-the-mill shooting of one young black dude by another.

But part of the blame also lies in the indisputable fact that too many so-called black leaders are loath to criticize blacks because they realize there is more political currency in blaming "racism" and "the man" than in holding up a mirror to our own pathologies.

Almost before poor Mr. Byrd's body was in the ground, Kweisi Mfume, Jesse Jackson and the usual cast of characters had assumed their usual places in front of TV microphones, sporting mournful countenances and expensive suits, decrying the "racist" war against black people.

There's a war going on, all right, and even though racism still lives, all too often the combatants on both sides are black. Every time a 5-year-old black boy is shot and paralyzed by some neighborhood punk with a gun, that's war. Ask some young lady who is afraid to walk to the corner store to get milk for her children who she fears more — three racist hillbillies in a pickup truck or a conscienceless black thug sucking on a 40-ounce malt liquor and carrying a gun?

True, the three retromingent ne'er-do-wells down in Texas allegedly committed an act of almost inconceivable barbarism against another human being merely because he was black. And it's also true that that was not the only such attack. But I am no more outraged by those attacks than I am when a black person is the perpetrator.

A few years ago, Jesse Jackson got in trouble for saying that he tenses up if a group of young black men is walking behind him on a dark street. He took lots of criticism from blacks for that, just as I know I will for writing that I see his point.

Don't get me wrong, now. I am happy that we have spokesmen to plead our case and express our collective outrage when injustices such as the Jasper horror occur.

But I'll be even happier when Jesse, Kweisi, et al., exhibit the same outrage for the cameras when those horrors are inflicted on us by us.

June 20, 1998

Shopping makes the man

I've got just one question for you: What the heck happened to men?

I thought things had hit rock bottom for us in the '80s, when the media glorified wusses like Alan Alda and Phil Donahue — males who were good at faking sincerity.

But things have deteriorated even more than I imagined, a point I discovered recently while at South Square mall in Durham with a buddy. I had pointed out to him a cool-looking jacket in a store window when he mentioned — actually, I think it slipped out — that his wife buys his clothes.

As any sensitive friend would do, I howled and taunted him mercilessly from one end of the mall to the other — pooh-poohing his contention that "that's life in the '90s."

"That's life for wimps in the '90s," I retorted, and set out to prove it by polling women.

I immediately wrote off the first woman we encountered, certain that her response wasn't typical.

"Why, yes, I buy all of his clothes," she said as she stood in the men's shoe department at Belk. "My husband doesn't even know what size underwear he wears."

That's sad, even sadder than the woman who a while ago bemusedly informed me that her husband once picked up a shirt in a store and asked, "Honey, do I like this?"

Dudes, how did it come to this? Clothes shopping, at least to me, is one of life's great pleasures — one I can't imagine relinquishing without a fight.

We've all seen the legion of blank-eyed men wandering aimlessly through malls or sitting docilely on benches clutching shopping bags. But I always assumed they were just chilling while the little woman browsed in Lane Bryant or Sharper Image. I did not know that they were sitting there like obedient little Beaver Cleavers while June picked their clothes for them.

There are certain things that just naturally fall under men's domain, things that we're supposed to teach our sons — like how to drink straight from the milk carton without getting caught, explaining the 24-second shot clock and buying your first pair of shoes that don't have "Nike" or flashing lights on them.

But how can a man impart to his son the joy of a well-hanging suit if he himself wears whatever his wife buys and lays out on the bed?

Wake up, men, before it's too late. Sure, I know marriage requires teamwork, and I don't knock guys who, for instance, dutifully sign their paychecks and hand them over to mama. I used to be that kind of chump — I mean man — when I was young and thought nothing of blowing my whole paycheck on albums, beer or tipping Miss Paradise over at the 14 Karat Dinner Theater.

But pal, I'm going to let you in on a secret: Your wife didn't buy you that purple, shiny, highwater suit because it makes you look good.

One of the joys of being single is having the freedom to put on whatever I want — even if it's my lime green, crushed velvet jumpsuit like the one Fred Williamson wore in "Hammer's Big Ripoff" — without wifeypoo standing there shaking her head and asking, "Are you really going to wear that out in public?"

So men, assert yourselves. Demand the right to dress yourselves. And if your wife doesn't like it, tell her she can continue buying yours if you can buy hers.

Of course, if men started buying their wives' clothes, we probably wouldn't need Miss Paradise.

June 22, 1998

Johnny, get your mower

If I were a gun nut, I'd be rejoicing right now over the story that appeared in The N&O recently.

It wasn't much of a story, about 3 inches long. But for people who sleep with their guns, name them and feel there is a liberal government conspiracy to take them, the story was their personal Magna Carta, Emancipation Proclamation and Declaration of Independence wrapped into one.

That would make Tim Grissinger their George Washington.

Grissinger is the Wendell man who, in the news story, was arrested and charged with assault with a deadly weapon.

Did he use an Uzi against his neighbor during the property dispute? A Glock? How 'bout a .357 Magnum?

Nope. He was way too creative for that. He used a John Deere,

police say. Or was it a Lawn-Boy? Police charged Grissinger with intentionally hitting Janet Perry Jones with his lawn mower during a confrontation. Grissinger's wife, Linda, denied that when I spoke with her.

"But, Saunders," I hear you asking incredulously, "what does a bound-
ary dispute involving a tree, a septic tank and a lawn mower in Wendell
have to do with gun control and gun lovers?"

A lot. You know how every time some kid goes ballistic and shoots
up a schoolyard full of classmates, there is a predictable cry for more
gun control?

Well, the National Rifle Association — to whom "gun control" means
using both hands — just as predictably resists those efforts. The Wendell
story provides some vindication to gun advocates, since it affirms one of
their basic tenets — that guns are not the problem, but hot—headed
people are.

If the gunshot that precipitated the Revolutionary War was "the shot
heard 'round the world," Grissinger's midday ride on his mower could
become known as the "crank heard 'round the world" if it tilts the argument over guns to the NRA's favor.

I'm sure somebody, probably Charlton Heston, will argue that this
story, if true, illustrates perfectly the danger of putting motorized lawn
equipment in the wrong hands. Yet, he'll bleat, you don't see the government running around trying to require waiting periods and background
checks for people who want to buy a Lawnboy, do you?

Just as gun lovers fret that any little voluntary concession on gun
ownership will lead to bigger, involuntary rules, I'm afraid that restrictions
on yard equipment will mushroom and lead us down an unmowed path,
as well.

Today motorized lawn mower, tomorrow weed-whackers.

Lawn mowers, like fire and, yes, guns, can be our friends if used
right. For instance, it was a lawn mower that allowed one of my heroes,
country singer George Jones, to drive to the liquor store after his wife
tried to enforce sobriety on him by taking his car keys.

Come to think of it that's what made him my hero.

In the future, pacifists won't be able to merely cite the biblical, anti-
violence injunction to beat swords into plowshares. I figure if a lawn
mower can be used as a weapon, why not a plow?

June 25, 1998

That list of 100 greatest movies? Give it the Shaft

Am I blue? Ain't these tears in these eyes telling you?

Y'all will have to excuse me if I'm not my usual, gleeful self lately.

Mr. Sunshine, which is what some people — OK, just me — call me, has been in a terrible funk for the past few days, ever since the American Film Institute released its list of the supposed 100 greatest films of all time.

The tears are because not a single one of my favorite movies made the list. Not even "Blacula."

Oh, sure, I agree that "The Godfather" and "Citizen Kane" should have been on the list. Both are masterpieces that I have watched countless times. I'll even grudgingly concede that "Gone With the Wind" deserves its No. 4 ranking, if only for the line where Rhett tells Scarlett — who has just asked him "Wherever shall I go? Whatever shall I do?" — "Frankly, my dear, I don't give a damn."

(I've always fantasized about saying that to a woman, but for some reason they always say it to me first.)

Even as I acknowledge that those are great movies, though, I have to bemoan the celluloid triumphs that were left off the list. For instance, where the heck is "Hell Up In Harlem"? Or "Carmen Jones"? Or even "Cleopatra Jones"?

I'm betting that the people who voted on these movies have never heard of Rudy Ray Moore, whose "Dolemite" trilogy is a true cinematic tour de force.

Lots of people have problems with "blaxploitation" flicks like "Superfly" that regrettably, glorified a cocaine dealer. But is that any worse than "Birth of a Nation," which made the list by glorifying the Ku Klux Klan?

I admit that the dialogue and story lines of most of these flicks aren't going to make anyone forget Ingmar Bergman or John Singleton at their scintillating best, but "Superfly" deserves recognition simply for the fashion revolution it spawned — dudes in wide-brimmed hats out to here, maxi-length coats, chrome-plated El Dorado Cadillacs that got six miles to the gallon. If you didn't run the air conditioner.

You know how some people wonder if the moon-landing was real or if Elvis is really dead? Well, I lie awake nights trying to figure out how "American Graffiti" made the list when "Cooley High" didn't.

After all, they both produced fabulous soundtracks and are about the same thing — high school nostalgia. The major difference is that one, the one that garnered the honors, is about white kids.

Now, I actually liked "American Graffiti," but it should have been left off the list for no other reason than that it was spun the dreadful, now-unwatchable television show "Happy Days."

Of course, "Cooley High" begat the equally dreadful "What's Happenin'" series, so maybe we're even.

But my favorite great movie that was left off the list was "Shaft."

I know, I know. The plot was not terribly believable and had holes in it big enough to drive Superfly's "Hog" — that's '70s lingo for Cadillac — through. Also, I've never figured out how Shaft got shot in the arm during the day and went rappelling through a 15th-story window that night with no noticeable ill effects.

But even if "Shaft" wasn't one of the 100 greatest movies of all time, it featured the second—greatest line of all time, next to Rhett Butler's.

It occurred when Shaft called his girlfriend Ellie — yes, Ellie — from a pay phone to check if he had any messages. (You see, this was in pre-answering machine days.)

Before hanging up to resume reading Ebony magazine, she said, "I love you, John Shaft."

His classic response: "Yeah, I know it, baby."

Now be honest, fellas. Who among you hasn't wished he could toss off a line like that without getting a telephone receiver jammed through his ear?

June 27, 1998

Kids today not so bad as reputed

I saw a lot of impressive stuff at the Festival for the Eno recently, not the least of which was the gigantic turkey leg I bought for $5.

The big ol' thing looked as though it might have come from a mutant strain of fowl that was raised next to the Chernobyl nuclear reactor or been something that our caveman ancestors would have used to club a saber-toothed tiger into submission.

But boy, was it tasty. Indeed, the only thing that filled me up more than the giant turkey leg was the general feeling of conviviality, a sense of fast-disappearing community, between the various burgs in the Triangle.

I met people from all around and heard all kinds of outstanding musical performers, each of whom connected with the crowd that strolled slowly past — as hot as it was, "slowly" was the only way to stroll.

But the most impressive event I witnessed at the annual festival, which drew more than 40,000 people over the weekend, was a private moment I shared with a young girl who stopped by The N&O's booth.

"Hey, li'l girl, you want to register to win one of these mountain bikes we're giving away?" I growled at the adolescent with my customary charm.

The li'l girl looked admiringly at the glistening bikes, then back at me. "Nah, I already have one," she said. "I'll give somebody else a chance to win one."

She turned and walked away, unaware of the impact her simple response had on me.

I know that encounter might seem like no big deal. But when I think of some of the selfish people I meet daily, her selfless act was an epiphany and it moved me.

Most people — OK, I — would have said, "Hmm, I'll win this one and give it to someone else," knowing full well that the odds of giving away a brand-new bike that I'd won were slim. If anything, I might've given away — or more likely sold — the old bike and kept the new one. But hey, that's just me.

Of course, I realize also that it could be that I'm just getting old, that the hinges on my mental gate need oiling and I'm therefore seeing profundity where none exists. Maybe that's why her small act of selflessness impressed me so.

But if that's the case, so be it. I prefer to think of it as further evidence that young people today are not as bad as we've too often portrayed them — or at least are no worse than previous generations.

Right about the time of the festival, I was driving down Main Street in Durham and saw a young kid with a lemonade stand in the sweltering heat. It was so sweltering that — impressed though I was by her entrepreneurial spirit — I didn't stop.

"I'll come back," I lied to myself.

I never did and I felt bad about it for the rest of the day. I felt even worse when I heard that the stand had been robbed.

Now, I have reversed my support of the death penalty. I figure if the murderous William Burmeister doesn't deserve the state-sponsored dirt nap, then no one does. But I think something pretty awful should happen to the louse who robbed that young'un's lemonade stand.

I wouldn't kill him, but I'd love to catch him alone with just him, me and one of those giant turkey legs.

July 13, 1998

An extra step for a thirsty dog

After reading the story about Lucille Rebecca Alexander, I just knew I had to go give that dog some water.

Miss Alexander, you recall, was the Durham woman whose body was recently found in her Ruth Street house.

Nothing unusual about that: Old people die every day. What was unusual, though, is that she had been dead for, oh, maybe 10 years and nobody had noticed. Or cared.

She was apparently a piece of work who antagonized and loathed her neighbors. Even though she appeared to be black, she obviously suffered from the same affliction as Michael and Janet Jackson: negrophobia. She threatened to shoot anyone who broached her property trying to be neighborly.

The loathing was reciprocated by her neighbors, which explains why none of them felt compelled to check on her. Her body might still be lying there today, buried under mounds of collapsed roof and pine needles, with a stocking cap clinging to her skull, if some neighborhood children hadn't stumbled across her remains.

Regardless of how unlovable she was — and interviews with people who knew her paint a picture of a pixilated, unlovable woman — nobody deserves such an inglorious death and resting place.

If she had been one of those Aunt Bea types who is always fixing cakes and pies for everybody and tending to strangers, her body would have been discovered within days, if not hours, of her demise.

Oh, she'd be just as dead, but I believe her soul would lie more peacefully knowing that somebody cared enough to check on her.

That's why I just had to give that dog some water.

For the past two days, the dog whose infuriating barks usually keep me awake 'til it's time to wake up has looked at me with what looks like desperate pleading in its eyes.

The neighbors who belong to the dog have been unseen by me for a couple of days, and I haven't seen anyone else tending to the mutt as it lies chained behind a fence. That means the dog had to survive temperatures in the high 90s without fresh water. One of my favorite blues songs goes "I wouldn't treat a dog the way you treated me." That kept playing in my head, but the words had become "I wouldn't treat a dog the way these people treat their dog." That's why, when I got home and saw that water dish in the same position it was in when I left for work, I marched right up there and filled it up.

I'm not applying for sainthood, because truthfully, I did it for selfish reasons: I'd have felt miserable if that dog had died because I chose to do nothing rather than possibly incur the wrath of my neighbors.

My reluctance to offer succor in the first place stemmed from the unneighborliness of my neighbors.

They're not mean and have never said an unpleasant word to me.

Indeed, they've never said anything to me — unless you count the few times I've almost forced them to acknowledge my persistent greetings. Even then, they acted as though they'd find eating a possum soaked in turpentine more pleasurable.

But as hot as it has been lately, I'd much prefer their wrath to the guilt and self-loathing I'd have felt had I not offered that dog a sip.

That reminds me. I wonder how Lucille Rebecca Alexander's neighbors feel right about now?

July 23, 1998

Capitol violence may bring change

Remember a few years ago when you darn near had to mortgage your home to buy a box of Cap'n Crunch?

Breakfast cereal is still no great bargain and ranks among the most expensive items on your grocer's shelves. But prices have dropped in recent years, and if you'll bear with me for a second, I'll show you how the story of the cereal price drop could prevent violence such as occurred in Washington, D.C., recently.

I heard a story, the authenticity of which I can't vouch for, about four congressmen who shared an apartment in Washington to cut down on expenses. For them, as for most single dudes, meals often consisted of cereal. One day, one congressman returned from the Safeway in a state of shock — sticker shock — over high cereal prices. He and his corn-flakes-crunching colleagues then started publicly throwing around words like "investigation" and "price-fixing," prompting the cereal companies voluntarily to reduce their prices lest Congress start snooping into their business practices.

The moral, Sherlock, is that as long as regular blokes such as you and I were spending a fortune on brightly colored boxes of brightly colored sugar, nothing happened.

But when politicians themselves felt the bite, well...

It's the same thing with guns. Now that Russell Eugene Weston Jr. has defiled the marbled sanctity of the U.S. Capitol and brought violence right up to Congress' door, I guarantee you that more politicians will start jumping out of bed with the National Rifle Association and proposing legislation making it tougher for angry madmen to arm themselves.

Now, all of you gun nuts out there, chill out. I'm not fixing to launch into a diatribe about how guns should be outlawed — because you'll just say, "Then only outlaws will have guns, blah, blah, blah." The issue isn't the "right" to bear arms, but the "desire" to do so. As Americans, we should have the right to bear arms or even to arm bears. But the person who does either worries me. No one, except maybe NRA toady Charlton Heston, could argue that the six-shooter Weston used was made to do anything but kill people. Isn't it ironic that fools such as Weston who waste their demented lives railing against the government can do so only because they are endowed by their creator with certain inalienable rights, rights which this government allows them to exercise?

Those truths, as the Constitution says, are self-evident. What isn't self-evident, at least not to me, is why doctors are laboring so mightily to save the diseased-brained Weston. I know all about the Hippocratic oath and such, but Hippocrates never had to clean up after a disgruntled paranoiac with a grudge and a gun. If Weston had been wheeled into my operating room, I'd have stared at him solemnly and said, "Sorry, Homeslice. I don't believe you're going to make it."

I know, I know. No one's going to confuse me with being a saint for expressing such a sentiment. Nor will anyone mistake me for Paul Revere, Crispus Attucks or any other fabled patriot we grew up reading about. Even so, I love this country. I get a lump right here whenever I hear Ray Charles sing "America the Beautiful." But since Weston's attack on the Capitol, I've felt a different kind of lump. In my heart.

July 27, 1998

Monica's motive? Historic preservation with an attitude

See there. That's precisely why I prefer full-grown, adult women who've been around — or even on — the block a few times.

Why? Because no full-grown woman in her right mind would keep an unclean dress for two years and then trot it out possibly to incriminate a man she'd had a consensual affair with.

But President Clinton was apparently less discriminating than I am and now finds his continued effectiveness as president hanging by a thread. Or, more literally, by the stains on a thread.

I proudly admit that for the past several weeks, my life has been a Monica-free zone. Anytime something about Lewinsky and her real or imagined trysts with the president comes on the tube, I turn to BET — where they're invariably playing the top 800 rap videos of the week — or to the Weather Channel. I once even watched Conan O'Brien's show to avoid a Monica update. Honest.

But despite my best efforts, I heard something about a navy blue dress that may have traces of Clinton's DNA, which, for the squeamish among you, stands for "Do Not Ask." I don't know how Lewinsky maintained the dress' "integrity" — whether she kept it in a hermetically sealed mayonnaise jar on Funk & Wagnall's front porch or else gave it to her mother with instructions to "drop this by the cleaners when you get a chance, please, Mom" — and mom just plain forgot.

Regardless of how Lewinsky kept the "integrity" intact — and regardless of what tests ultimately prove is on that dress — there are but two possible words to describe this young lady: Sinister or Trifling.

Either she had phenomenal foresight and orchestrated this whole scandal, knowing the dress could play a prominent role in giving her a huge payday — in which case, she and Linda Tripp are more alike than we initially thought — or she could just be trifling.

Don't look at me like that. What word would you use to describe someone who doesn't clean a dress for two years, regardless of what it is stained with?

And don't tell me that she really cared for the president and was keeping the Do Not Ask Dress as a loving keepsake.

Of course, some people still argue that Lewinsky's motives for holding onto the dress in its alleged state were neither sinister, trifling nor a sign of her unstable obsession with President Clinton. Yeah right.

What other possible reason could she have had for keeping it? As a conversation piece at parties? To donate to the Clinton Presidential Library in Little Rock? Not likely.

I was young once and remember holding onto things to remind me of certain women.

But I held onto normal stuff — like ticket stubs to the Parliament Funkadelic concert we attended, or the red, black and green ribbons Sweet Thang used to hold her Afro Puffs in place, or the first frying pan she ever threw at me. (OK, well, maybe everything wasn't normal.)

Now, that's love.

Anybody who has listened to an oldies radio station in the past 10 years is familiar with a great song by Dennis Yost and the Classics Four called "Traces of Love." It was about lovers' mementos and featured these beautiful lines:

Faded photographs, covered now with lines and creases,
Tickets torn in half, memories in bits and pieces...
Ribbons from her hair, souvenirs of days together,
The rings she used to wear,
Pages from an old love letter.

Now, that's romantic. There is nothing romantic about holding onto a possibly DNA-bearing dress.

That's just sinister. Or trifling.

August 15, 1998

Weaving a web of self-doubt

There are two ways to know summer vacation is over and kids are back in school:

First, you can hear the exploding champagne corks of celebrating parents. Second, you see lame-brained mothers buying hair weaves for their little girls.

I call such parents lamebrained because they seem totally unaware of — or maybe just unconcerned about — the very real damage they're doing to the psyches of little girls who go to bed baldheaded but wake up with hair down to here.

I was in the hair-care supply store recently buying some clippers to trim my beard (without the beard, I look too much like Denzel Washington) when I witnessed a disturbing scene. Six black mothers, with their young daughters in tow, were loading up on fake hair to strap to those babies' heads.

"When," I asked myself, "did hair weaves become a back-to-school essential the way notebooks, pencils and book bags are?"

Now, if grown women want to try to fool people into thinking they grew 12 inches of hair overnight, fine. They're grown and they can do what they want to do.

But slapping a foot or more of that synthetic stuff onto the head of little girls — and I've seen 'em as young as 4 years old — does nothing but cloud up their little mental skies with self-doubt about their attractiveness. Do these parents really think that a phony ponytail is going to raise their daughters' self-esteem and give them the self-confidence they need?

Think about it: When a mother drags her daughter off to the hair-care store for some weaves, what subconscious message does that convey? In essence, this: "Here, Keisha. You're not naturally pretty enough, so Mommy's going to make you look better with this 'near-hair.' "

What's next? Padded bras for underdeveloped pre-schoolers?

Who said every woman is supposed to have hair she can toss? Some of the most beautiful women I know have short hair.

Mothers need to understand that the most important asset with which they can imbue their daughters is not long, flowing locks, but knowledge and self-love. In other words, they'll help Tamika more by hanging out with her in the library than in the hair-care store.

I called Denise Barnes, a Triangle clinical psychologist, and asked her if hair weaves on prepubescent girls are just a harmless conceit or, as I think it is, an indirect way of telling your own daughter she's ugly.

"I think the moms are trying to boost their little girls' self-esteem,"

she said, "but they're not looking at the long-term repercussions of alter-
ing the girls' natural beauty."

In other words, once the weaves are removed — and they'll have to
be, unless you want to look like Stevie Wonder, whose hair line is headed
south of Tijuana — the girls will feel like Samson when he was shorn of
his locks: helpless.

A decade ago, during the reign of the dreaded, wet-headed jheri curl
hairstyle — which required a plastic bag to be worn on your head — I
heard Oprah admonishing people to "declare a moratorium on plastic
bags in public."

I, likewise, am asking mothers to declare a moratorium on hair
weaves. Because even if you buy a state-of-the-art, Janet Jackson-type
weave that fools everybody else, it won't fool you. Or your daughter.

August 20, 1998

Questions of taste in 'last meals'

No. Yes. No.

Those are the answers to the most frequently asked questions I
receive about my picture that goes with this column.

Here are the questions: Are you a pimp? Do you think you look good
in that stupid hat? Are you Andrew H. Brown's illegitimate son? (In case
you were born after World War II, Andy Brown was The Kingfish's dim-
bulb, derby-wearing sidekick on the "Amos 'n' Andy" show.)

Anyone who knows me will tell you that I am like a sensitive, easily
bruised flower. Reader insults of my appearance truly make my brown
eyes blue. Like when a recent caller said, "Damn, you ugly. Please, go
back to the cartoon."

But a letter I received two days ago hurt worse than that. It was
written by Wendell Flowers, who currently resides on death row inside
Central Prison. He was upset because he thought I'd made him the "butt-
end" of a joke. Thus he wrote, "From your picture, I can see how a sense
of humor would be handy ... You, with your bow-tie-wearing self, look like
a reject from an Orville Redenbacher popcorn commercial. Well, at least
you're trying to spread good cheer: I assume you wear those clothes to
make people laugh. I'll give you your props ... It takes a real man to wear
that ensemble. Or a complete nerd."

Flowers took exception to an exceptional column I wrote in May,
when he was initially scheduled to die for killing an inmate that his attorney and at least one other inmate insist he didn't kill.

I wrote that the state was guilty of cruel and unusual punishment for not killing Flowers after providing him a "last meal" of chitlins, cherry cheesecake, strawberry cheesecake and Cheerwine soda. Considering the war raging within his belly 'round about midnight, I wrote, Flowers was probably begging for that lethal injection.

The purpose of the column was not, as Flowers said, to poke fun at him but to show the socioeconomic disparity of the death penalty as evidenced by inmates' "last meals." Such repasts invariably consist of "po' boy" foods like chitlins, fried chicken from The Colonel and honeybuns. No wonder: Most of the people the state kills are — what else? — po' boys.

To my way of thinking, we won't have true death-penalty justice until someone is executed after a requested last meal of filet mignon or lamb chops in mint jelly.

Although it's not an issue I lie awake nights pondering, my own last meal would probably be a seven-course beauty: five cans of Vienna sausages, a pack of soda crackers and a Coca-Cola.

Flowers, though, suggested that I'd order rump roast, a portion of the pig my editor would only allow me to call "roasted mountain oysters" and a side order of corn flakes because, Flowers said, "you portray yourself to be a flaky pig's ass."

Ouch, dude.

He then promised me a "surprise" from his next "last meal" order.

I can hardly wait. But after hearing from his attorney and an inmate who contacted me this week, I'm beginning to wonder whether Flowers' next "last meal" should really be his last meal.

I'll check back with you on this one.

August 27, 1998

Wee hours of 'Titanic' madness

In the end, I decided that they're just too easy a target.

Here I was, all set to have some sadistic fun mocking the people who stayed up past midnight Monday to get a copy of "Titanic," when I was overcome by ... heck, I guess you could call it "conscience."

I was fixing to write them off as mindless, media-manipulated lemmings who had convinced themselves that life wasn't worth living if they weren't among the first in their neighborhood to possess a copy of the overhyped, movie.

(Truth be told, a dude I know was hawking cut-rate, bootleg copies a week after it came out last year. But let's not tell that to the thousands nationwide who descended upon Blockbuster stores this week.)

But after talking with customers at a Durham Blockbuster about

12:30 a.m. Tuesday, I decided they were not deserving of my scorn. Sympathy, perhaps, but not scorn.

Indeed, while talking to one young lady, I began to envy her giddiness at scoring a copy of the movie and four posters of its star. I remember thinking, "Geez, I haven't been that excited since Quick's Grill in Rockingham introduced the new lime-flavored M.D. 20/20 wine."

"I'm going to post them around the house," Christina Burton told me. "One in the bedroom, one in the bathroom, one in the kitchen ... I love the movie. I loooove it."

And what, I asked the Durham Tech student, did she "loooove" about it that made her come out alone at midnight for a copy?

"Leonardo," she said.

I couldn't relate to that, but I — and most other men — could relate to Jason Zaharis' reason for being at Blockbuster after midnight.

"My girlfriend," Zaharis answered when I asked why he stopped at Blockbuster after leaving his job as a federal correctional officer in Butner. "I was told not to come home without it."

Zaharis and others I spoke to deserve something less than scorn, but Blockbuster Entertainment, the company responsible for the shameless media event, deserve something more.

First, the company creates a media event by keeping its 10 million stores open until 2 a.m. to satisfy the "demand" for "Titanic," but then inexplicably forbids employees to answer any questions. (It couldn't have been out of concern for its customers' privacy and safety; if the company were really concerned, it wouldn't have lured them out after midnight.)

I saw something akin to terror on the faces of a couple of employees when I sauntered — actually, at that hour I stumbled — into the store about 1 a.m. and asked, "How's it going?"

Man, you would've thought I was Ken Starr coming in with a subpoena to find out if Monica Lewinsky had rented any movies on how to seduce a president.

"It's going well," they responded to each question — the company-approved line, I later learned.

How many videos have y'all sold tonight? I asked.

"It's going well."

Are most of the people coming in for "Titanic" men or women?

"It's going well."

Uh, are y'all going to stay open all night to satisfy demand for the re-release of "Blacula" next month?

"It's going well."

Now, that's something worth staying up all night for.

September 03, 1998

Manners displayed too late

Fourteen, 15, 16 ... oh, sorry.

Y'all caught me counting how many times now twice-convicted murderer Kawame Mays said "sir" during a two-minute stretch of his trial that ended Wednesday.

Two minutes. If you don't believe me, you can roll the videotape yourself: The case was broadcast nationally on "Court TV."

Mays didn't actually say "sir" when responding to prosecutors' questions: He said "suh," as though that would make him deserving of more sympathy, even pitiable, to jurors trying to decide whether he should die for killing Raleigh Police Detective Paul Hale.

Well, the final reviews are in, and the winner of the Oscar for best actor in a life-or-death situation is ... not Mays. Although a previous jury deadlocked on the first-degree murder charge, this one finally brought home the verdict most of you expected and, indeed, wanted.

But regardless of what you think of Mays, you have to admire his tour de force courtroom performance that still may keep him off Death Row.

Don't ask me how I know, but I can testify that standing before a stern-faced judge in a black robe brings out the politeness in the orneriest person alive. When Judgie-poo gives you that dirty look, the "yes, sirs" and "no, sirs" just tumble out of your mouth involuntarily.

I'm not saying Mays was putting on — which is the way country folk say "faking." Who knows? Maybe the soft-spoken, contrite, perpetually-on-the-verge-of-tears young man on "Court TV" was the real Kawame, although the obsequiousness he displayed in court was a far cry from the strutting, menacing dude prosecution witnesses describe when he has his 9 mm strapped on and is talking about "jacking" any cop foolish enough to try to arrest him.

But if I had to bet, I'd bet that the soft-spoken young man on television is closer to the real Mays than the one police and prosecution witnesses describe.

Naw, I'm not saying that Mays would be somewhere conducting a Bible study class or teaching Braille to the blind if he weren't probably on his way to the state-sponsored dirt nap. But on the streets where he and way too many other young boys grow old — which is not the same as growing up — courtesy and politeness are not negotiable currency. If anything, they are perceived as signs of weakness to be exploited.

Of course, this is nothing new, nor is it — as some would like to think — unique to black kids. We called it earning your "rep" — reputation — while every Mafia movie I've ever seen talks about young hoods "making their bones."

Regardless of what you call it, you achieve it by engaging in criminal, self-destructive conduct designed to impress like-minded peers.

And to do that, you have to play the macho hard-ass — even if the consequences land you on Court TV weeping for your life or strapped to a gurney awaiting a needle's deadly plunge.

Now tell me, how macho is that?

September 10, 1998

That Monica style, that attitude ... positively impeachy

Pinch me. No, really. Pinch me. That's the only way I'm going to believe what I just saw on television.

I was giving my thumb a workout by flipping through the channels of my dusty old Zenith when I came across Monica Lewinsky staring soulfully into some older man's eyes.

Nothing unusual there, you say, since the woman who has the president apologizing out of both sides of his mouth has been quite ubiquitous lately.

Only, this wasn't a news show. Nor, as it turned out, was it really Monica. It was merely an actress on a daytime soap opera who looked disturbingly similar to the notorious intern.

The TV actress wasn't quite as — hmm, what's a nice way to say this — fluffy as Lewinsky, but she had that same anachronistic, early Ricki Lake-late Patsy Cline hairdo thing working.

Coincidence? I think not. It was inevitable that some television writer or executive would conclude that any story line could be enlivened by having a character who looks like one of the most famous — or infamous, depending upon how you vote — women in the world right now.

Now, I realize that one actress on a soap opera doesn't make a trend, but what if that look catches on and a whole generation of young ladies starts wearing their hair like Monica?

Don't laugh. Remember a year or so ago when reliable surveys showed that 98 percent of all teenage girls were climbing into hairdressers' chairs across the country and asking for the "Jennifer Aniston" look — hoping to be mistaken for the "Friends" star?

Lewinsky looks like anything but a TV star, but because she is on TV, someone, somewhere, thinks she's cool. Or, perhaps, so uncool that she is cool.

Well, let me issue a warning, no, a plea, to the mothers of America: If your daughters come to you requesting money for a Monica-do, don't.

Sure, it worked for her and helped her snag a president, but I sus-pect that if the moon was right, the libidinous dude at 1600 Pennsylvania Ave. could have been snagged by an 88-year-old grandmother wearing spats.

There is already an organization — Monicas With Attitude — dedicat-ed to helping women with that name overcome the stigma Lewisky's notoriety has bestowed upon it.

"Monica," the organization's founder says, derives from the Latin word for "nun." Go figure.

Maestro, hit it:

Mamas don't let yer babies grow up to be interns.
Don't let 'em date presidents and then talk too much
Let 'em be doctors and lawyers and such...
Mamas don't let yer babies grow up to be interns.
Keep 'em away from the prez,
Believe nothing he says.
He just wants to get his swerve on...
Mamas don't let your babies grow up to be   interns.
Starr will ask have you seen her
Then send a subpoener.
And he won't quit 'til we're all dead.

September 19, 1998

You can't see the '70s from here

There are two reasons I love Chapel Hill.

First, Jesse Helms hated it. Second, Dean Smith coached there.

The latter reason is why, when I ran away from home at 16, I wan-dered Franklin Street for days, leaving only long enough to dash across UNC's leafy campus to see whether Smith's car was outside the gym.

For a weed-bending bumpkin from Rockingham, Franklin Street in the mid-1970s was exotic, like I imagine Berkeley, Calif., was in the 1960s. It seemed that everyone, from students to tambourine-wielding beggars, sported long hair and the official young folks' uniform of the day: jeans — dirty, ripped and baggy — and cheap flannel shirts. The smell of a popular herb — it wasn't oregano, pal — wafted on the air.

Now, the student uniform is khakis from the Gap and $150 Cole Haan shoes. And, after this week's assault on the homeless by Chapel Hill's Town Council, something else is wafting on the air: intolerance.

The council's desire to protect residents and merchants from aggres-sive, possibly violent panhandlers is laudable. But laws against intimidation already exist. Besides, by the time a normal person reaches the point in life where he is on the street pleading for "spare change," all fight has been knocked out of him.

For those who aren't normal — who are on the street rasslin' with their private inner demons as well as hunger — the threat of a $50 fine and two days in jail is laughable.

Chapel Hill Police Chief Ralph Pendergraph — no relation to '70s soul singer Teddy Pendergrass — put it perfectly to an N&O reporter. "This is not a police issue, it's a social issue," he said.

Despite the chief's enlightened attitude, the Town Council heaped yet another indignity upon the homeless: When the Tar Heels play football at home, fans receive notices to refrain from indulging those on the street. Well, hell, y'all, why not just put up signs like those at the zoo — to which Helms allegedly and famously compared the town? "Please don't feed the animals."

The misguided council, incredibly, is blaming the panhandling problem on an institution that helps the down-and-outers: the Inter-Faith Council. It seems to feel that if it weren't for the council providing the homeless a hot and a cot, they would all migrate to Durham.

If such municipal heavy-handedness had occurred in Charlotte or Cary — areas whose leaders take themselves way too seriously to begin with — we'd understand.

But repressive measures are uncharacteristic of Chapel Hill, which, along with Durham and its Ninth Street, has the closest thing to a bohemian strip in North Carolina.

Something dangerous — more dangerous than 1,000 bums a'bumming — is happening. It's the citification of our state, and it started, I swear, this year when the town of Wilson banned indoor furniture from front porches. Officials claim such furniture detracts from the town's aesthetics.

Now, the state's most liberal community adopts policies that ape its most conservative in the unspoken name of, you guessed it, aesthetics.

What's next? A Chapel Hill ordinance banning from Volvos and Saabs those bumper stickers that read, "I'm from North Carolina and I don't support Jesse Helms"?

October 01, 1998

A capital show on death row

There are two abiding principles by which I live. The first is, "Do unto others — and then run."

The second is, "Anything bad worth doing is worth doing badly."

That philosophy is directed at people who want to make the death penalty more humane by removing options for executions and permitting only lethal injections.

You see, some inmates, desiring to go out with a bang, have requested death by gas. But certain do—gooders in the state legislature are engaged in a ludicrous debate to deprive them of input in how they go out.

If they have their way, all inmates executed in North Carolina would have to die like sissies, stretched out on a gurney with needles sticking in their arms. What an undignified way to croak for someone who has perhaps murdered five people during a robbery.

It has been so long since anyone took the hot squat that Old Sparky, the state's electric chair, has grown cobwebs from inactivity, and the firing squad, stoning and hanging have gone the way of the guillotine.

Since those time-tested means of sending the deserving to perdition are regarded by many as unduly harsh, that makes you wonder just what method of execution they would condone? Tickling? Eating bad sushi? Listening to Kenny G. or Michael Bolton?

What's even more cruel and unusual than listening to Bolton sing "When a Man Loves a Woman" is the way some of these violent, conscienceless criminals are dispatched to the dirt nap.

One morning I was hanging out at Central Prison about 1, listening to official eyewitnesses describe the just-completed execution of an inmate by lethal injection. One of the witnesses said the man "raised his head, mouthed the words 'I love you' to his family and laid his head down as though dozing off to sleep."

Ahhh, how peaceful it all seemed, how humane, how utterly — hmm, what's the word I'm looking for here? — revolting. Because the executed man had kidnapped and raped a young woman before bashing her head in repeatedly with a cinder block.

I no longer support the death penalty, because that human snot rag James Burmeister didn't get it for gunning down two innocent people in Fayetteville. But I feel if you're going to do it, you might as well do it badly.

That, ironically, is also the way many death penalty opponents feel: They, too, favor the harsher methods, and some even want them shown on TV — with the assumption being that people will be so repulsed by the in-your-face brutality that they'll stop all executions.

For these TV death fests, they'd presumably have an announcer providing breath-by-breath coverage a la the World Wrasslin' Federation. All I can say is, "Cool."

Announcer: I don't know, folks. This could be it. The executioner has hit the electric switch, and smoke is rising from Jackson's scalp. Oh, boy! His breathing is becoming labored, and his head is drooping. Somebody stick a fork in him 'cos this turkey's done. No, wait! Jackson lifted his shoulder off the mat before the referee could pronounce him dead. What a fighter.

October 08, 1998

No laughing matter on UPN's own masterpiece theater

Memo to: Dean Valentine, President, UPN network.
From: Me.
Re: "The Secret Diary of Desmond Pfeiffer."
Dear Deano. Hey babe, I got that tape of "The Secret Diary. . ." and it was an absolute scream. I haven't laughed so hard since I watched "Saving Private Ryan," that screwball movie comedy in which thousands of soldiers get their faces blown off trying to save the world from that wacky fellow, Adolf Whatsisname.

But I do have a couple of suggestions that will make "Desmond" even funnier. Don't get me wrong, now. The show, about the fictitious escapades of a sex-crazed President Abraham Lincoln — as chronicled by his black aide, Desmond — is a "can't miss" hit. I mean, if the world isn't ready, in 1998, for a comedy about the good ol' days of slavery, then it'll never be.

Why, I'm predicting "Desmond Pfeiffer" will do for slavery what "Seinfeld" did for underemployed, aimless yuppies — make them funny and cool.

Sure, a few humorless radicals are going to reflexively protest against this inspired comedy, but hey, if they can't take a joke. . . well, you know the rest.

Besides, slavery was a long time ago. It ended, what, 133 years ago? Can't we all just laugh along?

I can see why some blacks are concerned, though. They, as I do, probably fear that "Desmond" will be the first step down a slippery slope toward the historical amelioration of slavery's true devastating, still-felt effects. I mean, syndicated columnist Robert Novak wrote recently that slavery "wasn't so bad," and lots of people — believe me, I hear from them — want to revise it as merely a time when we had full employment and slaves went home to their families on weekends.

But even despite such historical misrepresentations, the public battle against "Desmond" is not worth fighting. There are other affronts blacks can spend their time confronting — not all of them from whites. Let's try this, DV: Ask for a show of hands of those parents who were out picketing UPN studios who actually have read to their children or taken them to the library so they can learn about the real effects of the peculiar institution known as slavery. See what I mean.

Anyway, back to my suggestions to tweak the show a bit here and there: Remember that scene in the episode where Desmond has his feet propped up on a table in the White House kitchen and a witty character says "The slaves haven't been emancipated yet; get your feet off the table, Pfeiffer"? Well, Home Slice, I thought I was gonna die. I very nearly burst a gut.

But see, if you're going to make a comedy about slavery — and Disney has a movie comedy in production about a runaway slave called "Rufus" — you've got to really go for the jugular. Figuratively.

Like, I know you felt compelled to cut out that scene of the two men who'd been lynched in the first minutes of the first episode. You were quoted as saying you took it out because the scene was a "downer."

Nonsense. How could two dead men at the beginning of a comedy be considered a "downer"? Why, only a ninny wouldn't see the humor in that. But that's all blood under the dam now. You could still put in some funny bits about, say, a slave having his foot hacked off so he'll quit trying to escape. Now that's what I call cutting-edge humor. Get it: cutting edge. Ha ha.

Or, perhaps you could show a couple of disgruntled slaves swinging from a tree after ol' Massa caught 'em trying to learn to read.

But if you really want the belly laughs, how about showing a suckling infant being torn from his mother's breast so she can be shipped to a plantation in Virginia and the daddy to one in Georgia.

Just make sure you turn up the laugh track real loud so it'll drown out the agonizing screams that typically accompanied such business transactions.

Speaking of business, DV, what other historical comedies do you have in production to capitalize on the inevitable success of "Desmond"?

How about "The Secret Diary of Anne Frank," a coming-of-age comedy about a winsome little Jewish girl who, along with her family, sits out the Holocaust in an attic?

The comedic possibilities are limitless and I predict boffo ratings, DV.

October 10, 1998

Hate crime? Then get behind hate-crime legislation

This guy I know — OK, it was me — once responded to a question about his refusal to speak out for gay rights thusly: "I ain't got no dog in that fight."

At the time, I thought that was the proper response because I was already catching hell on two fronts. First as a black dude, and second as a dude who likes women who don't usually like me.

So why, I asked myself and the person questioning my commitment to gay rights, should I go jumping head first into somebody else's battle? Why should I care if gays were harassed or denied "special" protective legislation?

That was before what happened to Matthew Shepard happened. When I heard how that kid was beaten — so badly that the person who found him thought he was a scarecrow — and then tied to a fence on a cold Laramie, Wyo., prairie just because he was gay, well . . . my feelings about hate crime legislation changed: Anybody who is beaten that badly merely because of his sexual preference needs special protection. And anyone who would dole out such a beating for that reason needs special punishment.   Granted, adding hate-crime status to the crime of murder — which the suspects in Shepard's death have been charged with — would be superfluous. They already deserve the hot squat, so what would adding a hate crime designation to their despicable deed do? Allow Shepard's friends to stand there and call them bad names while the deadly electrical currents course through their carcasses?

In this case, that designation would do nothing. But in other cases that are not capital offenses, hate-crime laws would conceivably allow the judge to add an extra dollop of punishment onto the sentence. In other instances, they might even cause some cretin to stay his violent hand and walk on past the object of his hate or, in many cases, of his desire.

Don't look at me like that. You don't have to be Sigmund Freud to know that the people who are angriest at and most violent toward gays actually have concerns — "fears?" — about their own sexuality.

As a kid, I used to marvel at how guys would verbally and sometimes physically assault one of the few openly gay men in my little hometown — during the day and in public. Yet at night, I'd witness them tipping furtively to or away from his house after an . . . um . . . assignation.

Likewise, I'm sure some of the retromingent male slugs who buy into Republicans' attacks on gays and who incredibly wanted to protest against homosexuality at Shepard's funeral have, in the deepest recesses of their dark minds, glanced admiringly, maybe even wantonly, at other men and wondered how it would feel to . . . Well, you get the picture.

I wonder one thing, though. When they caught themselves entertaining these "evil" thoughts about entertaining another man, did they respond in typical fashion — by punching their own lights out?

Some people who are most resistant to hate-crime legislation claim that it restricts free speech. Well, they're right — if they mean you could no longer beat the crap out of someone while calling him "fag."

October 17, 1998

The man under the bridge

There's one good thing I can say about Earl, the man who sleeps under the bridge near my house: He's honest.

After talking with him for about an hour as he methodically devoured two sausage-and-egg biscuits I bought him for breakfast, I've concluded that that is also the only good thing one can say about him.

"Uh, how'd you end up sleeping under a bridge?" I asked gingerly, trying not to offend.

"Smokin' crack, man," he replied, as though the answer was written on his forehead and I couldn't read.

Later, I asked, "Well, if I help you find a place to stay and a job, will you keep it?"

"If I go out and get a job," he said after the briefest hesitation, "after that first paycheck, I'm going to go out and buy some crack."

Such honesty is refreshing, but it is nothing upon which anyone, regardless of how altruistic, wants to stake his reputation.

The "bridge" under which Earl sleeps is actually an Interstate 85 northbound viaduct that crosses over my street. I'd been wanting to talk to the dude for weeks, ever since I saw him curled up under a filthy blanket, his head on a pillow turned black by, presumably, both an infrequently washed head and automobile exhaust fumes.

I didn't consider his situation dire at first, not while the weather was warm. Heck, what man hasn't found himself sleeping outside at some point — either because Sweet Thang changed the locks or because the landlord didn't believe the check was in the mail?

But now that Old Man Winter is about to start blowing his horn — translation: It's fixing to turn cold — I became concerned, apparently more concerned than he is.

"I've done slept in the hawk before," he shrugged. "Nothin' new to me."

It took only a few minutes to realize that Earl doesn't want sympathy, maybe not even help. The youthful—looking 35-year-old makes it clear that he prefers the freedom of sleeping outside in the cold to the regimentation of a warm homeless shelter. "Who wants to be in by 8 and out by 6" in the morning? he asked.

Earl mentioned entering a drug treatment program to try to "get straight" for the fourth time. He quit one such program about a year ago because, he said, "I didn't want to sit around and listen to 20 or 30 people talking about their problems."

After some slight probing by me, he reiterated the real reason he opts to sleep under the bridge and roam the streets searching for odd jobs, working just enough to get high.

"I'm not going to lie to you. I've gotten lazy from smoking crack," he admitted.

As we parted, I had the disquieting feeling that I cared more about Earl's welfare than he did. That, to me, is unacceptable.

Thus, a line from "Harry Hippie," Bobby Womack's marvelous and haunting 1972 song, has been playing in my mind for the past few days. I suspect it'll be there days from now:

"I'd like to help a man when he's down,

"But how can I help him when he'd rather sleep on the ground?"

If you know the answer, tell me.

October 22, 1998

Upbraiding for the debs of AKA

I hereby sentence the very prim and proper sisters of Alpha Kappa Alpha sorority to six months without a straightening comb or hair relaxer, and to learn all the words to "Beauty's Only Skin Deep" and "Say It Loud (I'm Black and I'm Proud)."

Oops, y'all caught me wishing out loud — wishing I was a judge passing sentence on the leaders of the black sorority chapter in Raleigh who kicked a beautiful little girl out of their debutante ball for, in essence, looking too black.

No, really. Don't laugh. It's true.

You see, Michelle Barskile is an honor student at Garner High School, works two jobs where her hairstyle is not an issue and is being courted by several colleges where she can study medicine, her career goal. Yet, she was unceremoniously kicked out of the sorority's November ball because — get this — she wears her hair in dreadlocks.

Now, you can laugh.

This textbook example of racial self-denial, no matter how odious, is not without precedent. In the 1960s when everybody was saying "Black is beautiful," I'm guessing these same AKA sisters were the ones running around talking about "You'd better get yourself off that stage with that afro and get you a perm, girl." Or, even further back than that, they were the ones holding up a brown paper bag beside prospective sorors' skin and, if your skin was darker than that bag, saying, "Don't let the door hit you on the way out."

A spokesister at the sorority's national headquarters in Chicago — which I called to inquire about the intra-racial outrage in Raleigh — assured me that there was never a paper-bag test for membership. "I was just looking at some old pictures," she said proudly, "and half the sisters are dark-skinned."

She was not amused when I asked if perhaps she was looking at the negatives, not the pictures.

Michelle, to her credit, is not bitter, nor does she seem emotionally scarred by the foolishness of the black women who are rejecting her for sporting an ethnic hairstyle.

When we met, she made it clear that neither vanity nor the debs' scholarship money — a piddling amount, I assure you — compelled her to apply for the ball and spend a nonrefundable $500 on a gown.

She had two reasons, she said. "It was something I wanted to do to please my mother, because she was a debutante," she said, "and I wanted to dance with my father. You don't get many chances to dance with your father."

Gale Isaacs, the event's co-chair, whom I called to get the sorority's side of the story, said only, "Our side speaks for itself."

You know, I used to wonder how slaves, toiling for free under the hot sun and the overseers' whip, could sing — without irony or sarcasm — spirituals like: "Before I'll be a slave I'll be buried in my grave."

Now I know: The presence of chains doesn't make you a slave, nor, as the very prim and proper sisters of Alpha Kappa Alpha sorority in Garner have shown, does the absence of chains make you free.

October 26, 1998

Tempted by a legacy of song

OK, you can come out now. There is not one word about politics in this whole column.

Fact is, I just finished looking through my Bible, and for the life of me, I couldn't find "St. Otis" in there anywhere.

But if you watched, as I did, the televised mini-series on The Temptations singing group this week, you just know there has to be one. Because aside from showing the timelessness of the Temptations' music, the two-part movie showed just what a peach of a guy Otis Williams was. At least according to Otis.

While the other members struggled with well-documented personal problems involving drugs, alcohol and women, ol' Otis was presented as the rock that has held the group together through three decades. His only vice, according to the movie — which was based in large part on his autobiography — was that, goshdarnit, he just worked too hard, which made him a bit of an absentee father.

Of course, it is Williams' prerogative, as the last original Temp standing, to tell the story from his point of view. If it's true that no man is a hero to his valet, then it is equally true that every man is a hero to himself. That means we can forgive Otis the movie's excesses, even that eye-rolling one when the mother of a fellow Temp turned to Otis at the dinner table and said, "Thanks, Otis, for being what these boys needed."

I almost gagged on that one. But Otis' self-serving recollections don't really detract from the Temptations' legacy or from a wonderful performance by Leon, who portrayed the tormented lead singer, David Ruffin. If he doesn't win an Emmy, I'm going to be the one singing "Ball of Confusion."

Still, it is heart-rending that a group of dudes who brought such joy to the world brought such misery to their loved ones and themselves. It's a shame, and should be a crime, that the members of a group that made millions for Motown died broke — victims of their own profligacy and fiscal irresponsibility.

When they died, not one of them owned his own home, according to published reports. But I'm betting that a huge share of the blame had to do with the curious bookkeeping and accounting procedures of Motown's founder, Berry Gordy.

When Gordy signed The Temptations to his label, they were unsophisticated youngsters who probably did not know that the Cadillacs Gordy "bought" for them, the smooth costumes they wore on stage, even the salary for the choreographer who taught them their trademark steps, were all being deducted from their earnings.

Incredibly, the meter was running even when Motown artists went into the studio to rehearse and record songs for Motown.

The older one gets, the fewer things you find to be passionate about.

For me, the list has dwindled to a precious few: cheesy grits, reruns of "The Andy Griffith Show" and Temptations songs — played on a turntable, not a CD; that crackly, tinny sound you get from old records is as much a part of the Temptations' sound as that opening bass beat on "My Girl."

November 05, 1998

Bristling over a hair affair

I swear, I never thought I'd hear myself saying this to a woman, but here goes: "You can stop now!"

My plaintive plea is addressed to the members of the Alpha Kappa Alpha Sorority Inc., who have graciously bestowed upon me about 700 e-mail messages and telephone calls from across the country in the two weeks since I wrote about the shameful treatment a Garner high school student received from the Raleigh chapter of AKA.

Although some enlightened members of the Greek letter sorority agreed that the chapter showed execrable judgment in denying Michelle Barskile a spot in its debutante ball for refusing to abandon or camou-flage her ethnic hair style, most blamed me for "getting the story wrong" — which, of course, is highly unlikely — or for making public an issue they felt was nobody's business but their own.

They were offended because I suggested that the leaders of the Raleigh chapter — not the Garner chapter, as I incorrectly called it; OK, you can spank me now — were hung up on appearances.

I compared the chapter's rejection of the young lady's dreadlocks to the dreaded "paper bag test," which, once upon a time, some black social organizations — even churches — employed to keep out darker-skinned blacks. One reader wrote to me of her elderly aunt, an AKA, who still boasts of her membership in a group that accepted only those who were "light, bright and damned near white."

That is a shameful legacy of our history, to be sure, but not one I invented. No amount of historical revisionism will make it un-happen.

Yet, one soror was so upset that she wrote, "You, with your bowler, big-lipped, house-nigger-looking self, obviously have some racial issues of your own to deal with."

Two things: First, as dark as I am, there is no way I would have been in any massa's house during slavery. Second, after reading her response, who could think that that young lady was unduly concerned about appearances?

In writing about the hair incident, I was not making a universal con-demnation of all AKAs or even of all chapters. I was talking about a few arrogant members in one chapter. Period. I have since heard from count-less AKAs and others who extend their apologies to Michelle and who laud her willingness to stand up for what she believes in.

For instance, one AKA, a doctor in Atlanta, was impressed by Michelle's career interest in medicine and offered to be a mentor, and other sororities said they invite her to participate in their debutante balls — dreadlocks and all.

An AKA from New York, in a letter circulated on the Internet, wrote, "I hereby sentence you, sir, to get a life ... Clearly he is bitter. He probably tried to pledge undergrad and didn't make it ... Now, this article is his shining moment, a chance to get back at those Greeks" who didn't let him join.

Not true. Sure, I have been kicked out of or denied entry into many things, but I am philosophical about it. My philosophy is taken straight from Marx — Groucho, not Karl — who said, "I wouldn't belong to any club that would have someone like me as a member." So there.

November 09, 1998

It's always open season for growth

Leave me alone. The next time y'all see me eating a steak or a pork-chop sandwich or even a strip of bacon, don't say a @!#$#$$% word to me.

I'm giving fair warning to all of these so-called animal-rights people who like to castigate us for eating hot dogs, sausage or anything else that formerly had parents.

The same people who decry the inhumanity of boiling lobsters — "Oooh, you can hear them scream just like humans," they lament — sit silently by while an even more pernicious threat to animals exists: bull-dozers.

The bulldozers that are destroying this area's character do far more harm to animals than that cute little Oscar Mayer Wienermobile, but I haven't heard of People for the Ethical Treatment of Animals trying to derail the former as they do the latter.

Where, I want to know, are these activists when rampant develop-ment — make that rampant overdevelopment — destroys woodlands and sends countless animals fleeing to their deaths in front of 18-wheel-ers on our highways?

In recent weeks, I have seen so many dead deer lying by the side of Triangle roads that I wondered whether they were part of some mass animal suicide ritual — or whether perhaps they had been drinking and were returning from a night of wild animal partying when they stumbled from the woods into the path of traffic.

No. They were just victims of growth and of trying to find some woods in which to chill out.

State troopers, apparently seeking to blame the victims — in this case, the deer — warn motorists to watch out for deer each fall because the animals are seeking mates and fattening up for the long winter.

Hell, so am I, but you don't see me jumping in front of a speeding four-wheel-drive.

The sad fact is the deer are being killed by the unrestrained, seemingly unregulated growth that is destroying their natural habitat. It's funny, but whenever some good ol' boy wants to make like Elmer Fudd and hunt some deer and wabbits — or whenever some zookeeper doesn't bathe an elephant twice a day and read to it before tucking it in — PETA attacks like an enraged lion.

Yet, when some millionaire developer driving a Chevy Suburban conducts market research, decides that a certain area of the city just has to have yet another 7-Eleven and cuts down 10,000 trees, we hear not a peep of protest.

People scoff when hunters say they are being humane by "thinning the herd" of various animals. I scoffed, too, but now concede they might be onto something.

Think about it: What's more humane — to be chased from your natural environment by another strip mall and forced to rummage through garbage cans and eventually starve to death, or having a fighting chance against Elmer Fudd?

Me, I'd take the latter. Because Elmer Fudd might miss. Developers, as we see, never miss.

November 12, 1998

Mything with our minds

The woman who called me last week to warn of a deadly threat in the Triangle was genuinely concerned. It was obvious from her hushed yet breathless tone that she took the information she was imparting seriously. So seriously, in fact, that I didn't want to laugh.

But I couldn't help myself. You see, she was the third person this month — and probably the 20th in the past five years — to warn me of a Triangle gang initiation rite in which well-meaning motorists were shot for flicking their high-beams at oncoming cars whose headlights were off.

How horrible, you gasp — a gang initiation that requires young thugs-in-training to pop a good Samaritan for trying to save their life.

As bad as that story is, it would be even worse if true. Thankfully, it is not, and I chose not to write about it — despite desperate pleas from well-meaning readers — for fear of giving bad ideas to unimaginative, newspaper reading gangbangers.

Gangbanger No. 1: Yo, G. That idea is the bomb. Let's do it.

Gangbanger No. 2: Word, Dog.

But once I saw the story being debunked on local television news and in The N&O last week, I figured it was OK to declare open season on myths, much as the mythical gang declared open season on unsuspecting motorists.

Here's the deal: Police say the story of lead-slinging gangbangers is yet another urban myth foisted upon a gullible, paranoid public that is anxious and willing to believe anything if it is bad enough.

Urban myths — and rural ones, too — are nothing new. They've just become meaner. For instance, one making the rounds in Rockingham and, no doubt, other small towns in the late 1960s probably was started by a preacher trying to dissuade kids from fishing on Sundays. It seems an unfortunate little boy was out digging for bait but instead dug up a small, red devil.

That's rather benign, unless you're a 9-year-old boy with a hyperactive imagination who studiously avoided holes for months afterward. And everyone, I'm sure, knows someone who knows someone whose friend flushed a pet crocodile down the toilet, only for it to emerge — bigger and smellier — from someone else's toilet.

Such tall tales can be attributed to people with too much time on their hands. But other myths can hurt. For instance, about 10 years ago, a hot hip-hop clothes company went belly up when word was spread — probably by a competitor — that the company was a front for the Ku Klux Klan and that its name — TROOP — was an acronym for "To Rule Over Oppressed People."

Another myth making the rounds, primarily on the Internet, is being spread by seemingly sensible people and warns blacks of Congress' secret plan to revoke the 1964 Voting Rights Act in 2007.

How come there are no "good" urban myths, like, "I know a dude who went to a fast-food drive-through window and actually got what he ordered! And the server said, 'Thank you!' "

Hmmph. I guess some things are just too hard to believe.

November 19, 1998

Shaw picks wrong man to honor

All I can say to the folks at Shaw University is, "Y'all had better check the fine print."

That's my advice after learning that boxing promoter Don King pledged "millions" of dollars to the university at its Founder's Day Convocation on Friday. If King's reputation as a boxing promoter is any indication, Shaw could end up owing King millions and possibly renaming the school Don King U.

Just ask any of the scores of boxers who've been left broke, broken and shattered by his "pledges." Ask Mike Tyson why he is suing King for $100 million.

Of course, what Shaw bestowed upon King — an honorary doctorate degree in recognition of his "humanitarian efforts" — is invaluable, since it abets King's efforts to rewrite history and unsully his image for posterity. That effort began when he started writing checks to certain black schools and organizations and, voila, those same schools and organizations began giving him humanitarian awards like they were going out of style.

Anyone who knows me knows that I'd be the last person on earth to belittle someone's genuine efforts at contrition or their attempt to make up for a misbegotten past. Few pasts could have been more misspent than mine, and I am constantly trying to prove that the people — like Mr. James E. Hand in Rockingham — who bent over backward to help me weren't wrong.

But money alone shouldn't be the criterion for bestowing a humanitarian award. If Shaw wants to honor King's generosity — or his presumed generosity — fine. But to honor him as a "humanitarian" tarnishes an honor that has been bestowed upon such deserving people as Stokely Carmichael, one of the most significant, underappreciated men in modern history. Carmichael died last week after spending his life trying to make America live up to its creed of equality for all people. It's sad to think that King will now be mentioned in the same breath as he.

OK, answer me this: Would Shaw or anyone else have seen fit to honor King's "humanitarian efforts" had they not anticipated that a hefty pledge would be forthcoming?

Case closed. By no means is King the first to use money to try to rehab his image. If you look at some of this country's most beloved and famous families — well, you wouldn't want to look too closely. Perhaps one day King or his offspring will do something to enter the pantheon of those who've succeeded in canceling out unscrupulous pasts by present-day altruism. I wish him luck, but man, it should require more than writing a check.

Last year, when the NAACP gave King its highest honor, I called Flora Garrett, the widow of one of the two black men King has killed. He beat and stomped her husband to death over a gambling debt rumored to be $50 or $500. I asked her for her view of King's humanitarianism. "The man is a monster," she said. "My husband owed him some money, yes. But whether it was a dime or a million, you don't take a person's life for it."

Perhaps the Shaw alumni and students clamoring to bask in King's glow or to touch the hem of his garment — he did compare himself to Jesus during his speech — should have spoken with the widow Garrett first.

November 23, 1998

Too soon to write off old Wendell

There is a story, told as true, of a mysterious and elderly — although in our adolescent years those two words were synonymous — lady in Rockingham who was being transported to Nelson's Funeral Home in a hearse.

Only problem was, she wasn't dead. "What y'all doin' to me?" she asked weakly, lifting the sheet and rising in the back of the hearse.

That's probably the same question the town of Wendell is asking of townspeople who, likewise thinking their cute little town of 4,000 is dead, have embarked on a misguided, unwise attempt to "resuscitate" it.

For instance, its Chamber of Commerce hired a Florida jingle-writer to pen a song encouraging people to move there and bring their business along. The tune, which'll make no one forget Smokey Robinson or Bob Dylan, begins:

"Look out beyond your window
'Cause you're sure to find it there
That community you've always wanted
That has so much to share."
Make it funky, now. Good God.

Well, I've written a song for the people of Wendell, and it goes something like this: Maestro, hit it:

"Are y'all crazy? Are y'all crazy?
Can't you see what growth has done?
Just look at Raleigh if you think I'm lying.
There are now five houses where there used to be one.
Me and Sweet Thang used to walk down our street

Holding hands up under the stars.
But now there are so many people on our street
That we spend all of our time just dodging cars.
Newcomers say they love to hear the frogs croak
And they just looooove to see a pond full of ducks
But before you know it they're killing your frogs
And paving the pond to build a Starbucks.
And that, my friends, I'm sad to tell
Will be the death knell for the town of Wendell.
Gee, didn't we used to think this place was really swell?
Oh well."

Sure, big-city transplants to any pastoral little community will be enamored of its quaintness and extol the virtues of "country living." For about 15 minutes.

After that, they'll be griping about their inability to find the perfect Chardonnay for their dinner soirees, or yelping that the Piggly Wiggly's stock of gourmet vittles leaves much to be desired. "Do you realize, Muffy, that they hadn't a single jar of foie gras?"

Then someone will decide that what the town really needs is another video store.

Next thing you know, new residents will start complaining about — and then running for the town board and outlawing sofas on front porches, auto garages they find unsightly, maybe even eating Moon Pies in public.

OK, I just made that last one up, but ask the folks of Wilson and Holly Springs if you think I made up the other two.

December 21, 1998